GRADE **7**

McGraw Hill

Math

Third Edition

New York   Chicago   San Francisco   Athens   London   Madrid
Mexico City   Milan   New Delhi   Singapore   Sydney   Toronto

1 2 3 4 5 6 7 8 9   LWI   27 26 25 24 23 22

ISBN   978-1-264-28569-3
MHID   1-264-28569-8

e-ISBN 978-1-264-28570-9
e-MHID   1-264-28570-1

McGraw Hill products are available at special quantity discounts for use as premiums and sales promotions, or for use in corporate training programs. To contact a representative please visit the Contact Us pages at www.mhprofessional.com.

McGraw Hill is committed to making our products accessible to all learners. To learn more about the available support and accommodations we offer, please contact us at accessibility@mheducation.com. We also participate in the Access Text Network (www.accesstext.org), and ATN members may submit requests through ATN.

McGraw Hill thanks Wendy Hanks for her invaluable contributions to this new edition.

Table of Contents

Table of Contents

Letter to Parents and Students

Welcome to McGraw Hill's Math!

Parents, this book will help your child succeed in seventh grade mathematics. It will give your seventh grader:

- **A head start** in the summer before seventh grade
- **Extra practice** during the school year
- **Helpful preparation** for standardized mathematics exams

The book is aligned to **National and State Standards**. A chart beginning on the next page summarizes those standards and shows how each state that does not follow the national standards differs from those standards. The chart also includes comparisons to Canadian standards.

If you live in a state that has adopted Common Core standards, you won't need the information in this table, although you may find its summary of standards helpful. Parents who live in Canada or states that have not adopted Common Core standards will find the table a useful tool and can be reassured that most of these regions have standards that are very similar to the national standards. This book contains ample instruction and practice for students in **any state** or in **Canada**.

Students, this book will help you do well in mathematics. Its lessons explain math concepts and provide lots of interesting practice activities.

Open your book and look at the **Table of Contents**. It tells what topics are covered in each lesson. Work through the book at your own pace.

Begin with the **Pretest**, which will help you discover the math skills you need to work on.

Each group of lessons ends with a **Unit Test**. The results will show you what skills you have learned and what skills you may need to practice more. A **Posttest** completes your work in this book and will show how you have done overall.

Take time to practice your math. Practicing will help you use and improve your math skills.

Good luck!

Seventh Grade National and State Standards

Seventh Grade U.S. Common Core Standards	Texas*	Virginia	Indiana	South Carolina
Analyze proportional relationships and use them to solve real-world and mathematical problems.		More work on slope		This state's math standards for the Seventh grade align with the Common Core.
Apply and extend previous understandings of operations with fractions.				
Use properties of operations to generate equivalent expressions.				
Solve real-life and mathematical problems using numerical and algebraic expressions and equations.				
Draw, construct, and describe geometrical figures and describe the relationships between them.	Omits drawing	Omits drawing, plane sections, and scale drawings; includes transformations	Omits plane sections	
Solve real-life and mathematical problems involving angle measure, area, surface area, and volume.		Omits circles		
Use random sampling to draw inferences about a population.		No related standards		
Draw informal comparative inferences about two populations.				
Investigate chance processes and develop, use, and evaluate probability models.		Omits compound events	Omits compound events	

*Texas also has a section on personal financial literacy.

Minnesota	Oklahoma	Nebraska	Alaska	Canadian Provinces
				ON and WNCP omit fractional rates
			Also: convert among fractions, decimals, percents	
				ON omits graphing inequalities
Omits drawing & plane sections; Includes transformations	Omits drawing and plane sections; includes transformations	Omits scale drawings and plane sections		ON and WNCP omit plane sections
Omits angles	Omits angles			
No related standards	No related standards			
		More focus on circle graphs, less on distribution		ON and WNCP omit
Omits compound events	Omits compound events and models			ON and WNCP omit models

Name _____

Complete the following test items on pages 4–8.

1 Restate the number 4,587,902.453.

Expanded form: _____

Written form: _____

2 Cheryl's Department Store is having a sale. They have 145 coats in stock and are adding 55 more. If at the end of the sale they still have 25 coats in stock, how many coats did they sell? _____

3 Tracey pedals 16 miles a day on a stationary bicycle. How many miles does she pedal in the month of March? (Remember, March has 31 days.) _____

How many yards does she pedal? _____

Calculate.

4 $|-14| + 14 =$ _____

5 $\begin{array}{r} -11 \\ \times\ 59 \\ \hline \end{array}$

6 $\dfrac{5}{7} \div \dfrac{25}{28} =$ _____

7 $\$3.49 - 0.59 =$ _____

8 $0.34 + 1.86 + 0.02 =$ _____

9 $798 \div 0.38 =$ _____

10 $-3 - (-6) =$ _____

11 $-25\overline{)-155}$

12 Bailey bought $11\dfrac{1}{4}$ kilograms of bird feed. On the way home, he spilled $3\dfrac{5}{8}$ kilograms. How much bird feed does he still have left? _____

13 Margaret mixes 1400 centiliters of grape juice with $5\dfrac{2}{3}$ liters of seltzer and $\dfrac{2}{5}$ liters of orange juice. How many liters of punch will this make? _____

14 What is the volume of a rectangular box with length 12 cm, height 6 cm, and width 5 cm? _____

15 $-9 + 10 - (-8) + 6(-2) + \dfrac{6}{-2} =$ _____

16 Solve for x: $x - 9 = 18$ _____

17 Solve for x: $2x + 5 < 15$ _____

18 What property is represented by the following equation?
$4(5 + 6) = 4 \times 5 + 4 \times 6$

_____

19 What property is represented by the following equation?
$(3 + 6) + 6 = 3 + (6 + 6)$

_____

20 $|-9| + (2 + 3)^2 - (6 \div 3) + 4(8 \times 3) + 4(5 - 3) =$ _____

Pretest

21 Give the coordinates for the points.

A _____

B _____

C _____

D _____

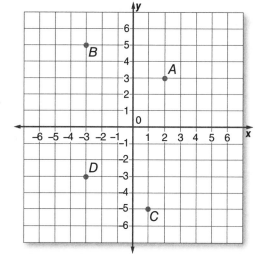

22 Restate in exponent form, then solve:

$4 \times 4 \times 4 + 2 \times 2 =$

_____

23 What is the area of the rectangle?

_____

What is the perimeter of the rectangle?

_____

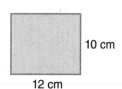

10 cm

12 cm

24 What is the area of the circle? (Use 3.14 for π.)

_____

What is the circumference of the circle?

_____

B 5 cm C

25 Identify the following angles as obtuse, acute, or right.

120°   90°   40°

_____   _____   _____

26 Identify the triangles as scalene, isosceles, or equilateral.

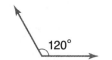 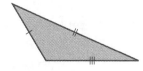

_____   _____   _____

27 Ramon spends $28.94 a month having pictures developed. He is working on a project that will take 19 months to finish. How much should he plan to spend on developing pictures for the project? _____

28 Restate 3.6 as an improper fraction and a mixed number. _____

29 Restate $4\frac{5}{8}$ as a decimal. _____

30 Is the following true or false? $\frac{5}{16} = \frac{60}{192}$ _____

31 $\sqrt{73}$ is between _____ and _____.

32 Drayson deposits $125 in a bank account that earns 4% simple interest. How much money will he have in the account after

1 year? _____

After 2 years? _____

33 What is the mode of the data distribution?

_____

What is the median?

_____

Stems	Leaves
1	3 5
2	3 6 9
3	3 8 8 8
4	4 4 5 6 6
5	3 4 6

34 $\frac{4}{7} \times 5\frac{4}{9} =$ _____

35 What is $\frac{3}{8}$ of 88%? _____

36 What is 30% of 0.675? _____

37 $0.15\overline{)0.235}$

38 $\frac{4}{3} + \frac{2}{3} + \frac{5}{3} - \frac{1}{3} - \frac{7}{3} =$ _____

39 Identify each quadrilateral as a square, rectangle, kite, rhombus, or trapezoid.

_____ _____ _____ _____ _____

40 Identify the following figures.

_____ _____ _____

41 Restate $5\frac{6}{13}$ as an improper fraction.

_____

42 Restate $\frac{43}{16}$ as a mixed number.

_____

43 What are the chances of choosing a black marker out of a bag containing 3 red markers, 5 blue markers, 3 yellow markers, and 4 black markers? What is the probability of choosing two black markers if the first marker is put back before the second is drawn?

_____

44 According to the graph, how many videos did Jamie watch in July?

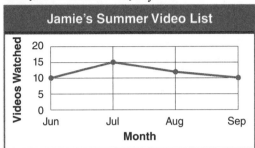

_____

45 During which week did Kelly and Heather swim the same distance?

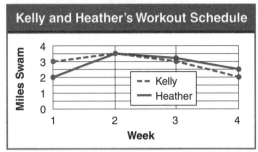

_____

46 What fruit is most preferred by the students?

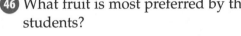

_____

47 Peggy's score was about 30 pins higher than whose score?

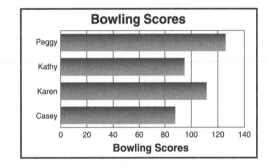

_____

48 What is the range of the data in the box-and-whisker plot below? What is the median of the data points shown?

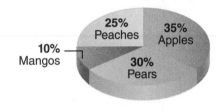

49 How much plastic wrap would you need to cover this rectangular solid?

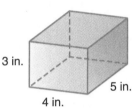

3 in.

5 in.

4 in.

_____

50 Name two line segments. _____

Name four rays. _____

Name a line. _____

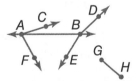

51 Fill in a Venn Diagram that displays the following data: There are two groups of students, 30 who take the bus to school and 25 who have a younger sibling in the school. There are 10 students who take the bus and who also have a younger sibling in the school.

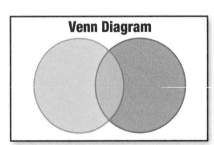

Venn Diagram

52 Are the rates in the table below proportional?

Car	Distance	Time
A	15 miles	20 minutes
B	20 miles	25 minutes

53 What is the unit rate for the price of grapes as shown on the graph below?

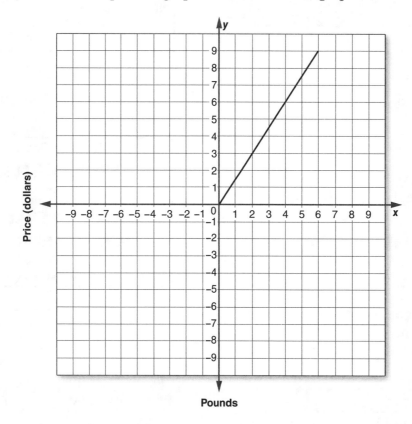

54 What is the best way to get a representative sample of the people at a baseball game for a survey about parking at the stadium?

(a) Choose one of the luxury boxes at random and survey all the people in that box.

(b) Survey the first 50 people to walk into the stadium.

(c) Choose 50 seat numbers at random and survey the people in those seats.

55 Complete the probability table below.

Outcome	Number	Probability
A	$\frac{23}{90}$	0.26
B		0.16
C	$\frac{53}{90}$	

Pretest

Answers and Explanations for Pretest

1. $(4 \times 1{,}000{,}000) + (5 \times 100{,}000) + (8 \times 10{,}000) + (7 \times 1000) + (9 \times 100) + (2 \times 1) + (4 \times 0.1) + (5 \times 0.01) + (3 \times 0.001)$; Four million five hundred eighty-seven thousand nine hundred two and four hundred and fifty-three thousandths

2. 175 coats $\qquad 145 + 55 - 25 = 175$

3. 496 miles; 872,960 yards $\qquad 16 \times 31 = 496$ miles; 496 miles $\times \dfrac{1760 \text{ yards}}{\text{mile}} = 872{,}960$ yards

4. 28 $\qquad |-14| = 14; 14 + 14 = 28$

5. -649
$$\begin{array}{r} -11 \\ \times 59 \\ \hline 99 \\ 550 \\ \hline -649 \end{array}$$

6. $\dfrac{4}{5} \qquad \dfrac{5}{7} \div \dfrac{25}{28} = \dfrac{{}^1\cancel{5}}{{}_1\cancel{7}} \times \dfrac{{}^4\cancel{28}}{\cancel{25}_{\,5}} = \dfrac{4}{5}$

7. $2.90
$$\begin{array}{r} \$\overset{2}{\cancel{3}}.\overset{1}{4}9 \\ -0.59 \\ \hline \$\,2.90 \end{array}$$

8. 2.22
$$\begin{array}{r} \overset{1}{0.34} \\ {}^1 1.86 \\ 0.02 \\ \hline 2.22 \end{array}$$

9. 2100
$$\begin{array}{r} 2100 \\ 0.38.\overline{)798.00} \\ \underline{76} \\ 38 \\ \underline{38} \\ 0 \end{array}$$

10. 3 $\qquad -3 - (-6) = -3 + 6 = 3$

11. 6.2
$$\begin{array}{r} +6.2 \\ -25\overline{)-155.0} \\ \underline{150\downarrow} \\ 50 \end{array}$$

12. $7\dfrac{5}{8}$ kg $\qquad 11 - 3 = 8; \dfrac{1}{4} - \dfrac{5}{8} = \dfrac{2}{8} - \dfrac{5}{8} = -\dfrac{3}{8}; 8 - \dfrac{3}{8} = 7\dfrac{5}{8}$

13. $20\dfrac{1}{15}$ L $\qquad 1400$ centiliters $= 14$ liters; $14 + 5 = 19; \dfrac{2}{3} + \dfrac{2}{5} = \dfrac{10}{15} + \dfrac{6}{15} = \dfrac{16}{15}; 19 + \dfrac{16}{15} = 20\dfrac{1}{15}$

14. 360 sq cm $\qquad 12 \times 6 \times 5 = 360$

15. $-6 \qquad -9 + 10 - (-8) - 12 + \dfrac{6}{-2} = -9 + 10 + 8 - 12 - 3 = -6$

16. $x = 27 \qquad x - 9 = 18; x - 9 + 9 = 18 + 9; x = 27$

17. $x < 5 \qquad 2x + 5 < 15; 2x + 5 - 5 < 15 - 5; 2x < 10; \dfrac{2x}{2} < \dfrac{10}{2}; x < 5$

18. Distributive Property of Multiplication over Addition

19. Associative Property of Addition

20. 136 $\qquad 9 + 5^2 - 2 + 4(24) + 4(2) = 9 + 25 - 2 + 4(24) + 4(2) = 9 + 25 - 2 + 96 + 8 = 136$

21. A(2,3); B(−3,5); C(1,−5); D(−3,−3)

22. $4^3 + 2^2 = 64 + 4 = 68$

23. Area = 120 sq cm; Perimeter = 44 cm $12 \times 10 = 120$; $12 + 12 + 10 + 10 = 44$

24. Area = 19.625 sq cm; Circumference = 15.7 cm $A = \pi r^2$; $A = \pi(2.5^2) = (3.14)(6.25) = 19.625$;
$C = \pi d$; $C = 3.14 \times 5 = 15.7$

25. Obtuse; right; acute $120° > 90°$; $90° = 90°$; $40° < 90°$

26. Scalene; equilateral; isosceles   all 3 sides different; all sides equal; 2 sides equal

27. $549.86 $28.94 \times 19 = 549.86$

28. $3\frac{3}{5}$ or $\frac{18}{5}$ $3.6 = 3\frac{6}{10} = 3\frac{3}{5} = \frac{18}{5}$

29. 4.625 $\frac{37}{8} = 37 \div 8 = 4.625$

30. True $\frac{60}{192} \div \frac{6}{6} = \frac{10}{32} = \frac{5}{16}$

31. 8 and 9 $\sqrt{64} = 8$ and $\sqrt{81} = 9$, so $\sqrt{73} \cong 8.5$

32. $130 after 1 year; $135.20 after two years $125 \times 0.04 = \$5$, so $130; $130 \times 0.04 = \$5.2$, so $135.20 in 2 years

33. Mode 38; median 38   38 appears 3 times; there are 17 values, so the median is value #9, which is 38

34. $3\frac{1}{9}$ $\frac{4}{7} \times \frac{49}{9} = \frac{4}{1} \times \frac{7}{9} = \frac{28}{9} = 3\frac{1}{9}$

35. 33% $\frac{3}{8} \times \frac{88}{100} = \frac{3}{1} \times \frac{11}{100} = \frac{33}{100} = 33\%$

36. 0.2025 $0.3 \times 0.675 = 0.2025$

37. 1.57

$$0.15.\overline{)0.23.500}$$

$$\begin{array}{r} 1.566... \\ \hline 15 \\ \hline 85 \\ 75 \\ \hline 100 \\ 90 \\ \hline 100 \\ 90 \\ \hline 10... \end{array}$$

38. 1 $\frac{4+2+5-1-7}{3} = \frac{3}{3} = 1$

39. Trapezoid; rhombus; square; rectangle; kite;

40. Heptagon; hexagon; pentagon

41. $\frac{71}{13}$

42. $2\frac{11}{16}$

43. $\frac{4}{15}$; $\frac{16}{225}$ There are 4 black out of 15 total, so $\frac{4}{15}$; $\frac{4}{15} \times \frac{4}{15} = \frac{16}{225}$

44. 15

45. Week 2

46. Apples   35% is the largest, so apples

47. Kathy   Peggy is about 125; $125 - 30 = 95$; Kathy is about 95.

48. 15; 12 $20 - 5 = 15$; 12 is marked as the median

49. 94 sq in.   surface area $= 2(3 \times 4) + 2(4 \times 5) + 2(3 \times 5) = 2(12) + 2(20) + 2(15) = 24 + 40 + 30 = 94$

50. Line Segments: $\overline{BD}$, $\overline{DB}$, $\overline{CA}$, $\overline{AC}$, $\overline{HG}$, $\overline{GH}$, $\overline{BE}$, $\overline{EB}$, $\overline{AB}$, $\overline{AF}$, $\overline{FA}$; Rays: $\overrightarrow{AC}$, $\overrightarrow{BD}$, $\overrightarrow{BE}$, $\overrightarrow{AF}$, $\overrightarrow{BA}$, $\overrightarrow{AB}$; Line $\overleftrightarrow{AB}$

51.

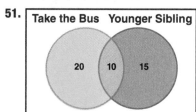

Take the Bus   Younger Sibling

20   10   15

52. No, Car A is going 45 miles per hour and Car B is going 48 miles per hour.

Car A: $\dfrac{15 \text{ miles}}{20 \text{ minutes}} = \dfrac{3 \text{ miles}}{4 \text{ minutes}} = \dfrac{\frac{3}{4} \text{ miles}}{1 \text{ minute}} \times 60 = 45$

Car B: $\dfrac{20 \text{ miles}}{25 \text{ minutes}} = \dfrac{4 \text{ miles}}{5 \text{ minutes}} = \dfrac{\frac{4}{5} \text{ miles}}{1 \text{ minute}} \times 60 = 48$

53. \$1.50   When $x = 1$, $y = 1.5$, so \$1.50

54. C   A random sample gives the most representative sample. B seems random, but the first 50 to arrive won't be representative of everyone who parks at the stadium.

55.

Outcome	Number	Probability
Win	$\dfrac{23}{90}$	0.26
Lose	$\dfrac{14}{90}$	0.16
Draw	$\dfrac{53}{90}$	0.58

B: $\dfrac{23}{90} + \dfrac{53}{90} = \dfrac{76}{90}$;

$1 - \dfrac{76}{90} = \dfrac{14}{90}$ C: $0.26 + 0.16 = 0.42$; $1 - 0.42 = 0.58$

Evaluation Chart

As you review your Pretest, check the chart below to see which lessons relate to the questions you missed. As you work through this book, pay special attention to those lessons!

1. Lesson 1.1
2. Lesson 1.2
3. Lesson 2.1 and 18.1
4. Lesson 5.2
5. Lesson 2.1 and 5.4
6. Lesson 8.3
7. Lesson 10.3
8. Lesson 10.1
9. Lesson 12.2
10. Lesson 5.3
11. Lesson 3.1 and 5.4
12. Lesson 6.6
13. Lesson 6.6 and 19.2
14. Lesson 18.6
15. Lesson 4.1
16. Lesson 17.3
17. Lesson 17.4
18. Lesson 4.3
19. Lesson 4.2
20. Lesson 4.1
21. Lesson 14.1
22. Lesson 16.1
23. Lesson 18.4 and 18.5
24. Lesson 26.4
25. Lesson 25.2
26. Lesson 26.1
27. Lesson 11.2
28. Lesson 9.3
29. Lesson 9.2
30. Lesson 13.2
31. Lesson 16.2
32. Lesson 15.5 and 15.6
33. Lesson 22.1 and 22.2
34. Lesson 7.3
35. Lesson 15.2
36. Lesson 15.3
37. Lesson 12.3
38. Lesson 6.3
39. Lesson 26.2
40. Lesson 26.3
41. Lesson 6.2
42. Lesson 6.1
43. Lesson 23.1 and 23.3
44. Lesson 21.2
45. Lesson 21.3
46. Lesson 21.4
47. Lesson 21.1
48. Lesson 22.3 and 22.1
49. Lesson 26.5
50. Lesson 24.2
51. Lesson 22.5
52. Lesson 13.3 and 13.2
53. Lesson 14.3
54. Lesson 22.6
55. Lesson 23.2

Place Value

Place value tells you what each digit in a number means. The value of the digit depends on the place it occupies.

> **Example:** In the number 375, the 3 is in the hundreds place, the 7 is in the tens place, and the 5 is in the ones place. So 375 means 3 hundreds + 7 tens + 5 ones.

USE A PLACE-VALUE CHART This place-value chart shows the places occupied by all the digits in the number 784,234,941.

Millions Period			Thousands Period			Ones Period		
Hundreds	Tens	Ones	Hundreds	Tens	Ones	Hundreds	Tens	Ones
7	8	4,	2	3	4,	9	4	1

In this number, the digit 7 is in the hundred millions place, the digit 8 is in the ten millions place, and so on. Places are organized into

periods, or groups of three. A long string of digits is hard to read, so periods are separated by commas.

DECIMAL PLACE VALUES Decimals have place values too. Look at this place-value chart.

Tens	Ones		Tenths	Hundredths	Thousandths
2	9	.	6	2	3

The number in the chart is 29.623. Read it like this: twenty-nine and six hundred twenty-three thousandths.

NUMBER FORMS There are three ways to write numbers:

- **Standard Form:** 8,297,345
- **Expanded Form:** $(8 \times 1,000,000) + (2 \times 100,000) + (9 \times 10,000) + (7 \times 1000) + (3 \times 100) + (4 \times 10) + (5 \times 1)$
- **Word Form:** eight million, two hundred ninety-seven thousand, three hundred forty-five.

Exercises SOLVE

1 In 231,739,465, the underlined digit is in which place? _____

2 In 92.609, the number 6 is in which place? _____

3 In 2,867,403, the underlined digit is in which place? _____

4 In 1.609, the number 1 is in which place? _____

5 The standard form of the number 7305.92 has the number 3 in which place? _____

6 Which digit is in the hundredths place in the number 4007.951? _____

7 In 58,601, the underlined digit is in which place? _____

8 The standard form of the number 987 has the number 7 in which place? _____

9 In 842.793, the number 9 is in which place? _____

Adding and Subtracting Whole Numbers

A **whole number** is a number that does not include decimals or fractions. Most people use *only* whole numbers when they count: 1, 2, 3 . . . up to as high as they need to go.

Example: Adding Whole Numbers

To add 372 + 49 + 2891, start by lining up the **addends**, the numbers you have to add, by place value. Add each place value, *starting in the ones place.* If the total for that place value has 2 digits, write the second digit and **carry** the first digit to the next column.

```
  1 2 1
    372
     49
+  2891
   3312
```

Example: Subtracting Whole Numbers

To subtract 723 – 514, start by lining up the numbers by place value. Subtract each place value number, *starting in the ones place.* How do you subtract 4 ones from 3 ones? You have to **regroup**. Borrow one ten from the tens place to make the 3 ones into 13 ones.

```
   113
   7̶2̶3̶
 - 514
   209
```

Remember...

When you add or subtract whole numbers, line up the numbers by place value. Then treat *each* place value as its own problem.

Exercises ADD OR SUBTRACT

1
```
   7
+  5
```

2
```
  33
+ 77
```

3
```
    21
+ 2100
```

4
```
  100
-  22
```

5
```
  5888
-  790
```

6
```
   544
   322
+ 1023
```

7
```
  10,000
-  8888
```

8
```
  1010
    11
+  311
```

9
```
  212
  355
+  22
```

10
```
  1001
-  988
```

11
```
     5
  1055
+  454
```

12
```
  7443
- 4567
```

Estimating Sums and Differences

What if you need only a *fairly good idea* of what a sum or a difference is? Do you still need to go through the whole process of adding or subtracting? No, you can estimate. To do that, start by **rounding** each number. Rounding changes one number into another close number that you can work with more easily.

After you decide on the digit to use for the rounding place, change *all* other digits in the number to 0. Repeat this process for all the numbers in the problem.

Your answer will *not* be exact, but it will be much better than a guess!

Example: Look at the highest place value. This is called the **rounding place**. Then look at the second highest place value. If the digit there is *less than 5*, keep the original digit in the rounding place. If the digit there is *5 or greater*, add 1 to the digit in the rounding place.

rounding place second highest place value

$$\begin{array}{r} 3611 \\ +\ 5299 \end{array} \quad \begin{array}{r} 4000 \\ +\ 5000 \\ \hline 9000 \end{array}$$

rounding place second highest place value

$$\begin{array}{r} 708 \\ -\ 593 \end{array} \quad \begin{array}{r} 700 \\ -\ 600 \\ \hline 100 \end{array}$$

Exercises ESTIMATE

1 122 + 82

2 249 + 357

3 25 + 78

4 239 + 555

5 31 + 131

6 45 + 21

7 147 + 97

8 333 − 203

9 2119 − 932

10 575 + 639

11 711 − 236

12 23 + 11

13 57,450 − 4997

14 4723 + 154

15 45 + 557 + 78

16 345 + 167

17 105,555 − 15,559

18 3454 + 549 + 777

19 10,329 − 5784

Multiplying Whole Numbers

Is multiplying more difficult than adding or subtracting? Not really—if you remember to line up the numbers by place value. Then multiply the *entire* top number by the ones place of the bottom number, and then by its tens place, and finally by its hundreds place. Think of it as doing a few single, simple problems one after the other. The answer to the entire multiplication problem is the **product**.

Example:

$$
\begin{array}{r}
356 \\
\times\ 294 \\
\hline
1424 \\
(+)\ 32040 \\
(+)\ 71200 \\
\hline
104664
\end{array}
$$

← placeholders

Remember...

Always use placeholder zeros in your multiplication exercises.

Exercises   MULTIPLY

1
$$\begin{array}{r} 5 \\ \times\ 12 \\ \hline \end{array}$$

2
$$\begin{array}{r} 32 \\ \times\ 11 \\ \hline \end{array}$$

3
$$\begin{array}{r} 7 \\ \times\ 19 \\ \hline \end{array}$$

4
$$\begin{array}{r} 44 \\ \times\ 13 \\ \hline \end{array}$$

5
$$\begin{array}{r} 41 \\ \times\ 21 \\ \hline \end{array}$$

6
$$\begin{array}{r} 55 \\ \times\ 52 \\ \hline \end{array}$$

7
$$\begin{array}{r} 3 \\ \times\ 547 \\ \hline \end{array}$$

8
$$\begin{array}{r} 444 \\ \times\ 92 \\ \hline \end{array}$$

9
$$\begin{array}{r} 72 \\ \times\ 33 \\ \hline \end{array}$$

10
$$\begin{array}{r} 1414 \\ \times\ 63 \\ \hline \end{array}$$

11
$$\begin{array}{r} 59 \\ \times\ 61 \\ \hline \end{array}$$

12
$$\begin{array}{r} 57 \\ \times\ 19 \\ \hline \end{array}$$

13 The local produce store received an order for 75 bags of potatoes. 30 potatoes can fit into each bag. How many potatoes will the store need to fill the bags?

_____

14 Steven is organizing his stamp collection into large envelopes. He plans to place 60 stamps in each envelope. If he can fill 22 envelopes, how many stamps are in Steven's stamp collection?

_____

Estimating Products

What if you want just a *pretty good* idea of the product?

Example:
$$515 \times 39$$

Step 1: Round both numbers. 500×40

Step 2: Ignore the zeros and multiply the digits.
$5 \times 4 = 20$

Step 3: Count the zeros and tack them onto the end of your product.
$515 \times 39 = $ about 20,000

Is that more or less than the real product? You do not know, because you rounded 515 *downward* and you rounded 39 *upward*. If you round both numbers *upward*, your estimate will be *greater* than the real product. And if you round both numbers *downward*, your estimate will be *less* than the real product.

Example: 39×58
That rounds to $40 \times 60 = 2400$. That product is definitely *greater* than the real product because you rounded both numbers *upward*.

Exercises   ESTIMATE

1 34×71

2 456×33

3 47×67

4 731×55

5 78×357

6 129×157

7 323×489

8 417×37

9 53×49

10 515×79

11 745×821

12 475×71

13 2701×23

14 77×74

15 521×555

16 303×251

17 727×462

18 92×177

19 42×420

20 499×55

Dividing Whole Numbers

Do you work a division problem differently than an addition, subtraction, or multiplication problem? Yes. In division, you work from left to right, *not* from right to left!

To understand what that means, you have to learn some terms used in division. The number to be divided is called the **dividend**. The number that goes into the dividend is called the **divisor**. The answer is called the **quotient**. It shows the number of times the divisor goes into the dividend. If you have a remainder, add a decimal point and a zero to the quotient and divide again. Keep dividing until there is no remainder or the decimal part of the quotient begins repeating.

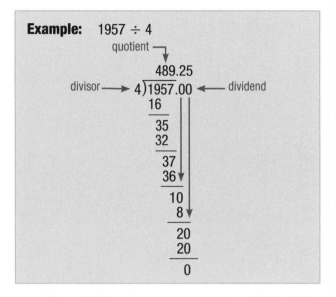

Example: 1957 ÷ 4

Remember...

Your remainder must be *less* than the divisor. If it is not, go back and check your work.

Exercises   DIVIDE AND ROUND TO THE NEAREST HUNDREDTH

1 7)395

2 21)950

3 12)9475

4 36)18,980

5 13)8307

6 44)2000

7 3)256

8 22)803

9 A tailor can repair about 20 garments in a day. How many days will it take him to repair 300 garments?

_____

10 Ms. Bailey is making information packets for all attendees at an education seminar. Each packet contains a total of 28 pages. If Ms. Bailey uses 1400 sheets of paper, how many people plan to attend the education seminar?

_____

Name _____

Estimating Quotients

What if you need only a *fairly good* idea of a quotient?

You do not use rounding to estimate a quotient. Instead, you find **compatible numbers**, numbers that you can work with easily in your head.

Example: 41297 ÷ 5

Step 1: Look at the two highest digits in the dividend, 41. This cannot be evenly divided by 5, so you will round to the closest compatible number, 40.

Step 2: 40 ÷ 5 = 8

Step 3: Add placeholder zeros to the estimated quotient for the place values you ignored in the original dividend.

41297 ÷ 5 is about 8000

Exercises   ESTIMATE

1 456 ÷ 8

2 2112 ÷ 11

3 674 ÷ 8

4 4657 ÷ 15

5 35,734 ÷ 12

6 4252 ÷ 9

7 67,891 ÷ 16

8 321 ÷ 19

9 682 ÷ 35

10 92,099 ÷ 34

11 678 ÷ 22

12 6578 ÷ 34

13 789 ÷ 28

14 4591 ÷ 17

15 7777 ÷ 44

16 456 ÷ 7

17 96,291 ÷ 31

18 91,111 ÷ 47

19 69,103 ÷ 41

20 13,401 ÷ 11

Order of Operations

What happens if you see a long string of mathematical calculations to perform? Is there some way to know where to begin? Yes, you can use a rule called **order of operations**. It tells you in what order you should do calculations in a long string.

There is even a simple word that can help you remember the order of operations: **PEMDAS**. That stands for **P**arentheses, **E**xponents, **M**ultiplication and **D**ivision, **A**ddition and **S**ubtraction.

Example:

Solve: $20 - 5 \times 2 + 36 \div 3^2 - (9 - 2) = ?$

You can solve this problem using order of operations. Remember PEMDAS.

Step 1: Parentheses
$(9 - 2) = 7$
$20 - 5 \times 2 + 36 \div 3^2 - 7 = ?$

Step 2: Exponents
$3^2 = 9$
$20 - 5 \times 2 + 36 \div 9 - 7 = ?$

Step 3: Multiplication and Division
$5 \times 2 = 10$
$36 \div 9 = 4$
$20 - 10 + 4 - 7 = ?$

Step 4: Addition and Subtraction
$20 - 10 = 10$
$10 + 4 = 14$
$14 - 7 = 7$

Exercises   CALCULATE

1 $(4 + 2) \times (4 - 2) - (2 \times 3) + 2^{4-2} =$

2 $(5 - 4) \times (10 - 6) - 2^2 + 4 =$

3 $(4 - 2)^3 + (4 - 2)^2 + 1 - 2 + 2^2 =$

4 $(4 + 2) \times (9 - 7) + 3^2 - (8 - 5)^2 =$

5 $(6 - 4)^3 - (6 - 4)^3 + 2 - (2 - 1) =$

6 $2^2 - (2^3 - 2) + (2^2 + 4) =$

7 $(5 - 2) + (6 - 4) - (3 - 1) =$

8 $(4 + 3) \times (5 - 2) \times (2 - 1)^2 =$

9 $(4 - 2) + (5 \times 2)^2 - 2 \times 12 - 4^2 =$

10 $(1 + 1 + 2) \times 7 - 4^2 =$

11 $(13 - 2) - 3^2 + 10 - (2 \times 4) =$

12 $7^2 + (4 - 1) \times 5 - 2 \times (3 - 1)^3 =$

4.2

Commutative and Associative Properties

Are there other rules to use that make math easier? Yes, you can learn the ways numbers behave, or the **properties** of numbers.

Commutative Property of Addition
You can add addends *in any order* without changing the sum.
$7 + 3 + 6 = 6 + 3 + 7$

Commutative Property of Multiplication
You can multiply factors *in any order* without changing the product.
$5 \times 2 \times 9 = 9 \times 5 \times 2$

Associative Property of Addition
You can group addends any way you like without changing the sum.
$(7 + 8) + 3 = 7 + (8 + 3)$

Associative Property of Multiplication
You can group factors any way you like without changing the product.
$(3 \times 12) \times 4 = 3 \times (12 \times 4)$

Exercises   IDENTIFY THE PROPERTY

1 $7 \times 4 \times 3 = 4 \times 3 \times 7$

_____

2 $2 + 9 + 22 = 22 + 9 + 2$

_____

3 $3 \times 4 \times 4 \times 2 = 3 \times (4 \times 4) \times 2$

_____

4 $4 \times 2 \times 3 \times 4 = 2 \times 3 \times 4 \times 4$

_____

5 $9 \times 2 \times 4 = 2 \times 4 \times 9$

_____

6 $9 \times 7 \times 9 \times 9 = (9 \times 7) \times (9 \times 9)$

_____

7 $9 + 7 + 1 = 7 + 9 + 1$

_____

8 $4 \times 11 \times 9 \times 4 = 4 \times 4 \times 9 \times 11$

_____

9 $2 + 8 + 6 + 4 = (2 + 8) + (6 + 4)$

_____

10 $6 \times 4 \times 2 = 4 \times 2 \times 6$

_____

11 $22 + 21 + 24 + 22 = 22 + (21 + 24) + 22$

_____

12 $6 \times 8 + 6 \times 0 = 8 \times 6 + 0 \times 6$

_____

The Distributive and Identity Properties

Do numbers have other properties, too? Yes!

The Distributive Property of Multiplication

To multiply a sum of two or more numbers, you can multiply by each number separately, and then *add* the products. To multiply the difference of two numbers, multiply separately and *subtract* the products.

Identity Elements are numbers in a problem that do not affect the answer. When adding, the identity element is 0, because any addend or addends + 0 will not change the total.

In multiplication, the identity element is 1, because any factor or factors × 1 will not change the product.

However, subtraction and division do not have identity elements.

Example:

$9 \times (2 + 5) = (9 \times 2) + (9 \times 5)$

You can also use the Distributive Property of Multiplication for dividing, but *only* if the numbers you are adding or subtracting are in the **dividend**.

$(28 + 8) \div 4 = (28 \div 4) + (8 \div 4)$

You *cannot* use the Distributive Property when the numbers you are adding or subtracting are in the **divisor**.

$28 \div (4 + 2)$ *does not* $= (28 \div 4) + (28 \div 2)$

Remember...

Addition and multiplication both have identity elements. Division and subtraction do not have identity elements.

Exercises SOLVE

1 $0 + 6 =$

2 $4(4 + 3) =$

3 $7 + 0 =$

4 $4(2 + 3 + 4) =$

5 $15(7 + 3) =$

6 $6(5 + 0) =$

7 $3 \times 4 + 2 \times 9 =$

8 $(4 + 8)4 =$

9 $34 + 0 + 7 =$

10 $35(2 + 3 + 0) =$

11 $0 + 7 + 7 + 0 =$

12 $5(33 - 11) =$

13 $(64 - 28)2 =$

14 $7 - 0 + 0 - 7 =$

15 $8(15 + 2 - 15) =$

Zero Property, Equality Properties

Do numbers have any other properties?

Yes, and learning them will make studying mathematics easier.

Zero Property of Multiplication:

Any number $\times$ 0 = 0.

Remember that an equation is a mathematical statement that two things are equal.

$(6 + 4) = (9 + 1)$

Equality Property of Addition: You can keep an equation equal if you add *the same number* to both sides.

$(6 + 4) + 3 = (9 + 1) + 3$

Equality Property of Subtraction: You can keep an equation equal if you subtract *the same number* from both sides.

$(6 + 4) - 5 = (9 + 1) - 5$

Equality Property of Multiplication: You can keep an equation equal if you multiply both sides by *the same number.*

$(6 + 4) \times 10 = (9 + 1) \times 10$

Equality Property of Division: You can keep an equation equal if you divide both sides by *the same number.*

$(6 + 4) \div 2 = (9 + 1) \div 2$

Remember, you may never divide by 0.

Exercises   SOLVE

1 $5 \times 0 =$

2 $0 (1 + 4) =$

3 $0 \times 1.111 =$

4 $7 (0 + 5) =$

5 $0 \times 0 \times 3 \times 9 =$

6 $233.31 \times 0 =$

7 $0 \times 200.893 =$

8 $0 \times 0 + 2 =$

9 $0 (2 + 0) =$

For questions 10–13, answer yes or no and briefly explain your answer.

10 If $8 + 1 = 6 + 3$, then does
$4 (8 + 1) = 4 (6 + 3)$?

_____

_____

11 If $6 \times 9 = 54$, then does
$4 + (6 \times 9) = 54 + 4$?

_____

_____

12 If $\frac{1}{5} = \frac{3}{15}$, then does
$\frac{1}{5} - 5 = \frac{3}{15} - 5$?

_____

_____

13 If $5 - 1 = 20 \times 0.2$, then does
$\frac{(5 - 1)}{22} = \frac{(20 \times 0.2)}{22}$?

_____

_____

Negative Numbers

Are any numbers less than zero? Yes. They are called **negative numbers**. To show a negative number, put a minus sign in front of the number.

On this number line, a negative number falls to the left of zero, while a positive number falls to its right. 0 is neither positive nor negative.

Notice that both −4 and 4 are four spaces away from zero, but in opposite directions on the number line. We say that −4 is the **inverse** of 4, and vice versa.

The Property of Additive Inverses:

When you add a negative number to its inverse, the total is 0. For example: −34 + 34 = 0.

Number Line

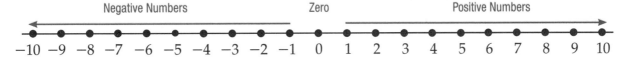

Negative Numbers   Zero   Positive Numbers

−10 −9 −8 −7 −6 −5 −4 −3 −2 −1 0 1 2 3 4 5 6 7 8 9 10

Exercises   ADD

1 $(-4) + 4 =$

_____

2 $(-110) + 210 =$

_____

3 $(-9) + 17 + 9 + (-17) =$

_____

4 $145 + (-125) =$

_____

5 $48 + (-38) =$

_____

6 $(-75) + 55 + 732 + (-712) =$

_____

7 $\frac{1}{4} + (-\frac{1}{4}) =$

_____

8 $541 + 641 + (-741) + (-641) =$

_____

9 $44 + (-77) + 0 =$

_____

10 $16 + \frac{1}{4} + (-\frac{1}{4}) + (-10) =$

_____

5.2

Name _____

Absolute Value

The absolute value of a number is that number's distance from zero on a number line. It does not matter whether the number is positive or negative. Absolute value is simply how far the number is from zero in either direction. For example, −3 and +3 have the same absolute value because they are both a distance of 3 away from zero on the number line. Absolute value is written as |−3| = 3 or |+3| = 3. An absolute value of 3 does not tell you whether the number is positive or negative; it just means that the number is 3 away from zero.

Examples:

$$|-2| = 2$$

$$|7.8| = 7.8$$

$$|-328.9| = 328.9$$

Exercises SOLVE

① $|-9| =$ _____

② $|-567| =$ _____

③ $|48| =$ _____

④ $|-0.24| =$ _____

⑤ $\left|\dfrac{-7}{8}\right| =$ _____

⑥ $\left|\dfrac{1}{3}\right| =$ _____

Compare using <, >, or =

⑦ $|-2|$ _____ $|-8|$

⑧ $|56|$ _____ $|-56|$

⑨ $|-12|$ _____ $|-3|$

⑩ $|-4|$ _____ $|567|$

⑪ $|35|$ _____ $|-98|$

⑫ $|6789|$ _____ $|6799|$

Solve

⑬ If Kim's bank account balance is $ −12.48, how much would she need to deposit in order to bring her balance to $100.00? _____

⑭ If gas prices were $1.20 above average in March and $1.36 below average in April, which month was further from its average price? _____

⑮ Bella's bank account balance is $15.00. If she spends $12.86 on a shirt and $3.24 on a bracelet, what is her new balance? _____

Adding and Subtracting with Negative Numbers

Can you add and subtract negative numbers? Yes, but to do this you have to know about **absolute value**. Absolute value is the number without its sign. It represents the distance between the number and 0 on the number line.

Examples:

$$-10 + 7 = -3 \qquad -6 + 8 = 2$$
$$(-3) + (-8) = -11$$

Remember...

To subtract one negative number from another, change the second number to its inverse and *add*.

To add two negative numbers, add their absolute values, and put a minus sign in front of the total. To add a negative and a positive number, find their absolute values, then subtract the smaller one from the greater one. Your answer will have the same sign as the number with the greater absolute value.

Examples:

$(-6) - (+7)$	equals	$(-6) + (-7) = -13$
$(-3) - (-8) = 5$	equals	$(-3) + (+8) = 5$
$(-8) + (+3) = -5$	equals	$(-8) - (-3) = -5$

Exercises ADD

1 $17 + (-3) =$ _____

2 $(-15) + 6 =$ _____

3 $1 + (-12) =$ _____

4 $75 + (-36) =$ _____

5 $110 + (-56) + 14 =$ _____

6 $95 + (-65) + (-1) =$ _____

7 $(-20) + (-20) + 7 =$ _____

8 $51 + (-33) + 20 =$ _____

9 $30 + (-22) =$ _____

10 $18 + 18 + (-18) =$ _____

11 $(-25) + 14 =$ _____

12 $80 + 13 + 29 + (-100) =$ _____

13 $57 + (-39) + 10 =$ _____

14 $(-23) + 63 + (-9) =$ _____

15 $4 + 2 + (-7) + (-1) =$ _____

16 $1 + (-9) + 9 =$ _____

Name _____

Multiplying and Dividing with Negative Numbers

Negative numbers can also be multiplied and divided. You need to remember these two rules:

- When two numbers have the same sign, either negative or positive, their product or quotient is *positive*.

- When two numbers have different signs, one negative and one positive, their product or quotient is *negative*.

Examples:

$5 \times 4 = 20$	$(-5) \times (-4) = 20$
$(-5) \times 4 = -20$	$5 \times (-4) = -20$
$6 \div 2 = 3$	$(-6) \div (-2) = 3$
$(-6) \div 2 = -3$	$6 \div (-2) = -3$

Exercises   **MULTIPLY OR DIVIDE**

1 $5 \times (-3) =$ _____

2 $13 \times (-10) =$ _____

3 $100 \times (-1) =$ _____

4 $23 \times (-3) =$ _____

5 $15 \times (-15) =$ _____

6 $(-12) \times 20 =$ _____

7 $(-2) \times (-4) =$ _____

8 $(-1) \times 1 =$ _____

9 $(-125) \times (-1) =$ _____

10 $(-3) \times 103 =$ _____

11 $(-20) \div 20 =$ _____

12 $(-22) \times 0 =$ _____

13 $(-3) \times (-1) =$ _____

14 $(-12) \div 4 =$ _____

15 $15 \div (-3) =$ _____

16 $(-27) \div (-9 \div \frac{1}{9}) =$ _____

Name _____

Challenge Questions

Let's see if you can apply your skills to a couple of really challenging questions. Ready?

1) The price of a loaf of bread at the corner store varies by no more than 5 cents from its original price of $2.29. Which of the following could be the total price for two loaves of bread?

$4.45

$4.57

$4.69

$4.75

2) $72 \div [3 \times (2 \times 6)] + (-7 \times 2)$

Answers and Explanations are on p. 220.

Lessons 1-5

Add or subtract.

1
```
  266
+  45
```

2
```
  447
+  58
```

3
```
  887
-  49
```

4
```
  1468
-  249
```

Round to the nearest thousand, then add or subtract.

5
```
    6234
+ 14,788
```

6
```
  12,661
  44,867
+  9059
```

7
```
  9870
- 1294
```

8
```
  17,650
-  3760
```

Unit Test

Lessons 1–5

Multiply or divide. Round to the nearest hundredth.

9   168
        × 19

10   276
        × 81

11   24$)\overline{504}$

12   16$)\overline{932}$

Round, then multiply or divide.

13   918
      × 84

14   9604
      × 31

15   77,453
      × 284

16   13,845
      × 366

17   79,867
      × 578

18   124$)\overline{383}$

19   175$)\overline{1025}$

20   95$)\overline{1885}$

21   73$)\overline{8898}$

22   96$)\overline{98,455}$

Name _____

Lessons 1–5

Give the place value of the number 7 for questions 23–26.

23 1,845,732   **24** 45.357   **25** 73,561,132.001   **26** 20.075

_____   _____   _____   _____

27 Parks Commissioner Davis is planning for the town's upcoming fiscal year. Last year the town had a total of 2435 visitors to its nature center, 7693 visitors to its children's park, and 9287 visitors to its arboretum. How many visitors did the town's parks have, in total, last year?

_____

28 Last year Trey had 435 coins in his collection. This year Trey added 124 more coins to his collection. How many coins does he now have in his collection?

_____

29 Edie's favorite magazine has a total of 1476 pages of advertising each year. If the magazine is published every month, about how many pages of advertising are in each issue?

_____

How many pages exactly?

_____

30 At 1776 feet in height, the new Freedom Tower in New York will be one of the tallest buildings in the world. What is the height of the building written in expanded form?

_____

31 What is the word form of the number 19,238,976?

_____

_____

Calculate using order of operations (PEMDAS).

32 $5 \times (7 - 3)^2 + (19 - 5) \times 2 + (6 - 3) \times 2 + 2^3$

33 $29 + (3 \times 5) \times 2 + (8 - 3)^2$

34 $63(0) + (63 + 0) =$

_____

Name _____

Lessons 1-5

Solve each equation and indicate the point on the number line that corresponds with the answer.

35 $-6 + 10 - 6 =$ _____

36 $-10 + 5 - 4 =$ _____

37 $-10 + (-4) + 8 =$ _____

38 $9 - 5 + (-8) =$ _____

Calculate.

39 -5×15

40 $-45 \div 9$

41 $63 \div (-7)$

42 $4 \times (-6) \div -3$

43 Calculate: $|-45| + |45|$ _____

44 Which is larger: $|-134|$ or $|-135|$? _____

45 If Noah arrives 23 minutes late for an appointment and Matthew arrives 28 minutes early, who arrived closer to the correct time? _____
_____

Unit Test

Answers and Explanations

1. 311
$$\begin{array}{r} {}^{1\,1}\\ 266 \\ +\ \ 45 \\ \hline 311 \end{array}$$

2. 505
$$\begin{array}{r} {}^{1\,1}\\ 447 \\ +\ \ 58 \\ \hline 505 \end{array}$$

3. 838
$$\begin{array}{r} {}^{1\,1}\\ 8\!\!\not{8}7 \\ -\ \ 49 \\ \hline 838 \end{array}$$

4. 1219
$$\begin{array}{r} {}^{5\,1}\\ 14\!\!\not{6}8 \\ -\ \ 249 \\ \hline 1219 \end{array}$$

5. 21,000
$$\begin{array}{r} {}^{1}\ \ 6000 \\ +\ 15,000 \\ \hline 21,000 \end{array}$$

6. 67,000
$$\begin{array}{r} {}^{1}\ 13,000 \\ 45,000 \\ +\ \ 9000 \\ \hline 67,000 \end{array}$$

7. 9000
$$\begin{array}{r} 10,000 \\ -\ \ 1000 \\ \hline 9000 \end{array}$$

8. 14,000
$$\begin{array}{r} 18,000 \\ -\ \ 4000 \\ \hline 14000 \end{array}$$

9. 3192
$$\begin{array}{r} {}^{6\,7}\\ 168 \\ \times\ \ 19 \\ \hline {}^{1}\ 1512 \\ 1680 \\ \hline 3192 \end{array}$$

10. 22,356
$$\begin{array}{r} {}^{6\,4}\\ 276 \\ \times\ \ 81 \\ \hline {}^{1}\ 276 \\ 22,080 \\ \hline 22,356 \end{array}$$

11. 21
$$\begin{array}{r} 21\ \ \ \\ 24\overline{)504} \\ 48\ \ \ \\ \hline 24 \\ 24 \\ \hline 0 \end{array}$$

12. 58.25
$$\begin{array}{r} 58.25 \\ 16\overline{)932.00} \\ 80\downarrow \\ \hline 132 \\ 128\downarrow \\ \hline 40 \\ 32\downarrow \\ \hline 80 \\ 80 \\ \hline 0 \end{array}$$

13. 72,000
$$\begin{array}{r} 900 \\ \times\ \ 80 \\ \hline 72,000 \end{array}$$

14. 300,000
$$\begin{array}{r} 10,000 \\ \times\ \ \ \ 30 \\ \hline 300,000 \end{array}$$

15. 24,000,000
$$\begin{array}{r} 80,000 \\ \times\ \ \ \ 300 \\ \hline 24,000,000 \end{array}$$

16. 5,600,000
$$\begin{array}{r} 14,000 \\ \times\ \ \ \ 400 \\ \hline 5,600,000 \end{array}$$

17. 48,000,000
$$\begin{array}{r} 80,000 \\ \times\ \ \ \ 600 \\ \hline 48,000,000 \end{array}$$

18. 3
$$\begin{array}{r} 3 \\ 125\overline{)375} \\ 375 \\ \hline 0 \end{array}$$

19. 6
$$\begin{array}{r} 6 \\ 175\overline{)1050} \\ 1050 \\ \hline 0 \end{array}$$

20. 20
$$\begin{array}{r} 20 \\ 95\overline{)1900} \\ 190 \\ \hline 0 \end{array}$$

21. 125
$$\begin{array}{r} 125 \\ 75\overline{)9000} \\ 72\ \ \\ \hline 180 \\ 144 \\ \hline 360 \\ 360 \\ \hline 0 \end{array}$$

22. 1000
$$\begin{array}{r} 1000 \\ 75\overline{)95,000} \\ 95\ \ \ \ \\ \hline 0 \end{array}$$

Unit Test

23. Hundreds

24. Thousandths

25. Ten millions

26. Hundreths

27. 19415 visitors

$$\begin{array}{r} {\scriptstyle 1\ 2\ 1}\\ 2435\\ 7693\\ +\ \ 9287\\ \hline 19,415 \end{array}$$

28. 559 coins

$$\begin{array}{r} 435\\ +\ 124\\ \hline 559 \end{array}$$

29. About 120 pages;

$$12\overline{)1440}$$ quotient 120

$$\begin{array}{r} 120\\ 12\overline{)1440}\\ \underline{12}\\ 24\\ \underline{24}\\ 0 \end{array}$$

123 pages

$$\begin{array}{r} 123\\ 12\overline{)1476}\\ \underline{12}\\ 27\\ \underline{24}\\ 36\\ \underline{36}\\ 0 \end{array}$$

30. $(1 \times 1000) + (7 \times 100) + (7 \times 10) + (6 \times 1)$

31. Nineteen million, two hundred thirty-eight thousand, nine hundred seventy-six

32. 122

$5 \times (4^2) + 14 \times 2 + 3 \times 2 + 2^3 =$

$5 \times 16 + 14 \times 2 + 3 \times 2 + 8 =$

$80 + 28 + 6 + 8 = 122$

33. 84

$29 + 15 \times 2 + 5^2 =$

$29 + 15 \times 2 + 25 =$

$29 + 30 + 25 = 84$

34. 63

$63(0) + (63) = 0 + 63 = 63$

35. D

36. C

37. B

38. A

39. -75

$$\begin{array}{r} {\scriptstyle 2}\\ -15\\ \times\ \ \ \ 5\\ \hline -75 \end{array}$$

40. -5

$\dfrac{-45}{9} = -5$

41. -9

$\dfrac{63}{-7} = -9$

42. 8

$4 \times -6 = -24;\ \dfrac{-24}{-3} = 8$

43. 90

$45 + 45 = 90$

44. $|-135|$

$134 < 135$

45. Noah

$|23| < |28|$

6.1

Changing Improper Fractions to Mixed Numbers

What words must you know to talk about fractions? You have to know that the number on the bottom is the **denominator**, which tells what kind of units the whole is divided into. The number on the top is the **numerator**, which tells how many of those units there are.

A fraction is less than 1 when the numerator is less than the denominator. A fraction is equal to 1 when the numerator is the same as the denominator. A fraction is *greater* than 1 when the numerator is greater than the denominator. Any fraction greater than 1 is an **improper fraction**. It can be changed into a **mixed number**, which is part whole number and part fraction.

Example: Change $\frac{13}{4}$ to a mixed number.

Step 1: $13 \div 4 = 3 \, R1$

So $\frac{13}{4} = 3\frac{1}{4}$

Exercises CHANGE TO MIXED NUMBERS

1. $\frac{44}{3}$

2. $\frac{91}{4}$

3. $\frac{5}{2}$

4. $\frac{22}{3}$

5. $\frac{55}{12}$

6. $-\frac{107}{11}$

7. $\frac{156}{16}$

8. $\frac{31}{8}$

9. $\frac{101}{21}$

10. $\frac{33}{2}$

11. $\frac{47}{11}$

12. $-\frac{202}{19}$

13. $\frac{78}{8}$

14. $\frac{47}{7}$

15. $-\frac{147}{12}$

16. $\frac{260}{16}$

17. $\frac{58}{3}$

18. $-\frac{77}{4}$

19. $\frac{133}{12}$

20. $\frac{345}{7}$

Changing Mixed Numbers to Improper Fractions

You know that you can change an improper fraction to a mixed number. You can also change a mixed number into an improper fraction. First, multiply the whole number by the denominator of the fraction. Then, add the numerator to that product. Finally, place the total over the denominator.

Example: Change $8\frac{3}{5}$ into an improper fraction

Step 1: $8 \times 5 = 40$

Step 2: $40 + 3 = 43$ So $8\frac{3}{5} = \frac{43}{5}$

Exercises   CHANGE TO IMPROPER FRACTIONS

1 $3\frac{1}{4}$ **2** $-5\frac{3}{7}$ **3** $12\frac{3}{11}$ **4** $14\frac{3}{5}$

5 $1\frac{2}{13}$ **6** $21\frac{3}{14}$ **7** $33\frac{1}{9}$ **8** $-4\frac{1}{17}$

9 $102\frac{1}{7}$ **10** $-32\frac{1}{2}$ **11** $29\frac{1}{29}$ **12** $37\frac{3}{8}$

13 $15\frac{2}{3}$ **14** $61\frac{5}{14}$ **15** $7\frac{2}{17}$ **16** $-6\frac{3}{22}$

17 $23\frac{2}{3}$ **18** $15\frac{4}{7}$ **19** $-13\frac{1}{13}$ **20** $4\frac{4}{44}$

Name _____

Adding Fractions with Like Denominators

Can you add fractions that have the same denominator? Two denominators that are exactly the same are called **like denominators**. They are easy to add, because you can ignore the denominators when adding!

Example: $\frac{5}{9} + \frac{2}{9}$

Step 1: Add the numerators. $5 + 2 = 7$

Step 2: Place the total over the like denominator.
So $\frac{5}{9} + \frac{2}{9} = \frac{7}{9}$

Exercises   ADD

1 $\frac{1}{2} + \frac{1}{2}$

2 $\frac{4}{5} + \frac{3}{5}$

3 $\frac{7}{8} + \frac{3}{8}$

4 $\frac{6}{7} + \frac{2}{7}$

5 $\frac{10}{11} + \frac{14}{11}$

6 $\frac{71}{17} + \frac{3}{17}$

7 $\frac{4}{9} + \frac{34}{9}$

8 $\frac{2}{3} + \frac{7}{3}$

9 $\begin{array}{r} \frac{4}{23} \\ + \frac{54}{23} \end{array}$

10 $\begin{array}{r} \frac{3}{37} \\ + \frac{54}{37} \end{array}$

11 $\begin{array}{r} \frac{3}{4} \\ + \frac{5}{4} \end{array}$

12 $\begin{array}{r} \frac{7}{11} \\ + \frac{5}{11} \end{array}$

13 $\begin{array}{r} \frac{5}{27} \\ + \frac{10}{27} \end{array}$

14 $\begin{array}{r} \frac{3}{4} \\ + \frac{13}{4} \end{array}$

15 $\begin{array}{r} \frac{23}{24} \\ + \frac{19}{24} \end{array}$

16 $\begin{array}{r} \frac{3}{37} \\ + \frac{10}{37} \end{array}$

Name _____

Subtracting Fractions with Like Denominators

Do you use the same kind of process to subtract fractions with like denominators? Yes, exactly! Ignore the denominator when doing your work.

To add or subtract fractions with like denominators, you only need to work with the numerators. Don't forget to put your total or difference over the same denominator.

Example: $\frac{14}{17} - \frac{9}{17}$

Step 1: $14 - 9 = 5$

So $\frac{14}{17} - \frac{9}{17} = \frac{5}{17}$

Exercises   SUBTRACT

1 $\frac{3}{4} - \frac{1}{4}$

2 $\frac{7}{8} - \frac{5}{8}$

3 $\frac{7}{4} - \frac{1}{4}$

4 $\frac{14}{5} - \frac{8}{5}$

5 $\frac{33}{7} - \frac{29}{7}$

6 $\frac{9}{11} - \frac{7}{11}$

7 $\frac{14}{3} - \frac{7}{3}$

8 $\frac{21}{19} - \frac{13}{19}$

9 $\frac{12}{5} - \frac{2}{5}$

10 $\frac{23}{7} - \frac{17}{7}$

11 $\frac{45}{8} - \frac{37}{8}$

12 $\frac{12}{51} - \frac{4}{51}$

13 $\frac{43}{13} - \frac{14}{13}$

14 $\frac{56}{17} - \frac{35}{17}$

15 $\frac{7}{4} - \frac{3}{4}$

16 $\frac{32}{37} - \frac{14}{37}$

Name ______________________________

Adding or Subtracting Fractions with Unlike Denominators

Can you add or subtract fractions if the denominators are different? Yes you can, but first you have to change your fractions so that they have a **common denominator**. This is another term for like denominator.

When you find a common multiple, take one fraction at a time. Multiply the original denominator to make it become the common denominator, and multiply the numerator by the same number. When you multiply the numerator *and* the denominator of a fraction by the same number, you do *not* change the value of the fraction.

Example: $\frac{5}{8} + \frac{1}{6}$

Step 1: Find a common multiple for both denominators. 24

Step 2: Multiply both the numerator and the denominator by the number that will make the denominator equal the common multiple. Do this for both fractions.

$\frac{5}{8} = \frac{5 \times 3}{8 \times 3}$ $\frac{1}{6} = \frac{4 \times 1}{4 \times 6}$

Step 3: Add the fractions. $\frac{15}{24} + \frac{4}{24} = \frac{19}{24}$

Remember...

Once you find a common denominator, the calculations are easy!

Exercises **ADD OR SUBTRACT**

1. $\frac{1}{4} + \frac{1}{5}$
2. $\frac{2}{7} + \frac{2}{3}$
3. $\frac{21}{20} + \frac{1}{3}$
4. $\frac{12}{13} - \frac{1}{2}$
5. $\frac{3}{4} - \frac{1}{7}$
6. $\frac{23}{21} + \frac{1}{5}$
7. $\frac{32}{11} - \frac{2}{3}$
8. $\frac{12}{7} + \frac{2}{3}$
9. $\frac{8}{15} - \frac{1}{3}$
10. $\frac{7}{8} - \frac{2}{5}$
11. $\frac{54}{11} + \frac{2}{7}$
12. $\frac{13}{12} - \frac{4}{5}$
13. $\frac{56}{13} - \frac{2}{3}$
14. $\frac{3}{4} - \frac{2}{5}$
15. $\frac{21}{4} - \frac{5}{2}$

Adding Mixed Numbers with Unlike Denominators

How do you add mixed numbers with unlike denominators? There are *two* ways to do this. In both ways, you will have to find a common denominator for the fractions.

One way is to change each mixed number to an improper fraction, then find the common denominator and add the fractions. The other way is even simpler. Just add the whole number parts first. Then find the common denominator for the fractions and add the fractions. Add the total fraction to your total whole number.

Example: $3\frac{2}{3} + 6\frac{1}{2}$

Step 1: Add the whole numbers. $3 + 6 = 9$

Step 2: Find a common denominator for the fractions. $\frac{2}{3} = \frac{4}{6}$ and $\frac{1}{2} = \frac{3}{6}$

Step 3: Add the fractions. $\frac{4}{6} + \frac{3}{6} = \frac{7}{6} = 1\frac{1}{6}$

Step 4: Add the sum of the fractions to the sum of the whole numbers.
$$3\frac{2}{3} + 6\frac{1}{2} = 9 + 1\frac{1}{6} = 10\frac{1}{6}$$

Exercises   ADD MIXED NUMBERS

1 $2\frac{1}{2} + 3\frac{1}{4}$

2 $3\frac{2}{3} + 4\frac{3}{7}$

3 $4\frac{5}{6} + 7\frac{3}{4}$

4 $3\frac{3}{4} + 2\frac{1}{3}$

5 $9\frac{1}{2} + 4\frac{1}{5}$

6 $54\frac{1}{2} + 14\frac{2}{3}$

7 $10\frac{5}{7} + 12\frac{2}{3}$

8 $4\frac{2}{9} + 3\frac{2}{7}$

9 $13\frac{4}{5} + 4\frac{3}{11}$

10 $23\frac{1}{6} + 57\frac{3}{13}$

11 $22\frac{3}{11} + 14\frac{2}{5}$

12 $4\frac{5}{7} + 3\frac{1}{3}$

13 $\begin{array}{r} 5\frac{1}{4} \\ + \ 7\frac{2}{15} \\ \hline \end{array}$

14 $\begin{array}{r} 102\frac{5}{6} \\ + \ 355\frac{1}{11} \\ \hline \end{array}$

15 $\begin{array}{r} 56\frac{1}{3} \\ + \ 89\frac{5}{14} \\ \hline \end{array}$

16 $\begin{array}{r} 21\frac{1}{2} \\ + \ 122\frac{3}{8} \\ \hline \end{array}$

Name _____

Subtracting Mixed Numbers with Unlike Denominators

How do you subtract mixed numbers with unlike denominators? You do the same thing you do when you add mixed numbers with unlike denominators. You find a common denominator for the fractions.

Example: $12\frac{5}{7} - 9\frac{2}{5}$

Step 1: Subtract the whole numbers. $12 - 9 = 3$

Step 2: Find a common denominator for the fractions. $\frac{5}{7} = \frac{25}{35}$ and $\frac{2}{5} = \frac{14}{35}$

Step 3: Subtract the fractions. $\frac{25}{35} - \frac{14}{35} = \frac{11}{35}$

Step 4: *Add* the difference of the fractions to the difference of the whole numbers.

$3 + \frac{11}{35} = 3\frac{11}{35}$

If the difference in step 3 is less than zero, then you *will subtract* that number from the difference of the whole numbers.

Exercises SUBTRACT MIXED NUMBERS

1. $5\frac{1}{2} - 2\frac{1}{4}$

2. $10\frac{3}{7} - 4\frac{2}{11}$

3. $21\frac{5}{9} - 4\frac{2}{5}$

4. $13\frac{5}{6} - 10\frac{2}{9}$

5. $14\frac{2}{3} - 5\frac{1}{6}$

6. $21\frac{3}{4} - 11\frac{5}{9}$

7. $13\frac{5}{6} - 3\frac{1}{7}$

8. $43\frac{4}{5} - 29\frac{3}{11}$

9. $\begin{array}{r} 10\frac{6}{11} \\ -\ 4\frac{1}{2} \\ \hline \end{array}$

10. $\begin{array}{r} 13\frac{2}{3} \\ -\ 11\frac{5}{9} \\ \hline \end{array}$

11. $\begin{array}{r} 77\frac{2}{3} \\ -\ 41\frac{2}{17} \\ \hline \end{array}$

12. $\begin{array}{r} 19\frac{5}{7} \\ -\ 3\frac{1}{14} \\ \hline \end{array}$

13. Janelle practiced playing the piano $2\frac{1}{2}$ hours on Saturday. On Sunday, she practiced for $3\frac{1}{4}$ hours. How many more hours did Janelle practice on Sunday than on Saturday?

_____

14. Robby is helping his father make a casserole for dinner. They purchased $1\frac{1}{4}$ pounds of potatoes, and used $\frac{2}{3}$ pounds of potatoes to make one casserole. Do they have enough potatoes left over to make the casserole a second time?

_____

Estimating Sums and Differences of Fractions and Mixed Numbers

FRACTIONS What if you only need a *fairly good idea* of the sum or difference of some fractions?

Example: Estimate $\frac{4}{7} + \frac{9}{10} + \frac{1}{16}$

Step 1: Round each fraction to the nearest half number and complete the problem.

$$\frac{1}{2} + 1 + 0 = 1\frac{1}{2}$$

MIXED NUMBERS Can you estimate subtraction of mixed numbers, too? Of course! First, estimate the difference of the whole numbers.

Then estimate the difference of the fractions. Add your two estimates together.

Example: Estimate $62\frac{15}{16} - 28\frac{4}{7}$

Step 1: Estimate the difference of the whole numbers. $60 - 30 = 30$

Step 2: Estimate the difference of the fractions. $1 - \frac{1}{2} = \frac{1}{2}$

Step 3: Add the difference of the fractions to the difference of the whole numbers. $62\frac{15}{16} - 28\frac{4}{7}$ is about $30\frac{1}{2}$

Exercises   ESTIMATE SUMS AND DIFFERENCES

1 $12\frac{5}{8} + 23\frac{5}{6}$

2 $57\frac{2}{3} + 34\frac{5}{8}$

3 $81\frac{1}{8} + 29\frac{4}{5}$

4 $202\frac{1}{9} - 34\frac{3}{9}$

5 $5501\frac{3}{4} - 456\frac{3}{5}$

6 $457\frac{8}{13} - 98\frac{8}{13}$

7 $67\frac{4}{19} + 53\frac{9}{23}$

8 $189\frac{4}{5} + 321\frac{6}{7}$

9 $547\frac{17}{19} - 44\frac{4}{11}$

10 $49\frac{5}{6} + 51\frac{1}{7}$

11 $67\frac{2}{3} + 46\frac{9}{23}$

12 $456\frac{6}{7} - 145\frac{5}{14}$

13 James has $32\frac{1}{8}$ ounces of dog food. If he feeds each of his three dogs $6\frac{3}{4}$ ounces of food, about how much dog food will be left?

_____

14 Sherry is making cookies for her family's holiday gift baskets. She has already made $5\frac{1}{4}$ dozen cookies. If Sherry makes an additional $3\frac{1}{2}$ dozen cookies, about how many dozen cookies will go into the gift baskets?

_____

7.1

Multiplying Fractions and Whole Numbers

Is there a simple way to multiply a fraction by a whole number? Yes. Multiply the fraction's *numerator* by the whole number. Then write that product over the fraction's denominator. If the final fraction is an improper fraction, you may need to change it to a mixed number.

Example: $17 \times \frac{2}{3}$

Step 1: Multiply the whole number by the numerator. Place your answer over the denominator. $\frac{17 \times 2}{3} = \frac{34}{3}$

Step 2: Change your answer to a mixed number. $\frac{34}{3} = 11\frac{1}{3}$

Exercises MULTIPLY

1. $3 \times \frac{1}{4}$

2. $15 \times \frac{2}{7}$

3. $12 \times -\frac{3}{8}$

4. $22 \times \frac{3}{11}$

5. $15 \times -\frac{3}{20}$

6. $31 \times \frac{2}{17}$

7. $6 \times \frac{7}{24}$

8. $14 \times \frac{10}{11}$

9. $16 \times \frac{5}{36}$

10. $7 \times \frac{2}{3}$

11. $16 \times -\frac{3}{5}$

12. $11 \times \frac{11}{12}$

13. $42 \times \frac{5}{7}$

14. $20 \times \frac{3}{40}$

15. $32 \times \frac{5}{8}$

16. $15 \times -\frac{1}{15}$

17. $16 \times -\frac{3}{16}$

18. $3 \times \frac{1}{3}$

19. $45 \times \frac{13}{15}$

20. $7 \times \frac{4}{7}$

Multiplying Fractions; Reciprocals

Is it complicated to multiply two fractions? No, it is easy if you know how to multiply whole numbers. Just multiply the numerators to get the numerator of the product. Then multiply the denominators to get the denominator of the product.

Example: $\frac{3}{5} \times \frac{8}{9}$

Step 1: Multiply the numerators and the denominators. $3 \times 8 = 24, 5 \times 9 = 45$

Step 2: $\frac{3}{5} \times \frac{8}{9} = \frac{24}{45}$

If the fractions are **reciprocals**, you do not even have to multiply at all! Reciprocals are two fractions that look like each other upside-down. The numerator of the first is the denominator of the second and the numerator of the second is the denominator of the first.

The product of reciprocals is *always* 1.

Example: $\frac{3}{4} \times \frac{4}{3} = \frac{12}{12} = 1$

When you multiply fractions, you can **reduce** before you multiply. Thanks to the commutative property of multiplication, if *either one* of the numerators shares a common denominator with *either one* of the denominators, you can reduce them.

Example: $\frac{\cancel{14}^{2}}{17} \times \frac{3}{\cancel{7}_{1}} = \frac{6}{17}$

Exercises MULTIPLY

1 $\frac{1}{2} \times \frac{2}{3}$

2 $\frac{5}{7} \times \frac{3}{8}$

3 $\frac{20}{21} \times \frac{2}{5}$

4 $-\frac{3}{2} \times \frac{3}{2}$

5 $\frac{2}{3} \times \frac{3}{2}$

6 $-\frac{7}{4} \times \frac{16}{3}$

7 $\frac{5}{9} \times \frac{90}{10}$

8 $\frac{4}{7} \times \frac{3}{28}$

9 $\frac{3}{11} \times \frac{11}{3}$

10 $\frac{12}{13} \times \frac{39}{2}$

11 $-\frac{3}{8} \times -\frac{2}{13}$

12 $\frac{7}{8} \times \frac{16}{3}$

13 $-\frac{81}{7} \times -\frac{1}{9}$

14 $\frac{7}{3} \times \frac{3}{14}$

15 $\frac{15}{16} \times \frac{3}{5}$

16 $\frac{10}{13} \times \frac{52}{7}$

Name _____

Multiplying Mixed Numbers; Reducing

How do you multiply mixed numbers? Change each mixed number into an improper fraction, then multiply the fractions.

Many fractions can be reduced. **Reducing** changes a fraction into its simplest form. To reduce, find a number that divides evenly into both the numerator and denominator. Then divide *both* the numerator and the denominator by that number. In Step 2 of the example, both the numerator and the denominator of the multiplication product can be divided evenly by 5. You don't always have to wait until you finish multiplying to reduce. Sometimes you

can reduce *before* you multiply. If you are multiplying two fractions, look at both numerators and then at both denominators. If you can divide *either* numerator by the same number as *either* denominator, you can reduce.

Example: $1\frac{7}{10} \times 3\frac{3}{4}$

Step 1: $1\frac{7}{10} = \frac{17}{10}$, $3\frac{3}{4} = \frac{15}{4}$

Step 2: $\frac{17}{10} \times \frac{15}{4} = \frac{255}{40} = \frac{51}{8} = 6\frac{3}{8}$

Exercises   MULTIPLY

1 $5\frac{1}{4} \times \frac{1}{2}$

2 $\frac{1}{3} \times 5\frac{1}{3}$

3 $-12\frac{1}{4} \times \frac{3}{2}$

4 $3\frac{1}{7} \times \frac{14}{3}$

5 $-\frac{1}{5} \times 1\frac{3}{4}$

6 $6\frac{5}{7} \times \frac{2}{3}$

7 $4\frac{2}{5} \times \frac{3}{8}$

8 $3\frac{1}{4} \times \frac{5}{8}$

9 $3\frac{2}{5} \times \frac{5}{9}$

10 $\frac{1}{4} \times 4\frac{1}{3}$

11 $3\frac{2}{3} \times 1\frac{2}{7}$

12 $-4\frac{1}{5} \times -2\frac{3}{14}$

13 $5\frac{1}{4} \times 3\frac{1}{3}$

14 $-2\frac{4}{5} \times -4\frac{2}{7}$

15 $3\frac{3}{4} \times 3\frac{3}{10}$

16 $3\frac{1}{3} \times 3\frac{3}{5}$

Dividing Fractions by Whole Numbers

To divide a fraction by a whole number, multiply the denominator by the whole number.

Example: $\frac{7}{9} \div 3$

Step 1: Multiply the whole number by the denominator. $9 \times 3 = 27$

Step 2: Place the numerator over the product.
$$\frac{7}{9} \div 3 = \frac{7}{27}$$

Exercises DIVIDE

1 $-\frac{1}{2} \div 4$

2 $\frac{3}{5} \div 4$

3 $\frac{6}{7} \div 3$

4 $\frac{1}{5} \div 11$

5 $\frac{5}{19} \div 2$

6 $-\frac{4}{5} \div 7$

7 $\frac{1}{9} \div 9$

8 $\frac{3}{11} \div 12$

9 $\frac{17}{18} \div 4$

10 $\frac{12}{13} \div 3$

11 $\frac{2}{3} \div 6$

12 $-\frac{5}{11} \div 20$

13 $\frac{3}{7} \div 11$

14 $-\frac{1}{3} \div 9$

15 $\frac{10}{11} \div 5$

16 $\frac{10}{13} \div 4$

17 $\frac{4}{5} \div 4$

18 $\frac{12}{13} \div 5$

19 $-\frac{2}{11} \div 4$

20 $\frac{3}{4} \div 7$

8.2

Name _____

Dividing Whole Numbers by Fractions

Why do you multiply to divide a whole number by a fraction? Actually, to divide a whole number by a fraction, you multiply the whole number by the reciprocal of the fraction.

Example: $5 \div \frac{2}{3}$

Step 1: Multiply the whole number by the reciprocal of the fraction.

$$5 \times \frac{3}{2} = \frac{15}{2} = 7\frac{1}{2}$$

Exercises   DIVIDE

1 $5 \div \frac{1}{4}$

2 $3 \div -\frac{4}{5}$

3 $7 \div \frac{1}{7}$

4 $9 \div \frac{4}{7}$

5 $2 \div \frac{1}{2}$

6 $4 \div \frac{2}{7}$

7 $15 \div \frac{5}{7}$

8 $4 \div -\frac{2}{9}$

9 $17 \div -\frac{2}{3}$

10 $5 \div \frac{3}{5}$

11 $6 \div \frac{2}{3}$

12 $9 \div \frac{2}{3}$

13 $5 \div \frac{1}{11}$

14 $14 \div \frac{7}{2}$

15 $3 \div -\frac{1}{9}$

16 $3 \div \frac{7}{2}$

Dividing Fractions by Fractions

How do you divide a fraction by another fraction? Can you multiply by a reciprocal in that kind of problem? Yes! You multiply the first fraction by the reciprocal of the second.

Example: $\frac{3}{10} \div \frac{2}{3}$

$$\frac{3}{10} \times \frac{3}{2} = \frac{9}{20}$$

Exercises   DIVIDE

1 $\frac{5}{7} \div \frac{3}{4}$

2 $\frac{2}{3} \div \frac{2}{7}$

3 $\frac{1}{9} \div -\frac{3}{7}$

4 $\frac{3}{4} \div \frac{1}{9}$

5 $-\frac{3}{13} \div -\frac{2}{9}$

6 $\frac{1}{9} \div \frac{1}{3}$

7 $\frac{2}{13} \div \frac{1}{5}$

8 $\frac{3}{13} \div \frac{2}{13}$

9 $\frac{4}{3} \div \frac{1}{4}$

10 $\frac{15}{4} \div \frac{4}{3}$

11 $\frac{6}{7} \div \frac{1}{7}$

12 $\frac{3}{17} \div -\frac{4}{17}$

13 $\frac{1}{11} \div \frac{22}{3}$

14 $-\frac{3}{7} \div -\frac{1}{21}$

15 $\frac{5}{14} \div \frac{1}{7}$

16 $\frac{3}{4} \div \frac{8}{3}$

Name _____

Dividing Mixed Numbers

How can you use a reciprocal to divide a mixed number by another mixed number? A mixed number can be changed into an improper fraction. So change both mixed numbers into improper fractions. Then multiply the first fraction by the reciprocal of the second.

Remember...

Do not forget to simplify if you can. If necessary, change your answer from an improper fraction back to a mixed number.

Example: $3\frac{3}{5} \div 2\frac{3}{6}$

Step 1: Change to improper fractions.
$3\frac{2}{5} = \frac{18}{5}$, $2\frac{3}{6} = \frac{15}{6}$

Step 2: Multiply the first fraction by the reciprocal of the second. $\frac{18}{5} \times \frac{6}{15}$

Step 3: $18 \times 6 = 108$, $5 \times 15 = 75$

Step 4: Reduce your answer and convert to a mixed number. $\frac{108}{75} = \frac{36}{25} = 1\frac{11}{25}$

Exercises   DIVIDE

1. $1\frac{1}{3} \div -2\frac{1}{2}$

2. $3\frac{3}{5} \div 1\frac{1}{8}$

3. $7\frac{1}{7} \div 3\frac{1}{3}$

4. $3\frac{4}{7} \div 2\frac{2}{5}$

5. $6\frac{4}{5} \div 3\frac{2}{5}$

6. $5\frac{1}{2} \div 3\frac{3}{4}$

7. $4\frac{2}{9} \div 2\frac{4}{9}$

8. $-9\frac{2}{7} \div -2\frac{1}{2}$

9. $5\frac{6}{17} \div 2\frac{2}{3}$

10. $5\frac{3}{13} \div 2\frac{3}{4}$

11. $1\frac{3}{4} \div -4\frac{3}{5}$

12. $9\frac{3}{8} \div 1\frac{1}{4}$

13. $-44\frac{4}{5} \div -4\frac{1}{2}$

14. $1\frac{1}{2} \div 3\frac{1}{2}$

15. $5\frac{3}{5} \div 1\frac{1}{3}$

16. $1\frac{2}{11} \div 3\frac{1}{3}$

Challenge Questions

Let's see if you can apply your skills to a couple of really challenging questions. Ready?

1) Emma Lee is buying candies at the candy store. She has a bag of red candies that weighs 1/5 pound and a bag of green candies that weighs 1/3 pound. Candy is sold by the half pound. How much more candy does she need to add to her bag?

2) Landon had a 3-day weekend. He spent 5/9 of his weekend playing video games, and of that time he spent 3/4 playing his newest game. What fraction of his weekend did he spend playing his newest game? How many hours did he spend playing it? (24-hours in a day, 2 days in a weekend)

Answers and Explanations are on p. 220.

Unit Test

Lessons 6-8

Change to mixed numbers.

1 $\dfrac{17}{7}$

2 $\dfrac{29}{6}$

3 $\dfrac{102}{17}$

4 $\dfrac{350}{33}$

Change to improper fractions.

5 $7\dfrac{6}{11}$

6 $5\dfrac{4}{13}$

7 $4\dfrac{15}{19}$

8 $7\dfrac{7}{16}$

Add or subtract, and reduce to simplest form.

9 $1\dfrac{3}{4} + \dfrac{3}{4}$

10 $\dfrac{17}{49} - \dfrac{11}{49}$

11 $1\dfrac{5}{11} + \dfrac{3}{11}$

12 $2\dfrac{23}{39} + \dfrac{24}{39}$

13 $\dfrac{34}{41} - \dfrac{13}{41}$

14 $\dfrac{11}{32} + \dfrac{19}{32}$

15 $\dfrac{55}{93} - \dfrac{28}{93}$

16 $\dfrac{36}{74} + \dfrac{33}{74}$

17 $5\dfrac{3}{17} - 4\dfrac{2}{17}$

18 $4\dfrac{23}{33} + \dfrac{17}{24}$

19 $\dfrac{4}{9} + \dfrac{4}{15}$

20 $\dfrac{14}{25} - \dfrac{13}{35}$

21 $1\dfrac{5}{9} + \dfrac{3}{11}$

22 $1\dfrac{7}{19} - \dfrac{2}{7}$

23 $\dfrac{3}{4} - \dfrac{19}{41}$

24 $2\dfrac{8}{13} + \dfrac{9}{17}$

Lessons 6-8

Estimate, then add or subtract.

25 $2\frac{14}{25} - 1\frac{17}{21}$ **26** $9\frac{22}{63} + 25\frac{43}{63}$ **27** $12\frac{23}{29} + 11\frac{17}{29}$ **28** $18\frac{3}{7} + 5\frac{1}{4}$

Multiply or divide, and reduce to simplest form.

29 $3 \times 3\frac{2}{11}$ **30** $\frac{1}{2} \times 55$ **31** $\frac{3}{4} \times 24$ **32** $\frac{14}{18} \times \frac{11}{28}$

33 $\frac{1}{3} \times 4\frac{7}{9}$ **34** $16 \times \frac{3}{11}$ **35** $\frac{16}{29} \div 48$ **36** $\frac{51}{47} \div 17$

37 $\frac{7}{3} \div 42$ **38** $\frac{4}{27} \div 3$ **39** $\frac{75}{83} \div 15$ **40** $39 \div \frac{6}{7}$

41 $125 \div \frac{25}{44}$ **42** $\frac{3}{4} \div \frac{16}{27}$ **43** $\frac{24}{17} \div \frac{24}{17}$ **44** $\frac{39}{76} \div \frac{52}{57}$

Unit Test

Name _____

Solve.

45 Elena jogs at a constant rate of $5\frac{1}{3}$ miles per hour. How far does she jog in 3 hours?

_____

46 To plant his vegetable garden, Randy needs to dig 24 holes that are each $4\frac{1}{2}$ inches deep. How many total inches does he have to dig?

47 Cassie has $\frac{5}{6}$ pound of sunflower seeds. She wants to divide the seeds among 3 people. How many pounds will each person get?

48 The temperature on Tuesday was $-3°$ F. On Wednesday the temperature was $4°$ F. What is the average temperature for the two days? On which day was the temperature closer to $0°$ F?

49 A cookie recipe calls for $\frac{3}{4}$ cup of sugar. If Aaron wants to make one and a half batches of cookies, how many cups of sugar will he need?

50 Vivi steps off a 10-foot-high diving board and goes $7\frac{3}{8}$ feet below the surface of the swimming pool, then back up to the surface. How far does she travel altogether?

52 Unit Test Lessons 6–8

Answers and Explanations

1. $2\frac{3}{7}$ $17 \div 7 = 2R3$, so $2\frac{3}{7}$

2. $4\frac{5}{6}$ $29 \div 6 = 4R5$, so $4\frac{5}{6}$

3. 6 $102 \div 17 = 6$

4. $10\frac{20}{33}$ $350 \div 33 = 10\ R20$, so $10\frac{20}{33}$

5. $\frac{83}{11}$ $\frac{7 \times 11 + 6}{11} = \frac{77 + 6}{11} = \frac{83}{11}$

6. $\frac{69}{13}$ $\frac{5 \times 13 + 4}{13} = \frac{65 + 4}{13} = \frac{69}{13}$

7. $\frac{91}{19}$ $\frac{4 \times 19 + 15}{19} = \frac{76 + 15}{19} = \frac{91}{19}$

8. $\frac{119}{16}$ $\frac{7 \times 16 + 7}{16} = \frac{112 + 7}{16} = \frac{119}{16}$

9. $2\frac{1}{2}$ $1 + \frac{3}{4} + \frac{3}{4} = 1 + \frac{6}{4} = 2\frac{2}{4} = 2\frac{1}{2}$

10. $\frac{6}{49}$ $\frac{17 - 11}{49} = \frac{6}{49}$

11. $1\frac{8}{11}$ $1 + \frac{5}{11} + \frac{3}{11} = 1 + \frac{8}{11} = 1\frac{8}{11}$

12. $3\frac{8}{39}$ $2 + \frac{23}{39} + \frac{24}{39} = 2 + \frac{47}{39} = 3\frac{8}{39}$

13. $\frac{21}{41}$ $\frac{34 - 13}{41} = \frac{21}{41}$

14. $\frac{15}{16}$ $\frac{11 + 19}{32} = \frac{30}{32} = \frac{15}{16}$

15. $\frac{9}{31}$ $\frac{55 - 28}{93} = \frac{27}{93} = \frac{9}{31}$

16. $\frac{69}{74}$ $\frac{36 + 33}{74} = \frac{69}{74}$

17. $1\frac{1}{17}$ $5 - 4 = 1$; $\frac{3}{17} - \frac{2}{17} = \frac{1}{17}$; $1\frac{1}{17}$

18. $5\frac{107}{264}$ $4 + \frac{23}{33} + \frac{17}{24} = 4 + \frac{184}{264} + \frac{187}{264} =$
    $4 + \frac{371}{264} = 5\frac{107}{264}$

19. $\frac{32}{45}$ $\frac{4}{9} + \frac{4}{15} = \frac{20}{45} + \frac{12}{45} = \frac{32}{45}$

20. $\frac{33}{175}$ $\frac{14}{25} - \frac{13}{35} = \frac{98}{175} - \frac{65}{175} = \frac{33}{175}$

21. $1\frac{82}{99}$ $1 + \frac{5}{9} + \frac{3}{11} = 1 + \frac{55}{99} + \frac{27}{99} = 1 + \frac{82}{99} = 1\frac{82}{99}$

22. $1\frac{11}{133}$ $1 - 0 = 1$; $\frac{7}{19} - \frac{2}{7} = \frac{49}{133} - \frac{38}{133} = \frac{11}{133}$; $1\frac{11}{133}$

23. $\frac{47}{164}$ $\frac{3}{4} - \frac{19}{41} = \frac{123}{164} - \frac{76}{164} = \frac{47}{164}$

24. $3\frac{32}{221}$ $2 + \frac{8}{13} + \frac{9}{17} = 2 + \frac{136}{221} + \frac{117}{221} = \frac{253}{221}$;
    $2 + \frac{253}{221} = 3\frac{32}{221}$

25. $\frac{1}{2}$ $2\frac{1}{2} - 2 = \frac{1}{2}$

26. 35 $9\frac{1}{2} + 25\frac{1}{2} = 35$

27. $24\frac{1}{2}$ $13 + 11\frac{1}{2} = 24\frac{1}{2}$

28. $23\frac{1}{2}$ $18\frac{1}{2} + 5 = 23\frac{1}{2}$

29. $9\frac{6}{11}$ $3\frac{2}{11} = \frac{35}{11}$; $\frac{3}{1} \times \frac{35}{11} = \frac{105}{11} = 9\frac{6}{11}$

30. $27\frac{1}{2}$ $\frac{1}{2} \times \frac{55}{1} = \frac{55}{2} = 27\frac{1}{2}$

31. 18 $\frac{3}{\cancel{4}_1} \times \frac{\cancel{24}^6}{1} = \frac{18}{1} = 18$

32. $\frac{11}{36}$ $\frac{\cancel{14}^1}{18} \times \frac{11}{\cancel{28}_2} = \frac{11}{36}$

33. $1\frac{16}{27}$ $4\frac{7}{9} = \frac{43}{9}$; $\frac{1}{3} \times \frac{43}{9} = \frac{43}{27} = 1\frac{16}{27}$

34. $4\frac{4}{11}$ $\frac{16}{1} \times \frac{3}{11} = \frac{48}{11} = 4\frac{4}{11}$

35. $\frac{1}{87}$ $\frac{16}{29} \div \frac{48}{1} = \frac{\cancel{16}^1}{29} \times \frac{1}{\cancel{48}_3} = \frac{1}{87}$

36. $\frac{3}{47}$ $\frac{51}{47} \div \frac{17}{1} = \frac{\cancel{51}^3}{47} \times \frac{1}{\cancel{17}_1} = \frac{3}{47}$

37. $\frac{1}{18}$ $\frac{7}{3} \div \frac{42}{1} = \frac{\cancel{7}^1}{3} \times \frac{1}{\cancel{42}_6} = \frac{1}{18}$

38. $\frac{4}{81}$ $\frac{4}{27} \div \frac{3}{1} = \frac{4}{27} \times \frac{1}{3} = \frac{4}{81}$

39. $\frac{5}{83}$ $\frac{75}{83} \div \frac{15}{1} = \frac{\cancel{75}^5}{83} \times \frac{1}{\cancel{15}_1} = \frac{5}{83}$

40. $45\frac{1}{2}$ $\frac{39}{1} \div \frac{6}{7} = \frac{\cancel{39}^{13}}{1} \times \frac{7}{\cancel{6}_2} = \frac{91}{2} = 45\frac{1}{2}$

41. 220 $\frac{125}{1} \div \frac{25}{44} = \frac{\cancel{125}^5}{1} \times \frac{44}{\cancel{25}_1} = \frac{220}{1} = 220$

42. $1\frac{17}{64}$ $\qquad \frac{3}{4} \div \frac{16}{27} = \frac{3}{4} \times \frac{27}{16} = \frac{81}{64} = 1\frac{17}{64}$

43. 1 $\qquad \frac{24}{17} \div \frac{24}{17} = \frac{\cancel{24}^{1}}{\cancel{17}_{1}} \times \frac{\cancel{17}^{1}}{\cancel{24}_{1}} = \frac{1}{1} = 1$

44. $\frac{9}{16}$ $\qquad \frac{39}{76} \div \frac{52}{57} = \frac{\cancel{39}^{3}}{\cancel{76}_{4}} \times \frac{\cancel{57}^{3}}{\cancel{52}_{4}} = \frac{9}{16}$

45. 16 miles $\qquad 5\frac{1}{3} = \frac{16}{3}; \quad \frac{16}{\cancel{3}_{1}} \times \frac{\cancel{3}^{1}}{1} = \frac{16}{1} = 16$

46. 108 inches $\qquad 4\frac{1}{2} = \frac{9}{2}; \quad \frac{\cancel{24}^{12}}{1} \times \frac{9}{\cancel{2}_{1}} = \frac{108}{1} = 108$

47. $\frac{5}{18}$ pounds $\qquad \frac{5}{6} \div \frac{3}{1} = \frac{5}{6} \times \frac{1}{3} = \frac{5}{18}$

48. $\frac{1}{2}°$F; Tuesday $\qquad \dfrac{-3+4}{2} = \text{avg.} = \dfrac{1}{2}°$;

$\qquad\qquad\qquad\qquad$ $|-3|$ is closer to $\circ$

49. $1\frac{1}{8}$ cups $\qquad 1\frac{1}{2} = \frac{3}{2}; \quad \frac{3}{4} \times \frac{3}{2} = \frac{9}{8} = 1\frac{1}{8}$

50. $24\frac{3}{4}$ feet $\qquad 10 + 7\frac{3}{8} + 7\frac{3}{8} = (10 + 7 + 7) + \left(\frac{3}{8} + \frac{3}{8}\right)$

$\qquad\qquad\qquad\qquad = 24 + \frac{6}{8} = 24\frac{3}{4}$

Place Value and Rounding

Understanding place value can help you work with decimals.

Look at the chart. Suppose you are asked to round a decimal to its highest whole number. You can do that by looking at the digit in the tenths place. If that digit is less than 5, round to the whole number that is there. If the digit in the tenths place is 5 or greater, add 1 to the whole number.

Tens	Ones		Tenths	Hundredths	Thousandths
1	5	.	4	0	7

You can also round a decimal to its nearest tenth, its nearest hundredth, its nearest thousandth, and so on. Just look at the digit to the *right* of the rounding place. If that digit is less than 5, keep the digit you see in the rounding place. If that digit is 5 or greater, add 1 to the digit in the rounding place.

Exercises   ROUND

Round to the nearest whole number.

1 45.7

2 77.4

3 145.6

4 1000.9

5 89.4

6 1501.1

Round to the nearest tenth.

7 14.37

8 125.51

9 149.49

10 33.35

11 275.77

12 212.99

Round to the nearest hundredth.

13 1435.344

14 3.555

15 111.119

16 32.756

17 999.989

18 954.376

Round to the nearest thousandth.

19 3.2378

20 329.3297

21 109.1090

22 8256.7835

23 49.4949

24 0.1138

Name _____

Changing Fractions to Decimals

What is the difference between a decimal and a fraction? Actually, a decimal *is* a fraction. It is just expressed in a different way. So $0.7 = \frac{7}{100}$, and $5.023 = 5\frac{23}{1000}$.

However, decimals are expressed only in tenths, hundredths, thousandths, and so on. So some fractions cannot be converted to simple decimals, but many fractions *can* be changed into decimals.

Every fraction represents its numerator divided by its denominator. So $\frac{5}{8} = 5 \div 8$. Set up a division problem. Add a decimal point and as many placeholder zeros as you need in your dividend. As you can see, $\frac{5}{8} = 0.625$, six hundred twenty-five thousandths.

Example: Change $\frac{5}{8}$ to a decimal.

$$\begin{array}{r} 0.625 \\ 8)\overline{5.000} \\ \underline{4.8} \\ 20 \\ \underline{16} \\ 40 \\ \underline{40} \end{array}$$

Exercises   CHANGE FRACTIONS TO DECIMALS

Round to the nearest ten-thousandth.

1 $\frac{5}{16}$

2 $\frac{4}{7}$

3 $\frac{15}{31}$

4 $\frac{3}{5}$

5 $\frac{1}{2001}$

6 $\frac{23}{25}$

7 $\frac{3}{4}$

8 $\frac{55}{66}$

Changing Decimals to Fractions

Can you also change decimals to fractions? Yes, and it is much easier to do than changing fractions into decimals.

Begin by looking at the place value farthest to the right. Use that as your denominator. The number becomes the numerator. After you have changed the decimal into a fraction, you might even be able to reduce it.

Example:

$$0.72 = \frac{72}{100} = \frac{18}{25}$$

Exercises CHANGE DECIMALS TO FRACTIONS

1 0.85

2 0.77

3 0.888

4 0.0125

5 0.678

6 0.6255

7 0.331

8 0.4545

9 0.876

10 0.3125

11 0.3435

12 0.7007

13 0.336

14 0.2141

15 0.56

16 0.0055

Name _____

Comparing and Ordering Decimals

How do you know which decimals are greater or less than others? If you look at place values, it is easy. Just as you can compare and order whole numbers, you can do the same with decimals. Make sure you line up the decimals so that the decimal points are all in the same column. As with whole numbers, each digit is one place value *higher* than the digit to its immediate right.

When comparing numbers with decimals, always look at the whole number parts first. If two whole numbers are the same, *then* compare moving right from the decimal point. To compare decimals like 0.07 and 0.072, you can imagine a placeholder zero to make them both fill the same number of places. So 0.07 = 0.070. That is less than 0.072.

Example:

Order these decimals:
5.62, 6.186, 0.2, 0.07, 5.65, 0.071, 0.009

> 5.62
>
> 6.186
>
> 0.2
>
> 0.07
>
> 5.65
>
> 0.071
>
> 0.009

The order, reading from highest to lowest is:
6.186, 5.65, 5.62, 0.2, 0.071, 0.009

Exercises   COMPARE

Each problem will have three numbers: a lowest, middle, and largest number. You will be told which of the three to select: lowest, middle, or largest.

1 4, 5, and 10   Lowest

_____

2 10.01, 10.10, and 10.11   Middle

_____

3 0.567, 0.5677, and 0.56   Largest

_____

4 45.45, 45.449, and 45.4449   Middle

_____

5 14.125, 14.0126, and 14.00126   Lowest

_____

6 21.21, 21.211, and 21.2121   Lowest

_____

7 11.1, 11.11, and 11.111   Largest

_____

8 12.12, 12.102, and 12.1023   Middle

_____

9 166.66, 166.60, and 166.6607   Middle

_____

10 144.32, 14.432, and 1.4432   Largest

_____

11 25.025, 25.205, and 25.502   Middle

_____

12 156.12, 157.01, and 158.32   Lowest

_____

Name _____

Adding Decimals

To add decimals, first line up your addends by place value. Once you do that, adding decimals is *exactly* the same as adding whole numbers. After you line up the decimal points, you can add placeholder zeros to even out your addends if you like.

Example: 79.46 + 8.65

```
  79.46
+  8.65
-------
  88.11
```

Remember...

Put a decimal point in its proper column in the total, too!

Exercises ADD

1
```
  45.45
+  2.1
```

2
```
  33.7
+ 41.22
```

3
```
  5.4
+ 8.54
```

4
```
  2.22
+ 3.001
```

5
```
  33.045
+  0.011
```

6
```
  9.0901
+ 13.245
```

7
```
  0.782
+  5.6
```

8
```
  454.32
+   2.111
```

9
```
  4.5
+ 9.5001
```

10
```
  63.1
+  5.46
```

11
```
  2.22201
+    7.38
```

12
```
  8.704
+ 18.0001
```

13
```
  4.147
+ 5.963
```

14
```
  9.46
+ 55.7222
```

15
```
  0.00152
+ 152.1522
```

16
```
  3.202
+ 2.3031
```

17
```
  9.781
+ 1.832
```

18
```
  2.2222
+ 8.888
```

19
```
  478.654
+   3.9702
```

20
```
  3.303
+ 19.0771
```

Lesson 10.1   Adding Decimals   59

10.2

Subtracting Decimals

When you subtract decimals, remember to line up the decimal points. Put in placeholder zeros, if you need to.

> **Remember...**
> The value of a number does *not* change if you add a decimal point at the end and then put in placeholder zeros. You can use as many placeholder zeros as you need.

Example: $243 - 178.961$

$$
\begin{array}{r}
243.000 \\
- 178.861 \\
\hline
64.139
\end{array}
$$

Exercises   SUBTRACT

1
$$
\begin{array}{r}
15.45 \\
- 7.82 \\
\hline
\end{array}
$$

2
$$
\begin{array}{r}
48.001 \\
- 5.62 \\
\hline
\end{array}
$$

3
$$
\begin{array}{r}
88.88 \\
- 2.97 \\
\hline
\end{array}
$$

4
$$
\begin{array}{r}
50.202 \\
- 2.5005 \\
\hline
\end{array}
$$

5
$$
\begin{array}{r}
10.3 \\
- 4.777 \\
\hline
\end{array}
$$

6
$$
\begin{array}{r}
100.111 \\
- 5.374 \\
\hline
\end{array}
$$

7
$$
\begin{array}{r}
565.002 \\
- 12.345 \\
\hline
\end{array}
$$

8
$$
\begin{array}{r}
7.701 \\
- 6.994 \\
\hline
\end{array}
$$

9
$$
\begin{array}{r}
5.5514 \\
- 4.61 \\
\hline
\end{array}
$$

10
$$
\begin{array}{r}
12.157 \\
- 5.2 \\
\hline
\end{array}
$$

11
$$
\begin{array}{r}
89.7 \\
- 63.63 \\
\hline
\end{array}
$$

12
$$
\begin{array}{r}
3.561 \\
- 2.9872 \\
\hline
\end{array}
$$

13
$$
\begin{array}{r}
4789.32 \\
- 555.55 \\
\hline
\end{array}
$$

14
$$
\begin{array}{r}
8.651 \\
- 6.98 \\
\hline
\end{array}
$$

15
$$
\begin{array}{r}
45.87 \\
- 33.999 \\
\hline
\end{array}
$$

16
$$
\begin{array}{r}
963.751 \\
- 8.8 \\
\hline
\end{array}
$$

17
$$
\begin{array}{r}
8.789 \\
- 1.79 \\
\hline
\end{array}
$$

18
$$
\begin{array}{r}
5.2 \\
- 3.571 \\
\hline
\end{array}
$$

19
$$
\begin{array}{r}
6.91 \\
- 2.84 \\
\hline
\end{array}
$$

20
$$
\begin{array}{r}
8.888 \\
- 2.913 \\
\hline
\end{array}
$$

Adding and Subtracting Money

Whenever you calculate amounts of money, you are adding and subtracting decimals. American money uses decimals, because a dollar is divided into 100 hundredths.

A hundredth of a dollar is "a cent." So if you have 21 dollars and 13 cents, you write it as $21.13, a decimal!

Example: $75 − $38.99

$$\begin{array}{r} \$75.00 \\ -\ 38.99 \\ \hline \$36.01 \end{array}$$

Remember...

You do not need to put a dollar sign next to all of the addends. However, you need to include a dollar sign in front of the total.

Exercises CALCULATE

1 $56
    + $32

2 $22.71
    + $5.20

3 $15
    − $12.40

4 $11.06
    + $0.32

5 $10
    − $7.21

6 $315.32
    − $297.61

7 $89.45
    − $3.50

8 $34
    − $4.77

9 $1000.03
    − $88.42

10 $45
    + $2.30

11 $89
    − $56.81

12 $813
    − $7.71

13 $5
    − $2.93

14 $71.45
    − $3.56

15 $8.55
    − $2.61

16 $3.21
    − $2

17 $1561
    − $87.87

18 $1987.23
    − $476.30

19 $81
    − $22.57

20 $45.60
    − $7

10.4

Estimating Decimal Sums and Differences

To estimate sums and differences of decimals, you round just as you would with whole numbers. However, you have to decide what rounding place is the best one to use. If you are estimating money, you may want to round to the nearest dollar. Or you may want to round even closer than the nearest dollar. You can round to the nearest half dollar, or 0.50. Look at the cents part and ask yourself: Is it closest to 0 dollars, to a $\frac{1}{2}$ dollar, or to 1 dollar?

Example: $12.46 + $11.39

Step 1: $12 + $11 = $23

Step 2: $\frac{1}{2}$ a dollar + $\frac{1}{2}$ a dollar = $1

Step 3: $23 + $1 = $24

Notice that you rounded *both* cents parts *upward* to $\frac{1}{2}$ a dollar. By doing this, you know that your estimated total is *higher* than the actual total.

Exercises ESTIMATE

1
$34.45
+ $22.52

2
$55.11
+ $22.73

3
$76.77
+ $ 2.31

4
$908.03
− $ 37.56

5
$32.77
− $21.99

6
$561.22
− $ 2.10

7
$77.55
− $55.77

8
$234.55
− $222.99

9
$45.32
+ $99.01

10
$10.08
− $ 1.07

11
$12.77
+ $ 2.39

12
$ 14.57
+ $217.66

13
$21.67
− $18.33

14
$2.33
− $1.87

15
$444.71
+ $ 67.33

16
$ 232.47
+ $1001.51

17
$ 67.89
+ $253.77

18
$ 7.52
+ $75.20

19
$2303.41
+ $ 223.67

20
$32.56
− $21.91

Name _____

Multiplying Decimals

Is multiplying decimals different from multiplying whole numbers? The technique is basically the same, except for *one* thing. You have to know the *total* number of decimal places in the numbers you multiply.

> **Example:** 33.2×0.46
>
> $$
> \begin{array}{r}
> 33.2 \\
> \times\ 0.46 \\
> \hline
> 1992 \\
> 13280 \\
> \hline
> 15.272
> \end{array}
> $$

Notice that you do *not* line up the decimal points when multiplying decimals. You just multiply as if there were no decimal points at all. Do not forget to add placeholder zeros if you need any. When you are finished multiplying, count the total number of decimal places in the factors, the numbers you have multiplied. Then, starting from the right of your product, count that number of places, and put your decimal point to the *left* of the last place you counted.

Exercises MULTIPLY

1
$$
\begin{array}{r}
32.5 \\
\times\ 0.5 \\
\hline
\end{array}
$$

2
$$
\begin{array}{r}
45.6 \\
\times\ 0.33 \\
\hline
\end{array}
$$

3
$$
\begin{array}{r}
-4.52 \\
\times\ 6.31 \\
\hline
\end{array}
$$

4
$$
\begin{array}{r}
789.3 \\
\times\ 6.8 \\
\hline
\end{array}
$$

5
$$
\begin{array}{r}
1.731 \\
\times\ 0.52 \\
\hline
\end{array}
$$

6
$$
\begin{array}{r}
10.01 \\
\times\ 1.01 \\
\hline
\end{array}
$$

7
$$
\begin{array}{r}
-89.89 \\
\times\ 23.23 \\
\hline
\end{array}
$$

8
$$
\begin{array}{r}
4.82 \\
\times\ 88.3 \\
\hline
\end{array}
$$

9
$$
\begin{array}{r}
-0.333 \\
\times\ 0.444 \\
\hline
\end{array}
$$

10
$$
\begin{array}{r}
5.5 \\
\times\ 77.76 \\
\hline
\end{array}
$$

11
$$
\begin{array}{r}
842.1 \\
\times\ 2.64 \\
\hline
\end{array}
$$

12
$$
\begin{array}{r}
63.4 \\
\times\ 36.5 \\
\hline
\end{array}
$$

13
$$
\begin{array}{r}
1.111 \\
\times\ 55.67 \\
\hline
\end{array}
$$

14
$$
\begin{array}{r}
51.02 \\
\times\ 3.91 \\
\hline
\end{array}
$$

15
$$
\begin{array}{r}
0.0013 \\
\times\ 0.0098 \\
\hline
\end{array}
$$

16
$$
\begin{array}{r}
-8.5 \\
\times\ 2.3 \\
\hline
\end{array}
$$

Name _____

Multiplying Decimals (cont.)

Is there an easier way to multiply decimals? Sometimes there is. Look at this place value chart.

Example:

$3.52 \times 1000 = 3520$ $3.52 \times 0.01 = 0.0352$

Thousands Period			Ones Period			?			
Hundreds	Tens	Ones	Hundreds	Tens	Ones	Tenths	Hundredths	Thousandths	Ten-thousandths
5	7	4,	2	3	2.	9	5	1	8

Each column represents a **power of 10**, which is 10 multiplied by itself one or more times. However, all you need to remember is that each place value is 10 times the place value of the number to its right.

If you keep powers of 10 in mind, you can use a trick. When you multiply a number by a power of ten greater than 1, move the decimal point of the number to the *right*, one place for each power of 10. If you need more places, add placeholder zeros.

When you multiply by a power of 10 that is less than 1, move the decimal point of the number to the *left* for each decimal place in the power of 10.

Exercises   MULTIPLY

1
```
   4.6731
×    0.1
```

2
```
   71.35
×    100
```

3
```
    0.58
×   1000
```

4
```
   16.45
×    0.1
```

5
```
   10.005
×    0.01
```

6
```
   1.112
× 1000
```

7
```
   0.593
×    10
```

8
```
   0.322
×   0.01
```

9
```
   1056.32
×      0.1
```

10
```
   28.90
×      1
```

11
```
   1.56
×  0.1
```

12
```
       2.1
× 10000
```

13
```
   58.31
×    10
```

14
```
   81.81
×   100
```

15
```
   0.973
×    10
```

16
```
   0.002
×  0.001
```

Multiplying Money

Since money is a decimal, you can multiply it the same way you multiply other decimals. However, you have to remember *two* important things.

First, you *cannot* multiply money by money. You can multiply money only by a whole number, a fraction, or a decimal.

Second, when you multiply money, the product is *also* money. So if your product has more than two decimal places, you have to round to the nearest hundredth, because money is *always* expressed in dollars and cents (hundredths of a dollar).

Example: $7.26 × 3.8

$$
\begin{array}{r}
\$7.26 \\
\times\ 3.8 \\
\hline
5808 \\
2178\mathbf{0} \\
\hline
27588 = \text{about } \$27.59
\end{array}
$$

Exercises   MULTIPLY

1
$$
\begin{array}{r}
\$5.65 \\
\times\ \ 3.2 \\
\hline
\end{array}
$$

2
$$
\begin{array}{r}
8.4 \\
\times\ \$96.25 \\
\hline
\end{array}
$$

3
$$
\begin{array}{r}
34.2 \\
\times\ \$2.25 \\
\hline
\end{array}
$$

4
$$
\begin{array}{r}
\$3.01 \\
\times\ \ 5.6 \\
\hline
\end{array}
$$

5
$$
\begin{array}{r}
6.3 \\
\times\ \$2.45 \\
\hline
\end{array}
$$

6
$$
\begin{array}{r}
\$5.57 \\
\times\ \ 0.15 \\
\hline
\end{array}
$$

7
$$
\begin{array}{r}
64.3 \\
\times\ \$7.88 \\
\hline
\end{array}
$$

8
$$
\begin{array}{r}
\$12.33 \\
\times\ 10.35 \\
\hline
\end{array}
$$

9
$$
\begin{array}{r}
\$13.50 \\
\times\ \ 85.3 \\
\hline
\end{array}
$$

10
$$
\begin{array}{r}
\$5.01 \\
\times\ 96.85 \\
\hline
\end{array}
$$

11
$$
\begin{array}{r}
\$45.55 \\
\times\ \ 3.25 \\
\hline
\end{array}
$$

12
$$
\begin{array}{r}
\$78.10 \\
\times\ \ 2.1 \\
\hline
\end{array}
$$

13
$$
\begin{array}{r}
\$89.99 \\
\times\ 0.011 \\
\hline
\end{array}
$$

14
$$
\begin{array}{r}
\$56.37 \\
\times\ \ 2.7 \\
\hline
\end{array}
$$

15
$$
\begin{array}{r}
\$85.14 \\
\times\ \ 6.62 \\
\hline
\end{array}
$$

16
$$
\begin{array}{r}
2.3 \\
\times\ \$9.63 \\
\hline
\end{array}
$$

Name _____

Estimating Decimal Products

Is there an easy way to estimate the products of decimals? If you know how to round, there is! Just round each factor to its highest place value, and then multiply the rounded amounts.

Example: 212.9×0.327
$200 \times 0.3 = 60.0$

That is a fairly good estimate. You even know something more about how the estimate compares to the *real* product. Did you notice that you rounded both numbers *downward*? This means your estimate is *less* than the actual product.

Exercises   ESTIMATE

1 505.2×-0.322

2 10.71×2.31

3 55.5×21.2

4 35.67×0.437

5 631.23×-1.61

6 2.87×950

7 7.3×0.51

8 111.159×0.23

9 81.453×-1.8

10 245.459×-0.37

11 93.7123×0.54

12 37.25×4.12

13 12.67×0.96543

14 1.111×-4.2519

15 5.51×0.50001

Dividing Decimals by Whole Numbers

Adding, subtracting, and multiplying decimals is similar to working with whole numbers. Is that also true for dividing decimals?

When you divide a decimal by a whole number, *only* the dividend has a decimal point. To calculate correctly, you must line up a decimal point in the quotient with the decimal point in the dividend. That is all there is to it!

Example: $92.4 \div 7$

$$
\begin{array}{r}
13.2 \\
7\overline{)92.4} \\
\underline{7} \\
22 \\
\underline{21} \\
14 \\
\underline{14}
\end{array}
$$

Exercises   DIVIDE

Round to the nearest ten-thousandth.

1 $5\overline{)45.7}$ **2** $4\overline{)29.34}$ **3** $11\overline{)78.9}$ **4** $-7\overline{)41.8}$

5 $14\overline{)745.2}$ **6** $7\overline{)41.9}$ **7** $18\overline{)22.56}$ **8** $-8\overline{)71.45}$

12.2

Dividing Whole Numbers by Decimals

Is dividing a whole number by a decimal different than dividing a decimal by a whole number? Only a little bit. However, you need to remember one simple trick. You want to move the decimal point of the divisor all the way to the right. So you must multiply the divisor by whatever power of 10 will do that. Then, you have to also multiply the dividend by that same power of 10.

You can put a decimal point at the end of the new dividend and add as many placeholder zeros as you need. If you do that, though, do not forget to put the decimal point in the quotient!

Example: $27 \div 0.08$

$0.08 \times 100 = 8$ $\qquad$ $27 \times 100 = 2700$

$$
\begin{array}{r}
337.5 \\
8{\overline{\smash{\big)}\,2700.0}} \\
\underline{24} \\
30 \\
\underline{24} \\
60 \\
\underline{56} \\
40 \\
\underline{40} \\
\end{array}
$$

Exercises   DIVIDE

Round to the nearest ten-thousandth.

1 $2.4{\overline{\smash{\big)}\,5}}$

2 $-9.1{\overline{\smash{\big)}\,6}}$

3 $6.3{\overline{\smash{\big)}\,55}}$

4 $23.1{\overline{\smash{\big)}\,654}}$

5 $8.9{\overline{\smash{\big)}\,72}}$

6 $-2.5{\overline{\smash{\big)}\,439}}$

7 $6.1{\overline{\smash{\big)}\,428}}$

8 $6.8{\overline{\smash{\big)}\,55}}$

Dividing Decimals by Decimals

Now you know how to divide a whole number by a decimal and a decimal by a whole number. Can you figure out how to divide a decimal by a decimal?

Example: $0.429 \div 0.05$

$0.05 \times 100 = 5 \qquad 0.429 \times 100 = 42.9$

$$\begin{array}{r} 8.58 \\ 5\overline{)42.90} \\ \underline{40} \\ 29 \\ \underline{25} \\ 40 \\ 40 \end{array}$$

If you said "multiply the divisor and the dividend by the same power of 10," you are correct. First, look at the divisor and find the smallest power of 10 that will move the decimal point all the way to the right. Then multiply both the divisor and the dividend by that power of 10.

Notice in this example that you have to add a placeholder zero to the dividend.

Remember...

You always want the divisor to be a whole number, so you must multiply it by a power of 10. Then, *always* multiply the dividend by the same power of 10.

Exercises DIVIDE

Round to the nearest ten-thousandth.

1 $-4.5\overline{)13.5}$

2 $2.5\overline{)5.7}$

3 $8.1\overline{)89.1}$

4 $2.1\overline{)4.2}$

5 $3.41\overline{)4.3648}$

6 $-2.11\overline{)6.752}$

7 $2.37\overline{)6.162}$

8 $5.55\overline{)6.38}$

Name _____

Dividing Money

Dividing money is *exactly* like dividing any other kind of decimal. However, you need to remember the following:

If you are dividing money, money *must* be in your dividend. If your divisor is also money, your quotient will *not* be money. If your divisor is *not* money, your quotient *will* be money.

Example 1: How many times does $4 go into $12?

$12 ÷ $4 = 3. Your divisor is money, so your quotient is *not*.

Example 2: How much is $12 ÷ 4?

$12 ÷ 4 = $3. Your divisor is *not* money, so your quotient is.

Remember...

If your quotient is money, you need to round it to the nearest cent (hundredth).

Exercises   DIVIDE

Round to the nearest cent.

1 $3)$\overline{\$15}$

2 $5)$\overline{\$56}$

3 $3.25)$\overline{\$89}$

4 $2.3)$\overline{\$10}$

5 $5.5)$\overline{\$45.45}$

6 $2.33)$\overline{\$5.01}$

7 $6.54)$\overline{\$89.25}$

8 $10.2)$\overline{\$9802.2}$

Estimating Decimal Quotients

There are *two* ways to estimate decimal quotients. Can you figure out what they are? In both methods, you need to drop the decimal.

Which way do you think will most often make your estimate closer to the actual quotient? The second way will *usually* get you closer.

Which estimate was better? Do the division problem and find out!

Example 1: Drop the decimals parts in both numbers and round as you would normally, looking for **compatible numbers**.

$$33.06 \div 4.1$$
$$33 \div 4$$
Compatible numbers $= 33 \div 3 = 11$

Example 2: Round **first** and then drop the decimals.

$33.06 \div 3.8$ 33.06 rounds to 33

3.8 rounds to 4 $33 \div 4 = 8.25 = 8$ (rounded)

Exercises   ESTIMATE

Use the estimating method from Example 1 to complete questions 1–8.

1. $313.2 \div 3.322 =$ 2. $10.71 \div 2.31 =$ 3. $33.3 \div 21.2 =$ 4. $33.67 \div 0.837 =$

5. $631.23 \div 1.61 =$ 6. $2.87 \div 1.31 =$ 7. $7.3 \div 2.31 =$ 8. $111.131 \div 5.23 =$

Use the estimating method from Example 2 to complete questions 9–17.

9. $13.7123 \div 4.38 =$ 10. $37.23 \div 8.12 =$ 11. $12.67 \div 1.86383 =$

12. $211.111 \div 8.2311 =$ 13. $43.31 \div 2.30001 =$ 14. $71.36 \div 3.33 =$

15. $66.2882 \div 10.101 =$ 16. $87.23 \div 9.1101 =$ 17. $78.3 \div 4.20101 =$

Challenge Questions

Let's see if you can apply your skills to a couple of really challenging questions. Ready?

1) Molly has a $20 gift card. She buys a shirt for $15.30 and spends the rest on candy bars that cost 50 cents each. How many candy bars does she get? How much is left on the gift card?

2) Jenna has 48.6 inches of ribbon. She is wrapping a box that is 22.4 inches around, and then she wants to divide the rest of the ribbon into four equal pieces to make a bow. How long is each piece for the bow?

Answers and Explanations are on p. 220.

Lessons 9–12

Round to the nearest tenth.

1 3406.997 _____

2 334,782.099 _____

3 65,529.0887 _____

4 12.94996 _____

Round to the nearest hundredth.

5 2,467,891.3554 _____

6 12.4532 _____

7 97.009 _____

8 17.61093 _____

Round to the nearest ten thousandth.

9 467,001.35545 _____

10 199.11115 _____

11 1,683,679.57344 _____

12 8.194301 _____

Convert decimals to fractions.

13 0.8 _____

14 0.875 _____

15 0.08 _____

16 0.625 _____

Convert fractions to decimals.

17 $\frac{3}{5}$ _____

18 $\frac{8}{15}$ _____

19 $\frac{3}{16}$ _____

20 $6\frac{1}{8}$ _____

Put the decimals in order from greatest to least.

21 0.122, 0.1145, 0.616, 0.6165, 0.513, 0.3132, 0.2126, 0.819

_____

22 0.217, 0.0217, 0.0133, 0.0487, 0.1243, 0.20413, 0.5257, 0.05257, 0.05205

_____

Unit Test

Lessons 9–12

Add or subtract.

23
$$1.157397$$
$$+\ 2.31542$$

24
$$3.10341056$$
$$+\ 3.431776$$

25
$$1.1564$$
$$2.1667$$
$$+\ 3.337833$$

26
$$4.15466$$
$$-\ 2.2355$$

27
$$1.892754$$
$$-\ 0.464043$$

28
$$2.4276$$
$$-\ 0.17813344$$

29
$$\$1.25$$
$$+\ \$5.5$$

30
$$\$1.89$$
$$+\ \$0.89$$

Multiply or divide.

31
$$0.4033$$
$$\times\quad 90$$

32
$$14.615$$
$$\times\quad 14$$

33 $25\overline{)\$2.67}$

34
$$4.539$$
$$\times\ 1.60$$

35
$$\$\ 0.56$$
$$\times\quad 1.64$$

36
$$1.7965$$
$$\times\quad 1.2$$

37
$$\$1.25$$
$$\times\quad 5.5$$

38 $24\overline{)35.4}$

39 $2.24\overline{)14.56}$

40 $0.23\overline{)\$2.69}$

41 $0.025\overline{)0.5805}$

42 $18\overline{)25.02}$

Estimate, then multiply or divide.

43
$$0.3134572$$
$$\times\qquad 0.34$$

44 $0.225\overline{)0.123143}$

45
$$1214$$
$$\times\ 0.25$$

46 $0.40\overline{)4802}$

47
$$60.50$$
$$\times\quad 1.5$$

48 $5.5\overline{)250.90}$

49
$$81.81$$
$$\times\ 3.765$$

50 $0.333\overline{)18.4545}$

Unit Test

Lessons 9–12

51 Flora went to the stationery store to buy tools for her art class. She spent $2.50 on colored pencils, $7.05 on a set of artist pallets, $4.59 for a used straight edge, $2.09 for a lined memo pad, and $5.28 for a new water bottle. How much did she spend altogether? _____

If Flora only brought thirty dollars with her, did she have enough money? _____

If so, how much change should she get back? _____

If not, how much more money does she need? _____

52 Thad and his chess club raised a total of $563.75 for the local homeless shelter. There are 11 people in the chess club. If each member raised the same amount of money, how much did each member raise? _____

53 Jane went to the store to buy food for a party of 8 friends. She spent $3.75 on each person for soup, $1.15 each for a warm beverage, and $.76 each for a piece of fruit. How much did she spend in total to buy the food? _____

She brought two $20-bills with her.

Did she have enough money? _____

54 Evelyn drives 14.25 miles each way to visit her aunt. What is the total distance she drives if she visits her aunt 3 times? _____

55 Brie has 14.7 inches of red licorice. She cuts off a piece that is 2.1 inches for herself and then divides the remainder between her 3 friends. How long is each piece her friends receive? _____

Unit Test

Answers and Explanations

1. 3407.0

2. 334,782.1

3. 65,529.1

4. 12.9

5. 2,467,891.36

6. 12.45

7. 97.01

8. 17.61

9. 467,001.3555

10. 199.1112

11. 1,683,679.5734

12. 8.1943

13. $\frac{4}{5}$ $\frac{8}{10} = \frac{4}{5}$

14. $\frac{7}{8}$ $\frac{875}{1000} = \frac{7}{8}$

15. $\frac{2}{25}$ $\frac{8}{100} = \frac{2}{25}$

16. $\frac{5}{8}$ $\frac{625}{1000} = \frac{5}{8}$

17. 0.6

$$5\overline{)3.0} \quad \begin{array}{r} 0.6 \\ \underline{3\,0} \\ 0 \end{array}$$

18. 0.5333

$$15\overline{)8.000} \quad \begin{array}{r} 0.533... \\ \underline{7\,5} \\ 50 \\ \underline{45} \\ 50 \\ \underline{45} \\ 5... \end{array}$$

19. 0.1875

$$16\overline{)3.0000} \quad \begin{array}{r} 0.1875 \\ \underline{1\,6} \\ 140 \\ \underline{128} \\ 120 \\ \underline{112} \\ 80 \\ \underline{80} \\ 0 \end{array}$$

20. 6.125 $6\frac{1}{8} = \frac{49}{8}$

$$8\overline{)49.000} \quad \begin{array}{r} 6.125 \\ \underline{48} \\ 10 \\ \underline{8} \\ 20 \\ \underline{16} \\ 40 \end{array}$$

21. 0.819, 0.6165, 0.616, 0.513, 0.3132, 0.2126, 0.122, 0.1145

22. 0.5257, 0.217, 0.20413, 0.1243, 0.05257, 0.05205, 0.0487, .0217, 0.0133

23. 3.472817

$$\begin{array}{r} 1.157\,397 \\ +\,2.315\,420 \\ \hline 3.472\,817 \end{array}$$

24. 6.53518656

$$\begin{array}{r} 3.103\,41056 \\ +\,3.43\,177600 \\ \hline 6.53\,518656 \end{array}$$

25. 6.660933

$$\begin{array}{r} 1.156\,400 \\ 2.166\,700 \\ +\,3.337\,833 \\ \hline 6.660\,933 \end{array}$$

26. 1.91916

$$\begin{array}{r} 4.15\,466 \\ -\,2.23\,550 \\ \hline 1.91\,916 \end{array}$$

27. 1.428711

$$\begin{array}{r} 1.892\,754 \\ -\,0.464\,043 \\ \hline 1.428\,711 \end{array}$$

28. 2.24946656

$$\begin{array}{r} 2.427\,60000 \\ -\,0.178\,13344 \\ \hline 2.249\,46656 \end{array}$$

29. $6.75

$$\begin{array}{r} 1.25 \\ +\,5.50 \\ \hline 6.75 \end{array}$$

30. $2.78

$$\begin{array}{r} 1.89 \\ +\,0.89 \\ \hline 2.78 \end{array}$$

31. 36.297

$$\begin{array}{r} 0.4033 \\ \times \quad\;\; 90 \\ \hline 36.2970 \end{array}$$

32. 204.610

$$\overset{1\,2}{1}\overset{2}{4}.6\overset{2}{1}5$$
$$\times \qquad 14$$
$$\overset{1}{5}\overset{1}{8}\,460$$
$$\overset{1}{1}46\,150$$
$$\overline{204.610}$$

33. $0.11

$$25\overline{)2.6700} \quad \text{quotient } 0.1068$$
$$\underline{25}$$
$$170$$
$$\underline{150}$$
$$200$$
$$\underline{200}$$
$$0$$

34. 7.2624

$$\overset{3\;2\;5}{4.539}$$
$$\times \qquad 1.6$$
$$2^{1}72^{1}34$$
$$4\,53\,90$$
$$\overline{7.2624}$$

35. $0.92

$$\overset{\;\;\overset{3}{2}}{0.56}$$
$$\times \; 1.64$$
$$224$$
$$3^{1}360$$
$$5\,600$$
$$\overline{0.9184}$$

36. 2.1558

$$\overset{1\;\;1}{1.79}{}^{1}6{}^{1}5$$
$$\times \qquad 1.2$$
$$3^{1}5^{1}930$$
$$1^{1}7965\,0$$
$$\overline{2.1558\,0}$$

37. $6.88

$$1^{1}.2^{2}5$$
$$\times \quad 5.5$$
$$625$$
$$6250$$
$$\overline{6.875}$$

38. 1.475

$$24\overline{)35.400} \quad \text{quotient } 1.475$$
$$\underline{24}$$
$$114$$
$$\underline{96}$$
$$180$$
$$\underline{168}$$
$$120$$
$$\underline{120}$$
$$0$$

39. 6.5

$$2.24.\overline{)14.56.0} \quad \text{quotient } 6.5$$
$$\underline{13\,44}$$
$$1120$$
$$\underline{1120}$$
$$0$$

40. $11.70

$$0.23.\overline{)2.69.000} \quad \text{quotient } 11.695\ldots$$
$$\underline{23}$$
$$39$$
$$\underline{23}$$
$$160$$
$$\underline{138}$$
$$220$$
$$\underline{207}$$
$$13\,0$$
$$\underline{11\,5}$$
$$15\ldots$$

41. 23.22

$$0.025.\overline{)0.580.50} \quad \text{quotient } 23.22$$
$$\underline{50}$$
$$80$$
$$\underline{75}$$
$$55$$
$$\underline{50}$$
$$50$$
$$\underline{50}$$
$$0$$

42. 1.39

$$18\overline{)25.02} \quad \text{quotient } 1.39$$
$$\underline{18}$$
$$70$$
$$\underline{54}$$
$$162$$
$$\underline{162}$$
$$0$$

43. 0.09 $\qquad 0.3 \times 0.3 = 0.09$

44. 0.6 $\qquad \dfrac{0.12}{0.2} = 0.6$

45. 300 $\qquad 1000 \times 0.3 = 300$

46. 120 $\qquad \dfrac{4800}{0.4} = \dfrac{480}{4} = 120$

47. 90 $\qquad 60 \times 1.5 = 90$

48. 50 $\qquad \dfrac{250}{5} = 50$

49. 320 $\qquad 80 \times 4 = 320$

50. 60 $\qquad \dfrac{18}{0.3} = \dfrac{180}{3} = 60$

51. $21.51; Yes; $8.49; N/A $2.50 + 7.05 + 4.59 + 2.09 + 5.28 = \$21.51$; Yes; $\$30 - \$21.51 = \$8.49$

52. $51.25

$$
\begin{array}{r}
51.25 \\
11\overline{)563.75} \\
\underline{55} \\
13 \\
\underline{11} \\
27 \\
\underline{22} \\
55 \\
\underline{55} \\
0
\end{array}
$$

53. $45.28; no $3.75 + 1.15 + 0.76 = \$5.66$ each; $\$5.66 \times 8 = \$45.28$; No; $40 < 45.28$

54. 85.5 miles $14.25 + 14.25 = 28.5$; $28.5 \times 3 = 85.5$

55. 4.2 inches $14.7 - 2.1 = 12.6$; $12.6 \div 3 = 4.2$

Ratios

A **ratio**, often expressed as a fraction, compares two numbers.

Examples:

Eight people want equal shares of one pie. You can set up a ratio.

$$\frac{1 \text{ pie}}{8 \text{ people}}$$

When you remove the words, you can see that each person should get $\frac{1}{8}$ of the pie. The ratio of pie to people is 1:8

You can compare *any* two numbers with a ratio. For example: Kira read 5 books last month, and Carmen read 4.

$$\frac{5 \text{ Kira books}}{4 \text{ Carmen books}}$$

The ratio of Kira's reading to Carmen's reading was 5:4 (say "five to four"). You can also express that as a mixed number. Kira read $1\frac{1}{4}$ times as many books as Carmen.

Exercises   COMPARE

1 Jennifer is making a cake that requires 2 cups of flour and 1 cup of milk. What is the ratio of flour to milk?

_____

2 At the movie theatre the manager wants to know which movie is selling the most tickets. He finds that movie A sold 150 tickets and movie B sold 100 tickets. What is the ratio of sales of movie A to movie B? Reduce your answer.

_____

3 Judy and Nancy have been swimming at the pool for one hour a day for the last month. Judy averages 25 laps every hour while Nancy averages 18. What is the ratio of Judy's average to Nancy's average?

_____

4 Michael and Leon get ice cream cones, Michael orders chocolate chip and Leon orders yogurt chip. They each count the number of chocolate chips and yogurt chips that they eat until they finish. Michael had 32 and Leon 17. What is the ratio of yogurt chips to chocolate chips in the ice cream?

_____

5 Joshua and Steve are erecting a fence around a pasture. Each day Steve erects 200 feet of fence while Joshua erects 150 feet. What is the ratio of work that Steve completes versus Joshua?

_____

Name _____

Ratios (cont.)

Now that you understand what a ratio is, let's look at how you can use ratios to solve problems. Ratios are often used to determine the particular amount of something that is needed. You can increase and decrease ratios as needed.

Examples:

To make shortbread cookies, you need 1 part sugar, 2 parts butter, and 3 parts flour. If you have 6 cups of flour, how much butter and sugar will you need? The easiest way to figure this out is to make a chart:

If we know any one of the actual numbers, we can find them all. Here is what we know so far:

	Ratio (parts)	Multiplier	Actual Amount
sugar	1		
butter	2		
flour	3		6 cups

A ratio can be multiplied by any number to increase it. Here, the ratio number for flour (3) is multiplied by 2 to get the actual number (6). The key is to multiply every part of the ratio by the same number to increase the ratio. Multiply 1 part sugar by 2 to get 2 cups and multiply 2 parts butter by 2 to get 4 cups. Here is the completed chart:

	Ratio (parts)	Multiplier	Actual Amount
sugar	1	2	2 cups
butter	2	2	4 cups
flour	3	2	6 cups
TOTAL	6 parts	2	12 cups

As you can see, a row for the total can also be added. This will tell you the total amount of the mixture and allow you to answer questions such as "What part of the mixture is butter?" Two parts butter out of six total parts is $\frac{2}{6} = \frac{1}{3}$.

Exercises   COMPARE

1. The ratio of students to teachers is 22:1. If there are 132 students altogether, how many teachers are there?

_____

2. Henri fills a bag of black, white, and red marbles in the ratio of 3:2:4. If he has 16 red marbles, how many marbles are there altogether?

_____

3. A can of mixed nuts has peanuts, almonds, and walnuts in a ratio of 6:2:3. If the can has 4 ounces of almonds, how many ounces of peanuts and walnuts does it have?

_____

4. Lemonade is made with 1 part sugar, 2 parts lemon juice, and 5 parts water. If you have 1 cup of lemon juice, how much sugar do you need?

_____

Proportions and Cross-Multiplying

Do you ever have to use more than one ratio to solve a problem? Yes. A **proportion** is a problem that contains two ratios that are equal. You set up a proportion problem when you do not know the value of one of the numerators or one of the denominators. This kind of problem is called an **equation**. An equation is a mathematical statement that two things are equal. In this example, q stands for the unknown number of *quarts*. Let's say that you are giving a party for 20 people. You know that two quarts of potato salad will be enough for 10 people.

Cross-multiplying is the way to find the missing number. Multiply the numerator of the first fraction by the denominator of the second fraction and write the product on one side of the equation. Then muliply the denominator of the first fraction by the numerator of the second fraction and write that product on the other side of the equation. To get the answer, look at the side that has both a known number and the unknown number. Divide *both* sides of the equation by that known number.

Remember...

If you divide both sides of an equation by the *same* number, they will still be equal.

Example: $\dfrac{2 \text{ quarts}}{10 \text{ people}} = \dfrac{\text{(how many quarts?)}}{20 \text{ people}}$

Step 1: Set up your equation. $\dfrac{2}{10} = \dfrac{q}{20}$

Step 2: Cross-multiply. $40 = 10q$
$$4 = q$$

Exercises   CROSS-MULTIPLY

Round to the hundredths place.

1 $\dfrac{x}{5} = \dfrac{30}{15}$

2 $\dfrac{z}{3} = \dfrac{24}{6}$

3 $\dfrac{14}{z} = \dfrac{100}{50}$

4 $\dfrac{56}{4} = \dfrac{y}{20}$

5 $\dfrac{45}{9} = \dfrac{w}{3}$

6 $\dfrac{14}{x} = \dfrac{70}{10}$

7 $\dfrac{33}{r} = \dfrac{11}{3}$

8 $\dfrac{72}{9} = \dfrac{24}{z}$

9 $\dfrac{3}{2} = \dfrac{x}{5}$

10 $\dfrac{700}{50} = \dfrac{35}{w}$

11 $\dfrac{36}{4} = \dfrac{x}{6}$

12 $\dfrac{84}{12} = \dfrac{q}{4}$

Proportions and Cross-Multiplying (cont.)

13 A drilling rig can drill to −5 meters below the ground in an hour. At that speed, how far has the rig dug in 12 hours?

_____

14 George likes to sweeten his iced tea. When he drinks an 8-ounce iced tea, he puts in two teaspoons of sugar. If he is making 36 ounces of iced tea, how many teaspoons of sugar should he add?

_____

15 The amount of vacation time earned varies directly with the time worked. If an employee has earned 3 hours vacation time for 2 weeks' work, how much will she earn in 8 weeks?

_____

16 The pet shop recommends that you add 50 tablespoons of salt to a 10-gallon saltwater fish tank. How many tablespoons should be added to a 25-gallon tank?

_____

17 In driver's education class, we learned that the distance to stop the car is directly proportional to the car's speed. It takes 200 feet to stop a car going 50 miles per hour. How many feet does it take to stop a car going 65 miles per hour?

_____

18 The value of y varies directly with x. If $y = 3$ when $x = 12$, what is the value of y when $x = 4$?

_____

Rates

What other kinds of problems can using proportions help you solve? Proportions can be used to solve a rate problem.

When you set up the equation, be sure that the numerators are the same units and the denominators are the same units. In this equation, the numerators are blocks and the denominators are minutes.

Example:

Your friend Becky can ride her bike at the rate of 6 blocks in 5 minutes. How many minutes will it take her to ride 30 blocks?

$$\frac{6}{5} = \frac{30}{m}$$

6m = 150

m = 25

Exercises SOLVE

1. Adam can eat 4 hot dogs in 7 minutes and David can eat 3 hot dogs in 5 minutes. Who eats hot dogs at a faster rate?

_____

2. WINK Inc. can make 2700 widgets in 5 hours. What is the rate in widgets per minute?

_____

3. If Alfredo can walk 2 miles in 40 minutes, how far can he walk in 30 minutes?

_____

4. The cost to fill a 12-gallon tank with gas is $22.50. What is the price per gallon?

_____

5. Five people working at the same rate can stack 9000 bricks in an hour. How many bricks could 7 people stack in an hour at the same rate?

_____

Name _____

Scale Factors

A scale factor is the ratio between the measurement of an object and the measurement of a representation of that object. Scale factors have many uses, including for making models, enlarging photos, or comparing similar geometric figures. If the representation of the object is larger than the object, the scale factor will be greater than one. If the representation of the object is smaller than the object, the scale factor will be less than one. You can find scale factors using proportions.

Example:

Triangles A and B are similar. If the base of triangle A is 4.5 centimeters and the base of triangle B is 9 centimeters, what is the scale factor for these similar triangles? If the height of B is 12 centimeters, what is the height of A?

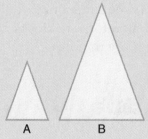

The measurements for triangle A are multiplied by some number to increase its size to that of triangle B. What number times 4.5 equals 9? $4.5 \times 2 = 9$, so the scale factor is 2. Once you know that, all you need to do to find the height of A is divide the height of B by the scale factor of 2: $12 \div 2 = 6$.

Exercises

1 The two rectangles are similar (proportional). Given the information about rectangle EFGH, what is the length of side CD?

_____

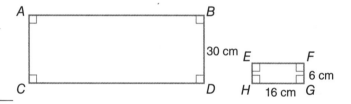

2 The two triangles are similar. Calculate the length of side s.

_____

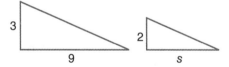

3 Chuck took a long hike where he started at point B and followed the path in the diagram shown. If Chuck wants to take a shorter hike where he starts at B and walks 4 miles east, turns and walks 3 miles north and then returns to point B, how long would his last leg be? Solve this problem using proportions even though you can solve it using the Pythagorean Theorem.

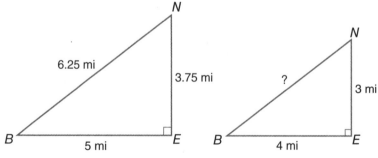

_____

Scale Factors (cont.)

4 On a map, the scale is 1 inch = 28 miles. If the distance between two cities is 10 inches, what is the actual distance?

_____

5 The blueprint for a house has a scale of 2 inches = 5 feet. What is the actual height of a wall in the house that is 5 inches on the blueprint?

_____

Name _____

Plotting Ordered Pairs

Can you make a graph that uses number lines? Yes. You can use one number line horizontally as the *x*-axis, and one number line vertically as the *y*-axis. On a graph, two numbers can express a point. Each of the two numbers can be positive or negative. The first number locates the point on the *x*-axis. The second number locates the point on the *y*-axis.

Example:

In this example, Point A is written as (3, 7). Point B is (−2, 1). And Point C is (0, −5).

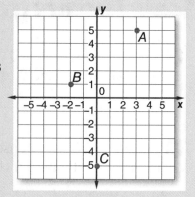

Exercises   PLOT ORDERED PAIRS

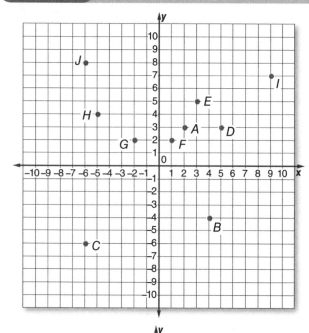

Give the coordinates for each point on the graph.

A _____   B _____

C _____   D _____

E _____   F _____

G _____   H _____

I _____   J _____

Plot the following ordered pairs on the graph:

A (3, 2)   B (7, −7)

C (−7, −7)   D (−7, 7)

E (7, 7)   F (9, 2)

G (6, 7)   H (−8, −6)

I (−2, 2)   J (−5, −5)

K (3, −4)   L (−2, −2)

Name _____

Graphing Relationships

You can create a graph to help you see how quantities relate to one another. Draw a graph with one quantity as the *x*-axis and the other quantity for the *y*-axis. Use the ratio, proportion, or rate as a point on your graph.

Example:

If a person walks at a rate of 2 miles per hour, draw a graph with distance on one axis and time on the other. Use the time 1 hour and the distance 2 miles as a point (1, 2) on the graph. You can plot other points as well. How far would that person walk in 2 hours? Use the point (2, 4) as a second point. How far would that person walk in 3 hours? Use the point (3, 6) as a third point. Now you can draw a line on the graph to show the rate.

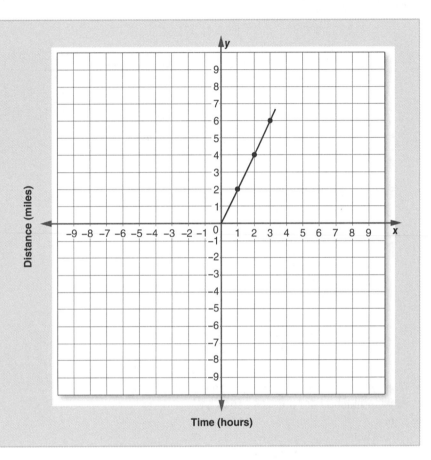

You can see that the distance and time are in a proportional relationship by observing that the line is straight and goes through the origin (0, 0). You can also see that the quantities are proportional by seeing whether the ratios are equivalent. Using the same values we used for the graph, you can show those as distance/time ratios of $\frac{2}{1}$, $\frac{4}{2}$, and $\frac{6}{3}$. All those ratios are equal to 2, so the relationship is proportional.

You can also use graphs to show relationships between different rates, ratios, and proportions. Plotting a rate for two people on the same graph allows you to easily compare them and draw conclusions about them.

Graphing Relationships (cont.)

Example:

After 1 hour, Jim has walked 2 miles and Laura has walked 3 miles. Each of them keeps walking at his or her same speed for a total of 3 hours. Draw a graph with distance on one axis and time on the other. Plot each of their rates on the graph.

Step 1: You need several values for each person to create a graph. Draw a function table to help you find values.

Time	Jim's distance	Laura's distance
1 hour	2 miles	3 miles
2 hours	4 miles	6 miles
3 hours	6 miles	9 miles

Step 2: Plot the values on a coordinate grid. Label each axis. Draw a line to show Jim's progress over the three hours and another line to show Laura's progress over the three hours. Be sure to use different colors or styles of line so that you can tell the difference. Include a legend to describe which line is for which person.

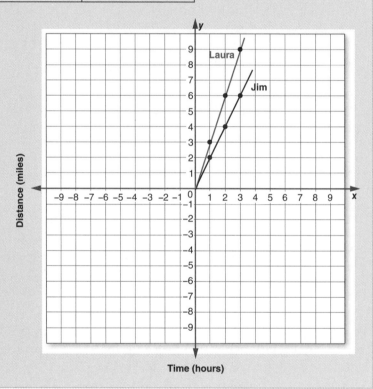

From this graph, you can see that Laura is walking much faster than Jim. They are 1 mile apart after 1 hour, 2 miles apart after 2 hours, 3 miles apart after 3 hours, and so on. Also notice that both lines are straight and go through the origin (0, 0). Whenever a rate is constant, the line will be straight and go through (0, 0).

Exercises SOLVE

Vicki can read 2 pages in 3 minutes. Bruce can read 4 pages in 3 minutes.

1 Complete the chart below to show this relationship.

Time	pages Vicki reads	pages Bruce reads
1 minute		
3 minutes	2	4
6 minutes		

2 Graph the relationship on the grid. Label each axis. Be sure to use different colors or styles of line so that you can tell the difference. Include a legend to describe which line is for which person.

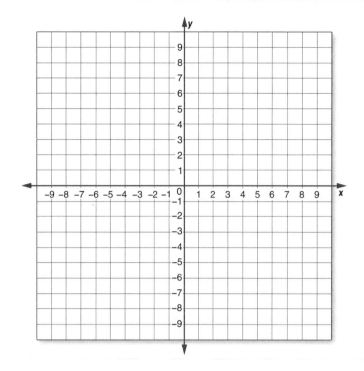

3 Which of the following correctly describes the relationship?

(a) Vicki reads twice as fast as Bruce.

(b) Bruce reads twice as fast as Vicki.

(c) Vicki's reading rate is one-third of Bruce's.

(d) Bruce reads half as fast as Vicki.

4 A store sells 5 pounds of potatoes for $1.00. How much would 1 pound cost? _____

Construct a graph for potato price on the grid below. Label each axis.

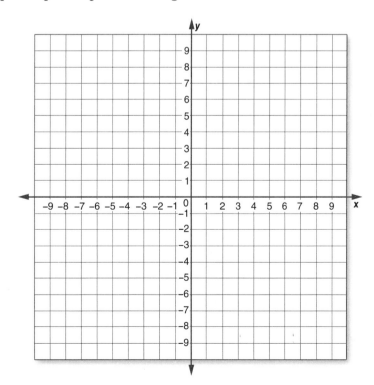

Name _____

Unit Rate

The value for y at which the x-coordinate = 1 is called the **unit rate**.

For Jim in the previous example, that point is (1, 2). We would say he walks at a rate of 2 miles per hour, so the unit rate is 2. For Laura, the point is (1, 3). She walks at a rate of 3 miles per hour, so her unit rate is 3.

You can find the unit rate for any ratio, proportion, or rate by finding how much per one of something.

Example:

If the ratio of teachers to students is 4:48, what is the unit rate?

Reduce the ratio to find how many students per 1 teacher. Divide 4:48 by 4 to reduce the ratio to 1:12. The unit rate is 12 students per teacher.

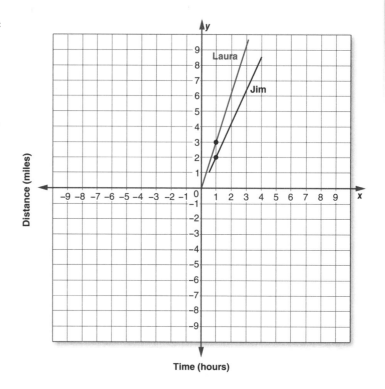

Exercises   SOLVE

The graph below shows the distance Isabella rides her bicycle over time.

1. Which coordinates (point) on the graph show the unit rate?

2. What is the unit rate shown in the graph?

3. If the graph also included a line to show how far Isabella walked over time at a rate of 3 miles per hour, would that line be above or below the one on the graph?

Price	Gallons of milk
$1.50	$\frac{1}{2}$
$3.00	1
$6.00	2

4. Are the quantities in the table above proportional?

5. What is the unit rate?

Name _____

Understanding Percent

Percents are special kinds of ratios, expressed as decimals. *Per* means *by,* and *cent* means hundredth. **Percents** compare numbers by looking at a whole as if it were divided into 100 parts.

Example:
$60\% = 0.60 = 0.6$
$6\% = 0.06$

Remember...

Every percentage can be displayed as a decimal or a fraction with a denominator of 100.

Exercises   WRITE DECIMALS AND FRACTIONS

Convert to a decimal and a fraction.

1 $7\% =$ _____ $=$ _____   **2** $16\% =$ _____ $=$ _____   **3** $100\% =$ _____ $=$ _____

4 $25\% =$ _____ $=$ _____   **5** $1\% =$ _____ $=$ _____   **6** $20\% =$ _____ $=$ _____

7 $44\% =$ _____ $=$ _____   **8** $99\% =$ _____ $=$ _____   **9** $23\% =$ _____ $=$ _____

10 $3\% =$ _____ $=$ _____   **11** $0\% =$ _____ $=$ _____   **12** $71\% =$ _____ $=$ _____

13 Out of 100 questions on an exam, Geraldine answered 89 questions correctly. What percentage of questions did Geraldine answer correctly?

_____

14 Frederick is dividing his birthday cake among 10 friends. If each person receives an equal 10% of the cake, how can Frederick use fractions to express a single slice of cake?

_____

15 How can Frederick use decimals to express a single slice of cake?

_____

Name _____

Percents and Fractions

Can you express percents in ways other than as a decimal?

Example:

What is 30% of 50?

$$\frac{30}{100} \times 50 = \frac{1500}{100} = 15$$

Just as you can with other decimals, you can change percents into fractions. The denominator of a percent is *always* 100, and the numerator will be the number of the percent.

$$\frac{2}{5} = ?\%$$

$$100 \div 5 = 20 \qquad 2 \times 20 = 40$$

$$\frac{2}{5} = 40\%$$

Some fractions can be turned into simple percents. If the denominator of the fraction can divide evenly into 100, find the quotient. Then multiply the numerator by the quotient, and add the percent sign. If the denominator of the fraction cannot divide evenly into 100, the fraction *cannot* be converted into a simple percent.

Remember...

Some fractions cannot be easily changed to percents. If 100 cannot be divided evenly by the fraction's denominator, you will not be able to convert the fraction to a simple percent.

Exercises CONVERT

Convert the fractions to a simple percentage, or state that the fraction cannot be converted to a simple percentage.

1 $\frac{1}{2} =$ _____

2 $\frac{3}{20} =$ _____

3 $\frac{7}{15} =$ _____

4 $\frac{3}{10} =$ _____

5 $\frac{2}{3} =$ _____

6 $\frac{3}{4} =$ _____

7 $\frac{6}{11} =$ _____

8 $1 =$ _____

9 $\frac{1}{32} =$ _____

10 $\frac{4}{25} =$ _____

11 $\frac{19}{50} =$ _____

12 $\frac{3}{50} =$ _____

13 $\frac{14}{10} =$ _____

14 $\frac{11}{20} =$ _____

15 $\frac{3}{25} =$ _____

16 $\frac{4}{9} =$ _____

17 $\frac{7}{20} =$ _____

18 $200 =$ _____

Percents and Decimals

How can you convert decimals with thousandths, ten-thousandths, and even smaller places into percentages? Simply move the decimal two places to the right and add a percent sign.

Example:

Convert 0.46072 to a percent.

0.46072 = 46.072%

In this example, move the decimal point two places to the right. Then add the percent sign.

Exercises **CONVERT**

Convert the decimals to a percentage. If the number is already a percentage, convert it to a decimal.

1 7% = _____

2 18.5% = _____

3 0.33 = _____

4 0.675 = _____

5 0.3356 = _____

6 0.01% = _____

7 2.34% = _____

8 3.45 = _____

9 2.145 = _____

10 0.3% = _____

11 33.29% = _____

12 2456 = _____

13 Taylor divided 6 shares of XYZ Corporation among 7 of her cousins. Each cousin received .8571 shares of XYZ stock. What percentage of a whole share did each cousin receive?

_____

14 Bill wants to take 15.43% of his earnings this year and put his money in his savings account. If Bill earned $100 this year, how much money will he put into his savings account?

_____

Multiplying Percents and Fractions

Can you multiply percents and fractions? Yes, you can. You learned that percents can be expressed as a fraction. So you need to convert the percent to a fraction and then multiply the two fractions.

An even simpler way to multiply a fraction by a percent is to multiply the percent *as if it were a whole number* times the fraction. The product will almost always be an improper fraction. Change that fraction into a mixed number and add the percent sign.

Example:

What is 50% of $\frac{2}{3}$?

$50\% = \frac{1}{2}$ $\frac{1}{2} \times \frac{2}{3} = \frac{1}{3}$

What is $\frac{1}{6}$ of 96%?

$\frac{1}{6} \times \frac{96}{100} = \frac{96}{600} = \frac{16}{100} = 16\%$

Remember...

Remember these two important points:

If you find a percent of a fraction, the product will be a fraction.

If you multiply a fraction by a percent, the product will be a percent.

Exercises MULTIPLY

1 $\frac{1}{2}$ of 40% =

2 $\frac{2}{3}$ of 60% =

3 50% of 18 =

4 12% of 400 =

5 $\frac{1}{4}$ of 8% =

6 20% of 75 =

7 39% of 300 =

8 $\frac{1}{9}$ of 45% =

9 $\frac{1}{3}$ of 90% =

10 25% of 60 =

11 $\frac{1}{3}$ of 27% =

12 18% of 50 =

13 120% of 35 =

14 100% of 37 =

15 $\frac{1}{4}$ of 36% =

Simple Interest

What does *simple interest* mean in a loan or a bank account? How do you calculate simple interest?

The amount you borrowed or deposited into the bank is called the **principal**. Simple interest is a percent of the principal that has to be paid by you if you borrowed the money, or by the bank if you deposited the money. In both cases, the interest is *added* to the principal.

Example:

How much simple interest would you earn on a deposit of $500 that remained in the bank for one year at 4% interest?

Principal = $500

Rate of Interest for one year = 4%

Principal (p) × Rate of Interest (r)

Interest $(i) = p \times r$

$i = \$500$ loan at 4% $= \$500 \times \dfrac{4}{100} = \$20$

Suppose you borrow the same amount of money at the same interest rate. How much would you have to pay back to the bank if the loan was paid in one year? You would have to pay $p + i = \$500$ (the principal) + $20 (the interest) = $520

Exercises   SOLVE

1 If the simple interest earned on $200 is $50, how much would you be earning on $700?

_____

2 A principal of $3000 will earn how much simple interest at 7.2%?

_____

3 Your uncle gives you $100 and deposits it into a savings account that pays simple interest of 6% per year. How much will you earn in interest for the year?

_____

4 At the beginning of the year you have $450 in your savings account and you are earning simple interest of 3.5% for the year. How much will you have at the end of the year?

_____

5 Simple interest at 7% on $5000 would be how much?

_____

6 Simple interest at 1% is how much for a principal of $10,000?

_____

7 If you have a principal of $4000 and earn simple interest of 5% for one year, how much will you have at the end of the year?

_____

8 How much will you earn in a year on $150 if the simple interest is paid at a rate of 11%?

_____

Name _____

Simple Interest for More or Less Than One Year

Does simple interest always have to be figured for exactly one year? No, you can calculate simple interest for longer or shorter time periods.

You still multiply the principal by the rate. But you *also* multiply by the number of years. It does not matter if the number of years is greater than, or less than 1!

Example:

Principal (Bank Account) = $250

Rate of Interest for one year: $6\frac{1}{2}\%$

Total number of years = 4

Interest = Principal (p) × Interest Rate (r) × Years (y)

Interest = $250 × 0.065 × 4 = $65

Principal (Bank Account) = $300

Rate of Interest for one year: 5%

Total number of years = $\frac{3}{4}$

Interest = Principal (p) × Interest Rate (r) × Years (y)

Interest = $300 × 0.05 × $\frac{3}{4}$ = $11.25

Exercises   SOLVE

Round all answers to the nearest cent.

1 How much simple interest would you earn if you had $10,000 and you were being paid 5% for 15 months?

_____

2 If you invest $5600 for 18 months at a simple interest rate of 7%, how much would you earn?

_____

3 What would be the total amount that you would have after 7 months if you started with $2700 and were paid simple interest of 5.5%?

_____

4 If you start with $6275 and earn simple interest of 14.75% for 37 months, what would be your total earnings for the period?

_____

5 You have a principal of $45,200 and will receive simple interest of 19.5% for 4 years. How much interest will you earn?

_____

6 What would be the simple interest earned on $2350 at 9.27% for 23 months?

_____

Percent Markups and Markdowns

Understanding how a percent is calculated will help you when you go shopping or out to eat. You will be able to calculate discounts, tax on a purchase, or a tip to leave in a restaurant. You will also be able to calculate commissions and fees or figure out by what percent an amount increased or decreased. To find a

markdown, such as a discount, multiply the percent off by the price and then subtract that amount from the price. To find a markup, such as a tax, tip, or fee, multiply the percent added by the price and then add that amount to the price.

Example:

Ryan has $15.00 and wants to be sure he has enough money to go to dinner at his favorite restaurant. He wants to order a hamburger for $8.00 and a soda for $1.00. There is 8% tax and then he wants to leave about a 20% tip. How much will his meal cost, including tax and tip?

Step 1: Find the total before tax. $8.00 + $1.00 = $9.00.

Step 2: Calculate the tax: $\frac{8}{100} \times 9 = \frac{72}{100} = 0.72$

Step 3: Add the tax to the total: $9.00 + 0.72 = $9.72.

Step 4: Calculate the tip. Since he wants to leave about 20%, you don't have to be exact. Let's round the total up to $10.00 to make the calculation simple.

$\frac{20}{100} \times \$10 = \frac{200}{100} = \$2$

Step 5: Add the tip to the total: $10.00 + $2.00 = $12.00.

Ryan has enough money.

Finding the percent increase or decrease between two amounts is a little bit different. Use this formula to make it easy:

$$\frac{\text{difference between the amounts}}{\text{original amount}} \times 100$$

Example:

The temperature today is 65 °F. Yesterday it was 60 °F. By what percent did the temperature increase?

Step 1: Find the difference between the two amounts.

$65 - 60 = 5$

Step 2: Use the formula to solve.

$\frac{5}{60} \times 100 = \frac{500}{60} = 8.33\%$

Exercises SOLVE

1 Valerie buys a book that costs $22.00, plus 8.25% sales tax. What does she pay for the book?

_____

2 Chris always tips his barber 30% for a haircut. If the haircut costs $25.00, how much will Chris leave for a tip?

_____

3 There is a 4% line fee added to cell phone bills in Bellville. If Erlene's bill before the fee is $56.80, what is her bill total after the fee is added?

_____

4 Bob earns a base salary of $500 per week, plus 6% commission on all his sales. If he sold $3240 this week, what will his salary be for this week?

_____

5 Last year, 32,500 people attended the county fair. This year, 45,800 people attended. What is the percent increase in attendance?

_____

6 Elba missed 7 out of 60 questions on a test. What percent did she get correct?

_____

7 A store is having a 15% off sale. What is the new price of a table that originally cost $200?

_____

8 A dress that was originally $89 is marked down to $75. By what percent was the price decreased?

_____

9 Only 12 people can ride a trolley at one time. This is 20% of the people waiting to ride. How many people are waiting to ride?

_____

10 Jack received $40 from his aunt for his birthday. He wants to buy a video game for $27.99, a hat for $7.99, and a candy bar for $.50. Sales tax is 8.5%. What would the total be for his purchases? Will he have enough money?

_____

Challenge Questions

Let's see if you can apply your skills to a couple of really challenging questions. Ready?

1) If the ratio of boys to girls in seventh grade is $2\frac{1}{2}:3$ and there are 40 boys in the seventh grade, what is the total number of students? What fraction of the seventh grade are girls?

2) It takes Kaveri 2 hours to sort 6 pounds of buttons and Ron 3 hours to do the same job. How many minutes will it take them to sort 12 pounds of buttons if they work together?

Answers and Explanations are on p. 220.

Unit Test

Name _____

Lessons 13–15

Determine if the following proportions are equal. (Write Yes or No.)

1 $\dfrac{5}{4} = \dfrac{24}{16}$ _____

2 $\dfrac{21}{12} = \dfrac{7}{36}$ _____

3 $\dfrac{12}{19} = \dfrac{36}{57}$ _____

4 $\dfrac{1}{4} = \dfrac{6}{24}$ _____

Solve for *x*.

5 $\dfrac{x}{10} = \dfrac{30}{20}$

6 $\dfrac{25}{x} = \dfrac{40}{100}$

7 $\dfrac{33}{96} = \dfrac{11}{x}$

8 $\dfrac{1}{10} = \dfrac{20}{x}$

Solve.

9 Create a ratio to compare the length of the side of a barn (140 ft) to the width of the barn (64 ft). _____

10 Create a ratio to compare the amount of unsaturated fat in salad dressing (5 grams) to the amount of carbohydrates (9 grams). _____

11 Wallace rides his bicycle at an average speed of 18 miles per hour. How many miles does he travel in $3\frac{1}{3}$ hours? _____

12 Jermaine can make 29 loaves of bread for every 3 batches he bakes. How many batches of bread does he need to bake in order to make 232 loaves? _____

13 Phyllis drinks $\frac{3}{4}$ of a pint of water after each mile she walks. How many pints of water will she drink if she walks $5\frac{3}{4}$ miles? _____

14 Ginny needs to check the air in her tires every 750 miles. How many times will she need to check her tires if she is taking a trip that is 6750 miles in length? _____

Unit Test

Lessons 13-15

Calculate.

15 30% of $1\frac{2}{5}$

16 40% of 440

17 $\frac{1}{4}$ of 48%

18 $\frac{2}{5}$ of 70%

19 $\frac{3}{8}$ of 340%

20 43% of 0.705

21 84% of 1.906

22 75% of 0.7575

23 Jessie deposited $824.25 of his babysitting money into an account that pays 4.5% interest. How much will he have in his account at the end of one year? _____

24 What is the annual rate of interest on a loan of $1500 if you have paid a total of $120 in interest after two years? _____

25 Chris bought a jacket that was marked $50 before tax. He paid $53.50 after tax. What percent tax did he pay? _____

If the jacket was on sale and was originally marked $75, by what percent did the price decrease? _____

Provide the ordered pairs for the points plotted on the graph.

26 A _____

27 B _____

28 C _____

29 D _____

30 E _____

31 F _____

32 G _____

33 H _____

34 I _____

35 J _____

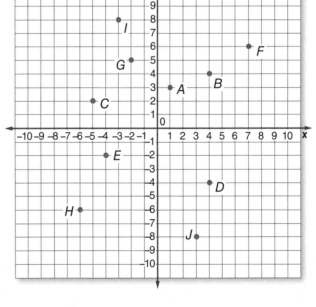

Unit Test

Lessons 13-15

Plot the following points on the grid provided:

36 A (1, 4)

37 B (4, 1)

38 C (3, 9)

39 D (−9, −3)

40 E (−4, 4)

41 F (−1, −4)

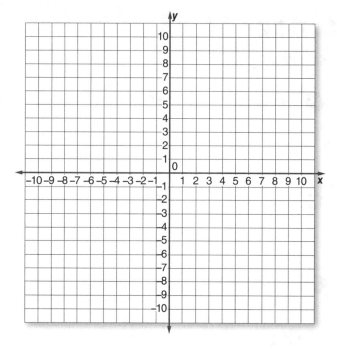

42 A train has 7 cars and can carry 224 people. If the train adds 2 extra cars, how many people can it carry?

_____

What is the unit rate per car?

_____

43 How fast is Car A going?

_____

44 How fast is Car B going?

_____

45 How far will Car A have gone after 5 minutes?

_____

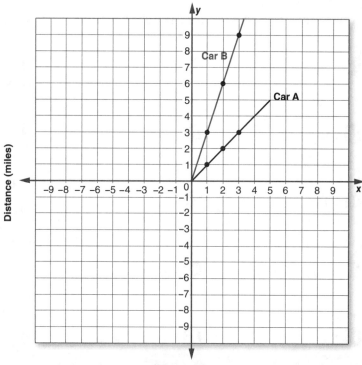

Unit Test

Answers and Explanations

1. No $5 \times 16 = 4 \times 24$; $5 \times 4 \times 4 = 4 \times 6 \times 4$; $5 \neq 6$

2. No $21 \times 36 = 12 \times 7$;
$3 \times 7 \times 3 \times 3 \times 4 = 3 \times 4 \times 7$; $9 \neq 0$

3. Yes $12 \times 57 = 19 \times 36$;
$3 \times 4 \times 3 \times 19 = 19 \times 3 \times 3 \times 4$; yes

4. Yes $1 \times 24 = 24$; yes

5. $x = 15$ $20x = (10)(30)$; $20x = 300$; $x = 15$

6. $x = 62.5$ $(25)(100) = 40x$; $2500 = 40x$;
$250 = 4x$; $x = 62.5$

7. $x = 32$ $33x = (11)(96)$; $3 \times 11 \times x = 11 \times 32 \times 3$;
$x = 32$

8. $x = 200$ $x = (20)(10) = 200$

9. $\dfrac{35}{16}$ $140{:}64 = \dfrac{140}{64} = \dfrac{35}{16}$

10. $\dfrac{5}{9}$ $5{:}9 = \dfrac{5}{9}$

11. 60 miles $\dfrac{18 \text{ miles}}{1 \text{ hour}} = \dfrac{m \text{ miles}}{\frac{10}{3} \text{ hours}}$; $18 \times \dfrac{10}{3} = 1 \times m$;
$6 \times 10 = m$; $m = 60$

12. 24 batches $\dfrac{29 \text{ loaves}}{3 \text{ batches}} = \dfrac{232 \text{ loaves}}{b \text{ batches}}$;
$29b = 3 \times 232 = 29b = 696$; $b = 24$

13. $4\dfrac{5}{16}$ pints $\dfrac{\frac{3}{4} \text{ pint}}{1 \text{ mile}} = \dfrac{p \text{ pints}}{\frac{23}{4} \text{ miles}}$; $\dfrac{3}{4} \times \dfrac{23}{4} = 1 \times p$;
$\dfrac{69}{16} = p$; $p = 4\dfrac{5}{16}$

14. 9 times $\dfrac{6750}{750} = \dfrac{675}{75} = 9$

15. $\dfrac{21}{50}$ $\dfrac{30}{100} \times \dfrac{7}{5} = \dfrac{210}{500} = \dfrac{21}{50}$

16. 176 $\dfrac{40}{100} \times \dfrac{440}{1} = 4 \times 44 = 176$

17. 12% $\dfrac{1}{4} \times 48 = \dfrac{48}{4} = 12$

18. 28% $\dfrac{2}{5} \times 70 = 2 \times 14 = 28$

19. 127.5% $\dfrac{3}{8} \times 340 = \dfrac{1020}{8} = 127.5$

20. 0.30315 $\dfrac{43}{100} \times \dfrac{0.705}{1} = \dfrac{43 \times 0.705}{100}$
$= \dfrac{30.315}{100} = 0.30315$

21. 1.60104 $\dfrac{84}{100} \times \dfrac{1.906}{1} = \dfrac{84 \times 1.906}{100}$
$= \dfrac{160.104}{100} = 1.60104$

22. 0.568125 $\dfrac{75}{100} \times \dfrac{0.7575}{1} = \dfrac{75 \times 0.7575}{100}$
$= \dfrac{56.8125}{100} = 0.568125$

23. $861.34 $824.25 \times 0.045 = \$37.09$;
$824.25 + \$37.09 = \$861.34$

24. 4% $120 = 1500 \times r \times 2$; $120 = 3000r$;
$r = 0.04 = 4\%$

25. 7%; 33% $53.50 - \$50.00 = \$3.50$ tax;
$\dfrac{x}{100} \times 50 = 3.50$; $\dfrac{1}{2}x = 3.50$;
$x = 7\%$ percent decrease
$= \dfrac{75 - 50}{75} = \dfrac{25}{75} = \dfrac{1}{3} = 33\%$

26. (1,3)

27. (4,4)

28. (−5,2)

29. (4,−4)

30. (−4,−2)

31. (7,6)

32. (−2,5)

33. (−6,−6)

34. (−3,8)

35. (3,−8)

36.–41.

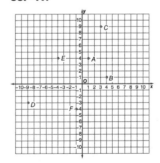

42. 288; 32 $\dfrac{7 \text{ cars}}{224 \text{ people}} = \dfrac{9 \text{ cars}}{p \text{ people}}$;
$7p = 224 \times 9$; $7p = 2016$; $p = 288$

43. 1 mile per minute

44. 3 miles per minute

45. 5 miles

Exponents

What if you want to multiply $3 \times 3 \times 3$? Or $5 \times 5 \times 5 \times 5$? Is there a simple way you can write that? Yes, you can use an **exponent**. The number you keep multiplying by itself is called the **base**. The exponent (written as a small number next to and slightly above the base) tells how many times you multiply the base by itself.

Examples:

$$\text{base} \rightarrow 2^{\overset{\text{exponent}}{4}} \qquad \text{base} \rightarrow 3^{\overset{\text{exponent}}{5}}$$

$2^4 = 2 \times 2 \times 2 \times 2 = 16$

$3^5 = 3 \times 3 \times 3 \times 3 \times 3 = 243$

You have already learned about **powers of 10**. Exponents represent powers. So 10^3 is 10 to the third power. Any number can be a base. For example, 3^5 is 3 to the fifth power. When a base is raised to the second power, we use the word "squared." 25^2 can be expressed as "25 to the second power," or "25 squared." When a base is raised to the third power, we often use the word "cubed." So 12^3 can be expressed as "12 cubed."

Here are two important things to know about exponents:

1. A base raised to the **first power** = the base.
   For example: $197^1 = 197$

2. A base raised to the **zero power** = 1.
   For example: $9592^0 = 1$

Exercises   CALCULATE

1 $12^2 =$ _____

2 $10^4 =$ _____

3 $7^3 =$ _____

4 $2^3 =$ _____

5 $4^4 =$ _____

6 $5^3 =$ _____

7 $41^2 =$ _____

8 $5^5 =$ _____

9 $6^7 =$ _____

10 $17^4 =$ _____

11 $0^{10} =$ _____

12 $101^0 =$ _____

13 $12^1 =$ _____

14 $24^0 =$ _____

15 $33^1 =$ _____

Exponents (cont.)

Is there a simple way to multiply and divide bases that have exponents? Yes. To multiply a base raised to a power by the same base raised to a power, simply add the exponents. To divide a base raised to a power by the same base raised to a power, simply subtract the exponents.

Examples:

Multiply	Divide
$3^2 \times 3^3 = 3^5$	$4^6 \div 4^4 = 4^2$
$2^4 \times 2^5 = 2^9$	$10^7 \div 10^3 = 10^4$

Exponents can be **negative**. A negative exponent creates a fraction. The numerator is 1. The denominator is the base raised to the power after the minus sign.

Can you multiply and divide a base raised to a negative power by the *same* base raised to a negative power? Yes, you can add and subtract negative exponents, just as you added and subtracted positive exponents. Ignore the negative sign while you add and subtract, but then make sure to include it in your answer.

Example:

For example: $6^{-2} = \dfrac{1}{6^2} = \dfrac{1}{6 \times 6} = \dfrac{1}{36}$

$2^{-6} = \dfrac{1}{2^6} = \dfrac{1}{2 \times 2 \times 2 \times 2 \times 2 \times 2} = \dfrac{1}{64}$

Exercises — MULTIPLY OR DIVIDE

1 $2^3 \div 2^{-5} =$ _____

2 $5^5 \times 5^{-6} =$ _____

3 $11^{11} \div 11^4 =$ _____

4 $54^4 \div 54^{-2} =$ _____

5 $3^2 \div 3^0 =$ _____

6 $8^1 \times 8^8 =$ _____

7 $15^5 \div 15^4 =$ _____

8 $8^6 \div 8^2 =$ _____

9 $18^7 \times 18^{21} =$ _____

10 $81^{10} \div 81^7 =$ _____

11 $19^{19} \times 19^{16} =$ _____

12 $21^2 \div 21^3 =$ _____

13 $15^{-5} \div 15^6 =$ _____

14 $10^{-8} \div 10^{-12} =$ _____

15 $17^{15} \div 17^{22} =$ _____

16.2

Square Roots

You have learned about exponents and know that the exponent shows how many times to multiply a number times itself. In 3^2, the exponent 2 means that you multiply the number 3 twice. This is also known as *squaring* a number. To square a number, you multiply the number by itself: $3^2 = 3 \times 3 = 9$. When you square an integer, the result is called a **perfect square**. The perfect squares up to 100 are: 1, 4, 9, 16, 25, 36, 49, 64, 81, and 100.

The **square root** of a number is the number that, when multiplied by itself, is equal to that number. A square root uses a radical sign, which looks like this: $\sqrt{\ }$. Square roots are always positive.

Example:

$\sqrt{9} = 3$ because $3 \times 3 = 9$.

Exercises   CALCULATE

Identify the square root.

1 $\sqrt{36}$ _____

2 $\sqrt{144}$ _____

3 $\sqrt{81}$ _____

4 $\sqrt{25}$ _____

5 $\sqrt{169}$ _____

6 $\sqrt{9}$ _____

7 $\sqrt{1}$ _____

8 $\sqrt{49}$ _____

9 $\sqrt{4}$ _____

10 $\sqrt{100}$ _____

11 $\sqrt{16}$ _____

12 $\sqrt{121}$ _____

13 $\sqrt{64}$ _____

14 $\sqrt{225}$ _____

Estimate.

15 $\sqrt{12}$ is between _____ and _____

16 $\sqrt{41}$ is between _____ and _____

Scientific Notation

It is difficult to write and read long numbers like 4,500,000,000 or 61,020,000. Is there a simpler way to express long numbers? Yes, you could use **scientific notation**. When you use scientific notation, notice that the decimal is always *greater than 1* but *less than 10*. You might think the difficult part is figuring out which power of 10 to use. However, that is not so hard. Look at the number in standard, or regular, notation. Imagine that there is a

decimal point to the right of that number. Move the decimal point to the left, one place value at a time, counting each time you move it. *Stop* when your number is greater than 1 but less than 10. Your count is the power of 10.

Examples:
$4{,}500{,}000{,}000 = 4.5 \times 10^9$
$61{,}020{,}000 = 6.102 \times 10^7$

Exercises   CONVERT

If the expression is in scientific notation, convert it to a number. If it is a number, convert it to scientific notation. Round all numbers to 6 places to the right of the decimal point when converting to scientific notation.

1 $5 \times 10^5 =$

_____

2 $478.23 =$

_____

3 $89{,}786 =$

_____

4 $6.721 \times 10^6 =$

_____

5 $2.9731 \times 10^{-2} =$

_____

6 $691{,}273 =$

_____

7 $5.9178 \times 10^{-3} =$

_____

8 $8.72345 \times 10^{10} =$

_____

9 $6{,}664{,}475 =$

_____

10 $0.0005123 =$

_____

11 $8.9 =$

_____

12 $100.235 =$

_____

13 $963{,}764 =$

_____

14 $4.6554 =$

_____

15 $789.23 =$

_____

16 $15{,}896{,}000{,}000{,}000 =$

_____

17 $8{,}999{,}345{,}000 =$

_____

18 $1.697324 \times 10^4 =$

_____

17.1

Understanding Variable Expressions

Is there a way to solve a problem when one number is unknown? Yes, there is. You need to use **algebra**. Algebra is a branch of math you can use to find the value of unknown numbers. Unknown numbers are called **variables**.

To find the unknown number, or variable, you will probably have to use algebraic expressions. An **algebraic expression** is a group of variables, numbers, and operations.

Some Algebraic Expressions

$$s + 32 \qquad\qquad (k - 31) \times 3$$

$$(45 \div y) + 9 \qquad\qquad z^2$$

$$\frac{j}{3} \qquad\qquad 4g$$

The last expression means $4 \times g$. When you multiply a variable, you do not need to write the $\times$ sign. Instead, you just use a **coefficient**, which is a number that multiplies a variable.

Exercises   EXPLAIN

Put into words what each expression is describing.

1 $\dfrac{a}{4}$

_____

_____

2 $y + 3$

_____

_____

3 $4b + 8$

_____

_____

4 $0.9q - 7$

_____

_____

5 $\dfrac{(x - 3)}{25}$

_____

_____

6 $8(2g + 6)$

_____

_____

7 $2n - 5$

_____

_____

8 $12(r - 14)$

_____

_____

9 $\dfrac{7}{h}$

_____

_____

10 $\dfrac{11 + b}{16}$

_____

_____

Understanding Inequalities

An inequality is similar to an equation, except instead of an equals sign, an inequality uses a sign to show that the expressions are *not* or *may not be* equal. These signs include:

>   greater than

≥   greater than or equal to

<   less than

≤   less than or equal to

Examples:

The inequality $x < 7$ means that a number is less than 7. Any real number less than 7 could be the value of x.

The inequality $2x \geq 14$ means that 2 times a number is greater than or equal to 14.

Exercises   EXPLAIN

Put into words what each expression is describing.

1 $3x < 6$

_____

_____

2 $p - 1 > 5$

_____

_____

3 $y \leq 4$

_____

_____

4 $s^2 \geq 25$

_____

_____

5 $\dfrac{f}{5} < 63$

_____

_____

6 $w + 9 < 12$

_____

_____

7 $643 < d + g$

_____

_____

8 $z + 2 \leq 15$

_____

_____

9 $4h > 17$

_____

_____

10 $1 - n \geq -63$

_____

_____

Name _____

Solving Equations and Inequalities by Addition and Subtraction

How do you use addition and subtraction to solve algebraic expressions? Refer back to Lesson 4.4 where you learned the Equality Properties of Addition and Subtraction. These rules help you solve equations and inequalities that use addition and subtraction.

In the first example, you subtract 6 from *both sides* of the equation to find *d*. In the second example, you add 4 to *both sides* of the inequality to find *w*.

Examples:

$d + 6 = 20$ Find *d*. $w - 4 > 10$. Find *w*.
$d = 12$ $w > 14$

Exercises   SOLVE

Solve for the variable shown in the expression.

1 $x + 6 = 17$

2 $17 = s + 9$

3 $14 + z = 49$

4 $17 - f < 14$

5 $c - 11 > 11$

6 $y + 23 = 25$

7 $107 = 5 + x$

8 $k + 36 = 64$

9 $15 + u \leq 43$

10 $59 - t = 22$

11 $9 - a = 3$

12 $75 + b > 101$

13 $49 - e = 24$

14 $16 + d \geq 39$

15 $w + 15 \leq 81$

16 $q - 23 = 35$

Solving Equations and Inequalities by Multiplication and Division

Can you use the Equality Properties of Multiplication and Division to solve algebraic expressions, too? Yes, you can. Before we look at these kinds of equations, you need to think about this: division and multiplication are opposites. If you multiply a number or a variable by a second number, and then you divide the product by that second number, you will end up with the original number or variable. For example: $7 \times 8 \div 8 = 7$, $h \div 2 \times 2 = h$. To solve a multiplication equation, divide both sides of the equation by the same number. To solve a division equation, multiply both sides of the equation by the same number. There is one important thing to remember: If you multiply or divide an inequality by a negative number,

reverse the direction of the sign. In other words, flip a "less than" sign around so that it becomes a "greater than" sign.

Examples:

$9p = 45$. Find p. $\quad \frac{u}{3} < 8$. Find u.

$p = 5$ $\quad\quad\quad\quad\quad u < 24$

In the first example, you divide *both sides* of the equation by 9 to find p. In the second example, you multiply *both sides* of the inequality by 3 to find u.

Remember...

You can keep an equation equal by performing the same operation on *both sides*.

Exercises SOLVE

1 $2y + 15 = 25$

2 $5 + 5p < 70$

3 $8c + 8 > 224$

4 $17 + \frac{w}{3} = 45$

5 $34 = 10 + 4q$

6 $42 = 7 + \frac{z}{5}$

7 $232 \le 8 + 8x$

8 $63 = 3 + 4g$

9 $12 = \frac{g}{9}$

10 $3k + 5 > 56$

11 $49 \ge 10 + \frac{p}{5}$

12 $2y + 5 = 74$

13 $8d + 130 = 210$

14 $33 + \frac{1}{3}c \le 66$

Challenge Questions

Let's see if you can apply your skills to a couple of really challenging questions. Ready?

1) If, $x^3 = 27$ and $x - y = 4$, what is the value of y?

2) Jacques wants to buy a new outfit consisting of a shirt that costs $15.99 and a pair of jeans that costs $38.49. He earns $7.50 per hour at his babysitting job. Write an inequality that expresses how many hours he must work in order to buy this outfit.

Answers and Explanations are on p. 220.

Unit Test

Lessons 16–17

Restate in exponential form then calculate.

1 $8 \times 8 \times 2 + 3 \times 3 \times 3$ _____

2 $2 \times 2 \times 4 \times 4 - 3 \times 3 \times 3$ _____

3 $5 \times 25 \times 2 \times 2 \times 4 \times 4 + 7 \times 7 - 5 \times 5$ _____

Restate using scientific notation.

4 13,654,764.011 _____

5 28,397.01 _____

6 0.100745 _____

7 21,194,668,041.1 _____

8 813.056 _____

Calculate.

9 3^3

10 8^4

11 $2^3 \times 2^{-2}$

12 $10^{-8} \div 10^{-9}$

13 $15^{11} \times 15^{-11}$

14 $\sqrt{49}$

15 $\sqrt{64}$

16 $\sqrt{16}$

17 $\sqrt{1}$

18 $\sqrt{25}$

Solve for x.

19 $x - 15 \leq 23$

20 $3 + x \geq 4$

21 $5x < 650$

22 $3x - 6 > 36$

23 $\frac{x}{4} \leq 8$

24 $6 + x = 13$

25 $x - 15 = 22$

26 $39 - x = 25$

27 $x + 60 = 90$

28 $6x + 3 = 33$

29 $4x - 5 = 19$

30 $6x + 3 = 45$

31 $2x + 14 = 42$

32 $4 - 4x = -48$

33 $\frac{x}{6} + 3 = 12$

34 $\frac{x}{2} - 5 = 30$

35 $\frac{1}{3}x - 4 = 16$

Unit Test

Name _____

Answers and Explanations

1. $8^2 \times 2 + 3^3 = 155$ $\qquad$ $8^2 \times 2 + 3^3 = 64 \times 2 + 27 = 128 + 27 = 155$

2. $2^2 \times 4^2 - 3^3 = 37$ $\qquad$ $2^2 \times 4^2 - 3^3 = 4 \times 16 - 27 = 64 - 27 = 37$

3. $5 \times 25 \times 2^2 \times 4^2$ $\qquad$ $5 \times 25 \times 2^2 \times 4^2 + 7^2 - 5^2 = 125 \times 4 \times 16 + 49 - 25 = 8000 + 49 - 25 = 8049 - 25 = 8024$
$+ \, 7^2 - 5^2 = 8024$

4. 1.3654764011×10^7

5. 2.839701×10^4

6. 1.00745×10^{-1}

7. $2.11946680411 \times 10^{10}$

8. 8.13056×10^2

9. 27 $\qquad\qquad\qquad$ $3 \times 3 \times 3 = 27$

10. 4096 $\qquad\qquad\quad$ $8 \times 8 \times 8 \times 8 = 4096$

11. 2 $\qquad\qquad\qquad$ $2^3 \times \dfrac{1}{2^2} = \dfrac{2^3}{2^2} = 2^1 = 2$

12. 10 $\qquad\qquad\quad$ $10^{-8} \div 10^{-9} = \dfrac{1}{10^8} \div \dfrac{1}{10^9} = \dfrac{1}{10^8} \times \dfrac{10^9}{1} = \dfrac{10^9}{10^8} = 10^1 = 10$

13. 1 $\qquad\qquad\qquad$ $15^{11} \times 15^{-11} = \dfrac{15^{11}}{1} \times \dfrac{1}{15^{11}} = \dfrac{15^{11}}{15^{11}} = 1$

14. 7

15. 8

16. 4

17. 1

18. 5

19. $x \le 38$ $\quad$
$$\begin{array}{rl} x - 15 \le & 23 \\ +15 \quad & +15 \\ \hline x \le & 38 \end{array}$$

20. $x \ge 1$ $\quad$
$$\begin{array}{rl} 3 + x \ge & 4 \\ -3 \quad & -3 \\ \hline x \ge & 1 \end{array}$$

21. $x < 130$ $\quad$
$$\begin{array}{l} \dfrac{5x}{5} < \dfrac{650}{5} \\ x < 130 \end{array}$$

22. $x > 14$ $\quad$
$$\begin{array}{rl} 3x - 6 > & 36 \\ +6 \quad & +6 \\ \hline \dfrac{3x}{3} > & \dfrac{42}{3} \\ x > & 14 \end{array}$$

23. $x \le 32$ $\quad$
$$\begin{array}{l} (4)\dfrac{x}{4} \le 8(4) \\ x \le 32 \end{array}$$

24. $x = 7$ $\quad$
$$\begin{array}{rl} 6 + x = & 13 \\ -6 \quad & -6 \\ \hline x = & 7 \end{array}$$

25. $x = 37$ $\quad$
$$\begin{array}{rl} x - 15 = & 22 \\ +15 \quad & +15 \\ \hline x = & 37 \end{array}$$

26. $x = 14$ $\quad$
$$\begin{array}{rl} 39 - x = & 25 \\ +x \quad & +x \\ \hline 39 = & 25 + x \\ -25 \quad & -25 \\ \hline 14 = & x \end{array}$$

27. $x = 30$ $\quad$
$$\begin{array}{rl} x + 60 = & 90 \\ -60 \quad & -60 \\ \hline x = & 30 \end{array}$$

28. $x = 5$ $\quad$
$$\begin{array}{rl} 6x + 3 = & 33 \\ -3 \quad & -3 \\ \hline \dfrac{6x}{6} = & \dfrac{30}{6} \\ x = & 5 \end{array}$$

29. $x = 6$ $\quad$
$$\begin{array}{rl} 4x - 5 = & 19 \\ +5 \quad & +5 \\ \hline \dfrac{4x}{4} = & \dfrac{24}{4} \\ x = & 6 \end{array}$$

30. $x = 7$ $\quad$
$$\begin{array}{rl} 6x + 3 = & 45 \\ -3 \quad & -3 \\ \hline \dfrac{6x}{6} = & \dfrac{42}{6} \\ x = & 7 \end{array}$$

31. $x = 14$ $\quad$
$$\begin{array}{rl} 2x + 14 = & 42 \\ -14 \quad & -14 \\ \hline \dfrac{2x}{2} = & \dfrac{28}{2} \\ x = & 14 \end{array}$$

32. $x = 13$ $\quad$
$$\begin{array}{rl} 4 - 4x = & -48 \\ -4 \quad & -4 \\ \hline \dfrac{-4x}{-4} = & \dfrac{-52}{-4} \\ x = & 13 \end{array}$$

33. $x = 54$ $\quad$
$$\begin{array}{rl} \dfrac{x}{6} + 3 = & 12 \\ -3 \quad & -3 \\ \hline (6)\dfrac{x}{6} = & 9(6) \\ x = & 54 \end{array}$$

34. $x = 70$ $\quad$
$$\begin{array}{rl} \dfrac{x}{2} - 5 = & 30 \\ +5 \quad & +5 \\ \hline (2)\dfrac{x}{2} = & 32(2) \\ x = & 70 \end{array}$$

35. $x = 60$ $\quad$
$$\begin{array}{rl} \dfrac{1}{3}x - 4 = & 16 \\ +4 \quad & +4 \\ \hline (3)\dfrac{1}{3}x = & 20(3) \\ x = & 60 \end{array}$$

114 $\quad$ Unit Test $\quad$ Lessons 16–17

Customary Units of Length

Length is customarily measured in inches (in.), feet (ft), yards (yd), and miles (mi). You can compare them to each other, and even change one to another by simple calculations.

1 foot = 12 in.

1 yard = 3 ft

1 mile = 1760 yd or 5280 ft

Exercises   CALCULATE

1 12.5 feet is how many yards? _____

2 1 mile is how many feet? _____

3 144 inches is how many yards? _____

4 3 miles is how many yards? _____

5 128 inches is how many feet? _____

6 10,560 yards is how many miles? _____

7 15.5 yards is how many feet? _____

8 3.25 miles is how many inches? _____

Name _____

Customary Units of Liquid Volume

When you buy a fruit juice or when you add a liquid to a recipe, you often measure in units of **liquid volume**. Liquid volume is the amount of liquid a container can hold. Liquid volume is measured in cups (c), pints (pt), quarts (qt), and gallons (gal). And, as with units of length, you can compare these units to each other, and change one to another by simple calculations.

1 pint = 2 cups

1 quart = 2 pints

1 gallon = 4 quarts

Exercises   CALCULATE

1 4 gallons is how many pints?

_____

2 A 33-gallon gas tank has how many quarts? _____

3 64 quarts is how many gallons?

_____

4 36 pints is how many gallons?

_____

5 2000 cups is how many quarts?

_____

6 300 pints is how many cups?

_____

7 64 gallons is how many pints?

_____

8 42 quarts is how many cups?

_____

Customary Units of Weight

Weight is customarily measured in ounces (oz), pounds (lb), and tons (T). As with units of length and liquid volume, you can compare units of weight to each other, and change one to another by simple calculations.

1 pound = 16 oz   1 ton = 2000 lb

Exercises   CALCULATE

1 20 pounds is how many ounces?

_____

2 5.2 tons is how many pounds?

_____

3 4 tons is how many ounces?

_____

4 196 ounces is how many pounds?

_____

5 Three 200-pound men weigh how many tons?

_____

6 A 13.5-ton elephant weighs how many pounds?

_____

7 A $1\frac{3}{4}$ ton truck can carry $1\frac{3}{4}$ of a ton of materials in its bed. How many pounds is that?

_____

8 If there are 1050 students at school and each eats 3 ounces of turkey burger for lunch, how many pounds of turkey burger is that?

_____

Name _____

Perimeter

Imagine that you want to find the distance around a figure. This is the **perimeter**.

Example:

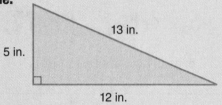

The perimeter of this triangle is
5 + 12 + 13 = 30 in.

You could change this total number into feet by dividing the number of inches by 12.

$$\frac{30}{12} = 2\frac{1}{2} \text{ ft}$$

Example:

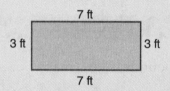

The perimeter of this rectangle is
7 + 3 + 7 + 3 = 20 ft.

You could change this total into inches by multiplying by 12.

20 × 12 = 240 inches

Remember...

Right triangles are usually marked with a special symbol.

90°

Exercises ▸ SOLVE

1 Which has a longer perimeter, a triangle with sides of 26 feet or a hexagon with sides of 18 feet?

_____

2 If Trent walks east for 25 feet, then north for 30 feet, then west for 25 feet, how long would he have to walk to get to his starting point and how long did he walk in total?

_____

3 If you have a 120-foot piece of fencing wire, how long would each side of a square-shaped corral be if all the fencing is used?

_____

4 If you want to put a ribbon around a rectangular box with sides of 5 and 10 inches, how much ribbon would you need?

_____

5 What is the perimeter of the figure shown?

_____

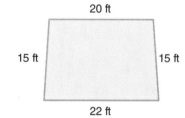

Area

To calculate a figure's **area**, you need to know what to call those units. The units used in describing area are: square inches, square feet, square yards, or even square miles. Remember, however, that a square foot does *not* equal 12 square inches; and a square yard does *not* equal 3 square feet; and a square mile does *not* equal 1760 square yards.

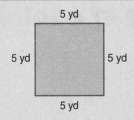

5 yd × 5 yd = 25 sq yd

A square is a special kind of rectangle, with all of its sides equal in length.

You may remember that a number to the second power, or a number multiplied once by itself, is called "squared."

Examples:

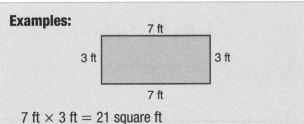

7 ft × 3 ft = 21 square ft

The area of a rectangle is its length (l) × its width (w).

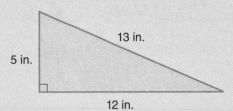

$\frac{1}{2}$ × 5 in. × 12 in. = 30 sq in.

The area of a triangle is $\frac{1}{2}$ × its base (b) × its height (h).

Exercises   SOLVE

1 How many people can you allow on a beach if the lifeguards want to have 30 sq ft per person and the beach is 1000 ft long and 200 ft wide? Round to a whole number.

_____

2 A square that has sides of 25 ft is split in half down the middle. What is the area of each of the pieces?

_____

3 A right triangle has a base of 24 feet and a height of 7 feet. What is its area?

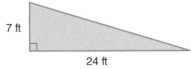

_____

4 Which has a larger area, a triangle with a base of 15 ft and a height of 25 ft or a square with sides of 14 ft?

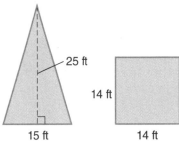

_____

Name _____

Volume of a Solid

The **volume** of a solid figure is measured by
cubic inches, cubic feet, cubic yards, and cubic miles.

Example:

To find the volume of a rectangular solid, multiply
length × width × height (h).

Volume = 5 yd × 2 yd × 3 yd = 30 **cu yd**

Volume of a rectangular pyramid = $\frac{1}{3}$ × Base Area × Height

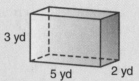

3 yd   5 yd   2 yd

Exercises   **SOLVE**

1 What is the volume
of a cube with sides of
10 inches?

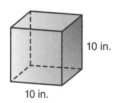

10 in.

10 in.

_____

2 A shoe box has dimensions of 12 inches
by 8 inches by 6 inches. How many cubic
feet is it?

_____

3 A rectangular solid with sides of 9 ft by
5 ft by 13 ft has what volume?

_____

4 A cube that has sides of 120 inches has
how many cubic yards of volume?

_____

5 A storage container in the form of a
rectangular solid has dimensions of
12 inches by 30 inches by 16 inches. If
the crate is only half full, what is the
remaining volume?

_____

6 A parking lot measures 420 ft long and
162 ft wide. If a construction company is
told that it needs to have 3 feet of asphalt
under the parking lot for proper drainage,
how many cubic yards do they need to
order?

_____

Time

You know how to tell time, but have you ever thought about the units you use to tell time?

Remember that some months have different overall lengths. Some months have 30 days, while others have 31. February has only 28 days, except in a leap year, when it is 29 days long. Because of the extra day added to February, a leap year has 366 days.

A few other terms you need to know to talk about time:

a.m. = *ante meridiem*, "before the middle of the day"

The middle of the day is noon, so a.m. hours are between midnight and noon.

p.m. = *post meridiem*, "after the middle of the day"

Those hours are between noon and midnight.

1 minute = 60 seconds	1 hour = 60 minutes	1 day = 24 hours
1 week = 7 days = 1 month = 28, 29, 30, or 31 days		
1 year = 12 months = 52 weeks = 365 (or 366) days		
1 decade = 10 years	1 century = 100 years	

Exercises   CALCULATE

1   36 hours = _____ seconds

2   25 days = _____ hours

3   35 days = _____ minutes

4   96 hours = _____ days

5   32 days = _____ minutes

6   125 minutes = _____ hours

7   If you get paid $700 and you worked 3.2 days, approximately how much did you make per hour (assume an 8-hour day of work)?

_____

8   The production rate for widgets in the factory is 8 per second. How many widgets should you make in a 9-hour shift?

_____

9   What is the maximum of different centuries that a person can live in if he lived to be 110 years?

_____

10   If you get paid $8.00 per hour and you work 5400 minutes, how much will you earn?

_____

Name _____

Metric Units of Length

You may have heard of metric units. In America, we do not usually measure with these units, but they are much easier to work with mathematically than customary units. That is because metric units are all based on the powers of 10. The metric units of length are millimeters (mm), centimeters (cm), meters (m), and kilometers (km).

Remember...

To make calculations simpler for yourself, learn these prefixes:

milli = thousandth   centi = hundredth   kilo = thousand

| 1 centimeter = 10 mm | 1 meter = 100 cm | 1 kilometer = 1000 m |

Exercises   CALCULATE

1 335 cm = _____ m

2 6235 mm = _____ m

3 5.761 km = _____ cm

4 725.02 km = _____ mm

5 335 cm + 550 mm = _____ m

6 2.611 km = _____ cm

7 12 cm + 12 mm = _____ m

8 6.872 m = _____ mm

Metric Units of Liquid Volume

The basic metric unit of liquid volume is the liter (L). There are also milliliters (mL) and kiloliters (kL).

1 liter = 1000 mL
1 kiloliter = 1000 L

Exercises   CALCULATE

1 2.1 L = _____ mL

2 1700 L = _____ kL

3 3.456 L = _____ mL

4 350 L = _____ mL

5 A $\frac{3}{4}$ liter bottle of water is a common size. How many of these bottles of water would it take to fill a 20-liter container?

_____

6 If the reservoir has 200,000,000,000 centiliters of water in it, how many kiloliters does it contain?

_____

7 If you are providing beverages for 25 students and family members at the school outing and each person expects to drink 1500 centiliters, how many liters of beverages will you need?

_____

8 If an aquarium holds 60 liters of water, and each cup of water holds 250 milliliters, how many cups of water does the aquarium hold?

_____

Name _____

Metric Units of Mass

The basic metric unit of mass is the gram (g). Remember the prefixes milli- = thousandth, centi- = hundredth, and kilo- = thousand.

1 cg = 10 mg
1 g = 100 cg
1 kg = 1000 g

Remember...

Metric units of mass are easy to work with because they are also based on the powers of ten.

Exercises   CALCULATE

1 354 g − 346 mg = _____ g

2 4300 g + 3300 mg = _____ kg

3 5300 g − 2430 mg = _____ g

4 12.34 kg + 1.66 kg = _____ g

5 2 mg + 4 g + 5 kg = _____ kg

6 300 kg + 300 g + 300 cg = _____ mg

7 142 g + 258 mg = _____ cg

8 65 g + 6500 g = _____ kg

Metric Perimeter, Area, and Volume of a Solid

You can use metric units to calculate perimeters, areas, and the volumes of solids. You have to remember that you are working with metric units, and your answers will be expressed in metric units.

Perimeter is expressed in mm, cm, m, or km.

Area is expressed in sq mm, sq cm, sq m, or sq km.

The volume of a solid is expressed in cu mm, cu cm, cu m, or cu km.

Remember...
Do not change from metric to customary units.
For example, 1 **sq km** *does not* = 1000 **sq miles**

Exercises   CALCULATE

1 What is the perimeter of a square with sides of 7 cm?

7 cm

7 cm

_____

What is the area?

_____

2 The perimeter of this figure with 6 equal sides is 48 millimeters. What is the length of each side?

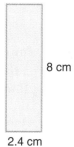

_____

3 A cube has sides of 6 cm. What is the volume of the cube?

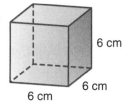

6 cm

6 cm

6 cm

_____

What is the surface area of the whole figure?

_____

4 A rectangle has sides of 2.4 cm and 8 cm. What is the perimeter of the rectangle?

8 cm

2.4 cm

_____

What is the area of the rectangle?

_____

5 What is the perimeter of this rectangle with sides of 14 meters and 6 meters?

14 m

6 m

_____

What is the area?

_____

6 Damian designed a course around his neighborhood to race his bicycle with friends. His neighborhood is in the shape of a regular pentagon with 5 equal sides measuring 500 meters each. What is the total length of the course?

_____

7 Anabelle is buying a new rug for her living room. The rug store prices the rug by the square meter. If Anabelle needs a rug with dimensions of 3.7 meters long and 2 meters wide, and the rug store charges $12.00 per square meter, how much will she pay for a new rug?

_____

What is the perimeter of the rug?

_____

8 What is the volume of the rectangular solid?

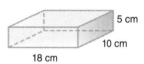

_____

9 What is the area of the triangle?

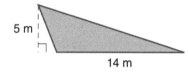

_____

10 How much water can a swimming pool with a flat bottom hold? It is 12 meters long, 8 meters wide, and 2.5 meters deep.

_____

11 What is the area of the triangle?

_____

12 What is the area of this rectangle?

_____

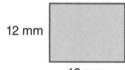

Name _____

Temperature

The units used to describe temperature are called degrees. Degrees are written with a small circle to the top right of a number: 30 degrees = 30°. Customary degrees are measured on the **Fahrenheit** scale. You must add the word Fahrenheit (or just **F**), because other temperature scales that are *not* customary are also used to describe temperature.

The metric unit to describe temperature is called the **Celsius** degree (or just **C**). This is also sometimes referred to as Centigrade.

Celsius	Fahrenheit	
0° C	32° F	Freezing point of water
100° C	212° F	Boiling point of water
35° C	95° F	Hot air temperature
37° C	98.6° F	Human body temperature

The Celsius scale is used in scientific work and is easier to use than the Fahrenheit scale. Even though both are expressed in degrees, a Celsius degree *does not* equal a Fahrenheit degree!

You can change Celsius to Fahrenheit temperatures, or Fahrenheit to Celsius temperatures. To do so, you must use the following equations:

$$(F - 32) \times \left(\frac{5}{9}\right) = C \qquad C \times \left(\frac{9}{5}\right) + 32 = F$$

Example:
Convert 98.6° F to Celsius.

Step 1: Set up the equation:
$$(98.6 - 32) \times \left(\frac{5}{9}\right) = C$$

Step 2: Calculate: $66.6 \times \frac{5}{9} = 37$
$$98.6° F = 37° C$$

Exercises   CONVERT

1. 200° C = _____ F
2. 132° F = _____ C
3. 81° F = _____ C

4. 32° C = _____ F
5. 214° F = _____ C
6. 320° F = _____ C

7. 10° F = _____ C
8. 45° C = _____ F
9. 75° F = _____ C

10. 90° C = _____ F
11. −15° F = _____ C
12. 130° F = _____ C

13. 37° C = _____ F
14. 2000° C = _____ F
15. 244° C = _____ F

16. Sarah has a fever and is running a temperature of 39° C. What is her temperature in Fahrenheit?

_____

17. Jared is baking cookies for a bake sale. His recipe calls for him to set the oven to a temperature of 350° F. If his oven only displays temperature in Celsius, then to what temperature should Jared set his oven?

_____

20.1

Changing from Customary Units to Metric Units

Can you change customary units to metric units? Yes. Here
are a few charts to guide you. Keep in mind that some of
the metric units are not exact, but they are fairly close.

Length	Liquid Volume	Weight or Mass
1 inch = 2.54 centimeters	1 cup = 0.237 liters	1 ounce = 28.35 grams
1 foot = 0.305 meters	1 pint = 0.473 liters	1 pound = 0.454 kilograms
1 yard = 0.914 meters	1 quart = 0.946 liters	1 ton = 907.18 kilograms
1 mile = 1.609 kilometers	1 gallon = 3.785 liters	
	1 fluid ounce = 29.574 milliliters	

Exercises — CONVERT

1. The weight limit on a bridge is 16,000 pounds. What is the weight limit in kilograms?

_____

2. The directions on a plant fertilizer bag recommend using 3 pounds for a 4 × 10 garden. How many grams is that?

_____

3. A 2-ton truck weighs how many kilograms?

_____

4. A car with a 23-gallon gas tank holds how many liters of gas?

_____

5. A 24-ounce fruit juice bottle contains how many liters of fluid?

_____

6. Jasmine has a 150-ft length of rope. Does she have enough rope to reach the bottom of a 40-meter cliff?

_____

7. A 3-pound lobster weighs how many kilograms?

_____

8. Would you rather have 2.4 pounds or 1000 grams of gold?

_____

9. About how many meters tall is a 100-ft tree?

_____

10. How many meters tall is a 9.5-foot tree?

_____

Changing from Metric Units to Customary Units

Since customary units can be changed to metric units, you can obviously reverse this process. Again, remember that some of the numbers on the charts below are not exact. However, they are fairly close.

Length	Liquid Volume	Weight or Mass
1 millimeter = 0.039 inches 1 centimeter = 0.394 inches 1 meter = 39.37 inches 1 kilometer = 0.621 miles	1 liter = 1.056 quarts 1 kiloliter = 263.2 gallons	1 gram = 0.035 ounces 1 kilogram = 2.205 pounds

Exercises   CONVERT

1 If each person on a hike is supposed to carry 1.75 liters of water, how many gallons of water would you need to bring for a group of 45 people?

_____

2 Every camper is served .15 kilograms of cereal each morning. If there are 12 campers, how many pounds of cereal will you need to bring for a 7-day trip?

_____

3 11 kilograms is about how many ounces?

_____

4 A 3-meter diving board is how many feet above the pool?

_____

5 A 15-meter length of rope is how many feet long?

_____

6 A dog weighs 22 kilograms. How many pounds is that?

_____

7 A 50-meter pool is the standard size for the Olympics. What is that length in feet?

_____

8 A reservoir contains 11,250,000 kiloliters of water. How many gallons is that?

_____

9 The local middle school sponsored a 6-kilometer race for everyone to run. What is the length of the race in miles?

_____

10 A jet that travels at 4200 kilometers per hour is traveling how many miles per hour?

_____

11 How many inches is 300 centimeters?

_____

How many feet?

_____

12 The average defensive lineman on the football team at Bloomingdale High School weighs 110 kilograms. The average offensive lineman weighs 240 pounds. Which position has a lower average weight?

_____

Challenge Questions

Let's see if you can apply your skills to a couple of really challenging questions. Ready?

1) Each side of a regular polygon measures 57.5 centimeters, and the total perimeter is 2875 millimeters. How many sides does the polygon have?

2) Rachel ran 19,272 feet on Saturday and twice that far on Sunday. What is the total distance she ran in miles?

Answers and Explanations are on p. 220.

Unit Test

Lessons 18-20

1 Armando is going to replace the trim around all of the doors in his house. The outside of each door measures $18\frac{1}{2}$ feet. If he has 9 doors, how many inches of trim does he need to replace?

_____

2 Ashley wants to empty her fish tank before she cleans it. The fish tank holds 34 gallons. She is using a one-quart container to empty the tank by hand. How many full containers will she need to empty the tank?

_____

3 Annika weighed boxes for shipping books to customers. The first box weighed 160 ounces, the second box weighed $10\frac{3}{8}$ pounds, and the third box weighed $\frac{1}{200}$ ton. Which box weighed the most?

_____

4 Mandie wants to fence in her corral, and needs to know how much fencing to purchase. The corral has an irregular shape, with sides of $25\frac{1}{4}$ feet, 330 inches, 6 yards, one foot, $\frac{3}{160}$ of a mile, and 9 feet. How much fence material will she need?

_____ feet

5 What is the area of a rectangle with a length of 20 feet and a width of 144 inches?

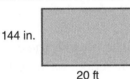

144 in.

20 ft

_____ square feet

6 What is the area of a right triangle with sides of 6 feet, 8 feet, and 120 inches?

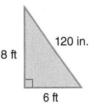

8 ft

120 in.

6 ft

_____ square feet

7 What is the volume of a rectangular box with sides of 48 inches and $3\frac{1}{2}$ feet, and a height of 30 inches?

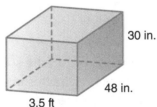

30 in.

48 in.

3.5 ft

_____ cubic feet

8 A modern spacecraft must travel 8.1 miles per second in order to reach the planet Mars. How far does the spacecraft travel in a minute?

_____

in an hour? _____

in a day? _____

Lessons 18–20

9 If the distance to the moon from the earth is 248,000 miles, how long does it take the spacecraft in the previous exercise to travel to the moon? _____

How many times a day could the spacecraft go back and forth between the moon and the earth?

_____

10 The world record for the shot put is 23.12 meters. The world record for the discus throw is 74.08 meters. How many centimeters longer is the record for the discus throw than the record for the shot put?

_____

11 Stacey is measuring fabric for her grandmother, who is going to make a rectangular banner for the school. The banner will be 6.5 meters in length and 2350 millimeters in width. How much fabric will Stacey's grandmother need to buy?

_____ sq cm

12 Sharon has three cans of latex paint to recycle. One can holds 2957 milliliters of paint, the second can holds 105.6 centiliters of paint, and the third can holds 3.9 liters of paint. How much paint, in total, will Sharon be recycling?

_____ liters

13 What is the area of a triangle with sides of 8 cm, 8 cm, a base of 4 cm, and a height of 6 cm?

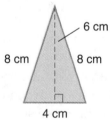
6 cm
8 cm   8 cm
4 cm

_____ sq cm

14 Jerrie walked around the entire rectangular school parking lot, which measures 106 meters by 7500 centimeters. How far did Jerrie walk?

_____ meters

15 How much topsoil can fit into a rectangular dump truck that measures 3.6 meters in width, 6.5 meters in length, and 3.5 meters high?

_____ cu meters

16 The average player on the soccer team measures 5 feet, 11 inches tall. About how tall is that in centimeters?

_____

Lessons 18–20

17 The average taxicab has a gas tank that holds 85 liters of gasoline. How much is that in quarts?

_____ quarts

In gallons?

_____ gallons

18 Pauline measured a rectangular box and found that its dimensions were 55 inches by 32 inches by 20 inches tall. What is the total outside surface area in square inches?

_____ sq in

In square feet? _____ sq ft

19 A body temperature of 103.6° F is considered an extremely high fever. What temperature is that in Celsius?

_____

20 In track and field, the standard middle distance event is the 5000 meters. About how many feet is 5000 meters?

_____ feet

21 What is the volume of the rectangular pyramid?

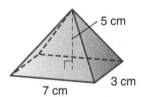

22 What is the volume of the triangular solid?

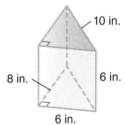

_____

23 The air conditioning company suggests that people keep the temperature in their homes between 23 and 26 degrees Celsius during the summer. What is that range in degrees Fahrenheit?

_____

24 The distance of a flight from Boston to Chicago is about 1200 miles. The average ground speed for a commercial airliner is about 850 kilometers per hour. About how long will it take to fly from Boston to Chicago?

_____ hours

Answers and Explanations

1. 1998 inches of trim

$18.5 \times 9 = 166.5$; $166.5 \times 12 = 1998$ in.

2. 136 quart containers

$34 \times 4 = 136$

3. The second box weighs the most

Box 1: $160 \div 16 = 10$ lbs; Box 2: $10\frac{3}{8}$ lbs; Box 3: $\frac{1}{200} \times 2000 = \frac{2000}{200} = 10$

4. 179.75 ft

330 in. $\div 12 = 27.5$ ft; 6 yd $\times 3 = 18$ ft; $\frac{3}{160}$ mile $\times 5,280 = 99$ ft;
$25.25 + 27.5 + 18 + 1 + 99 + 9 = 179.75$ ft

5. 240 sq ft

144 in. $\div 12 = 12$ ft; $12 \times 20 = 240$ sq ft

6. 24 square ft

$A = \frac{1}{2}bh$; $A = \frac{1}{2}(6)(8) = \frac{1}{2}(48) = 24$ sq ft

7. 35 cu ft

48 in. $\div 12 = 4$ ft; 30 in. $\div 12 = 2.5$ ft; $V = lwh$; $V = (4)(2.5)(3.5) = 35$ cu ft

8. 486 miles in a minute;
29,160 miles in an hour;
699,840 miles in a day

$8.1\frac{\text{miles}}{\text{second}} \times 60\frac{\text{seconds}}{\text{minute}} = 486\frac{\text{miles}}{\text{minute}}$; $486\frac{\text{miles}}{\text{minute}} \times 60\frac{\text{minutes}}{\text{hour}}$
$= 29,160\frac{\text{miles}}{\text{hour}}$; $29,160\frac{\text{miles}}{\text{hour}} \times 24\frac{\text{hours}}{\text{day}} = 699,840\frac{\text{miles}}{\text{day}}$

9. 8.5 hours;
about 3 times

$\frac{29,160 \text{ miles}}{1 \text{ hour}} = \frac{248,000 \text{ miles}}{x \text{ hours}}$; $29,160x = 248,000 \times 1$;
$x = \frac{248,000}{29,160} = 8.5$; $24 \div 8.5 \approx 3$

10. 5096 cm

$74.08 - 23.12 = 50.96$ m; 50.96 m $\times 100 = 5096$ cm

11. 152,750 sq cm

6.5 m $\times 100 = 650$ cm; 2350 mm $\div 10 = 235$ cm;
$650 \times 235 = 152,750$ sq cm

12. 7.913 liters

2957 mL $\div 1000 = 2.957$ L; 105.6 cl $\div 100 = 1.056$ L;
$2.957 + 1.056 + 3.9 = 7.913$ L

13. 12 sq cm

$A = \frac{1}{2}bh$; $A = \frac{1}{2}(4)(6) = \frac{1}{2}(24) = 12$ sq cm

14. 362 meters

7500 cm $\div 100 = 75$ m; $106 + 106 + 75 + 75 = 362$ m

15. 81.9 cu m

$V = lwh = 3.6 \times 6.5 \times 3.5 = 81.9$ cu m

16. 180.2 cm

$5 \times 12 = 60$; $60 + 11 = 71$; $71 \div 0.394 = 180.2$

17. 89.8 quarts;
22.4 gallons

$85 \times 1.056 = 89.76$ qt; $89.76 \div 4 = 22.44$ gal

18. 7000 sq in;
48.61 sq ft

$SA = 2(55 \times 32) + 2(55 \times 20) + 2(20 \times 32) = 2(1760) + 2(1100) + 2(640)$
$= 3520 + 2200 + 1280 = 7000$ sq in; $7000 \div 144 = 48.61$ sq ft

19. 39.78° C

$(103.6° \text{ F} - 32) \times \frac{5}{9} = (71.6) \times \frac{5}{9} = 39.78°$ C

20. 16,393 ft

5000 m $\div 0.305 = 16,393$ ft

21. 35 cu cm

$V = \frac{1}{3}$ base area $\times H = \frac{1}{3}(7 \times 3)(5) = \frac{1}{3}(21)(5) = (7)(5) = 35$ cu cm

22. 144 cu in.

$V = $ base area $\times H = \frac{1}{2}(b \times h)(H) = \frac{1}{2}(6 \times 8)(6) = \frac{1}{2}(48)(6) = (24)(6)$
$= 144$ cu in.

23. 73.4–78.8° F

$23°$ C $\times \frac{9}{5} + 32 = 41.4 + 32 = 73.4°$ F; $26°$ C $\times \frac{9}{5} + 32 = 46.8 + 32 = 78.8°$ F

24. $2\frac{1}{4}$ hours

1200 m $\times 1.609 = 1930.8$ km; $\frac{850 \text{ km}}{1 \text{ hr}} = \frac{1,930.8 \text{ km}}{x \text{ hr}}$; $850x = 1 \times 1930.8$;
$x = 2.2715$

Name _____

Bar Graphs

In order to remember facts, some people need to be able to visualize them. Is there some way you can picture numerical information?

A **Bar Graph** uses bars to display **data**, or information, comparing two or more people, places, or things. The bars can be compared to one another because each one represents a number.

For example, there are 50 students in the seventh grade at Thomas Jefferson Middle School. Each student voted for a favorite vegetable. The vertical axis shows the number of students, and the horizontal axis show the various vegetables.

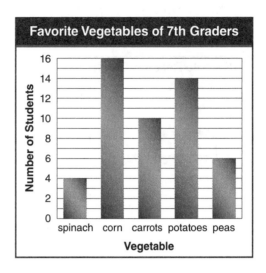

Exercises) INTERPRET

① Your neighborhood diner is preparing breakfast for 100 hungry customers. Using the information in the chart below, what type of eggs should the cook prepare the least of?

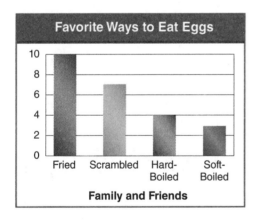

② You are responsible for ordering food for all of the animals at the shelter. Using this chart, which two groups of animals would you order the least amount of food for?

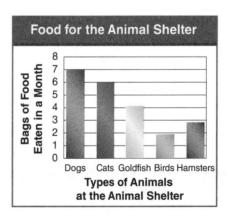

3 According to the chart below, which aspect of the Sample Reading Profile gave students the most difficulty?

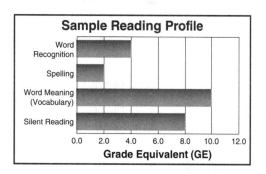

_____

4 According to the chart below, what student won the ice cream eating contest?

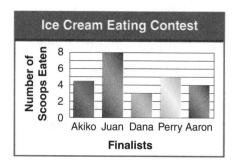

_____

5 The chart below shows the years of teaching experience for Pleasant Hill High School. Where do the majority of teachers fall?

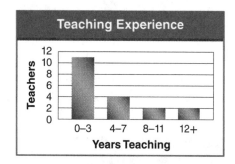

_____

6 What two letter grades in the chart below had the lowest percentages of students receiving that grade?

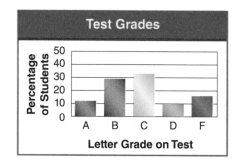

_____

7 What conclusion can you make about student performance at Fitchburg State College from the chart below?

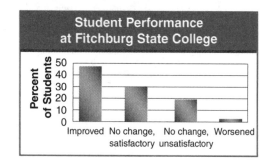

_____

_____

8 Can you make any conclusions about the trend of temperatures by looking at the chart below?

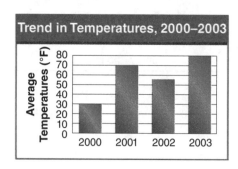

_____

_____

Line Graphs

Can you show data for something that changes as time passes? You might use a **Line Graph**, which shows how information changes over time.

The numbers on the horizontal axis are dates. The distance from one date to another is shown in **intervals** of 5 days. When the line segment connecting intervals is steep, there is a great deal of change. A less steep line segment shows less change during that interval.

Looking at this graph, in what time periods did Mr. Jones do the most driving? The least driving?

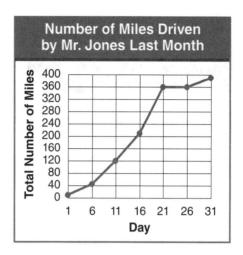

Number of Miles Driven by Mr. Jones Last Month

Exercises   INTERPRET

1 The guide at the Abracadabra Falls Visitor Center tells you that their tourist season lasts all year, not just in the winter or summer. Does the graph shown support this? Why or why not?

_____

_____

_____

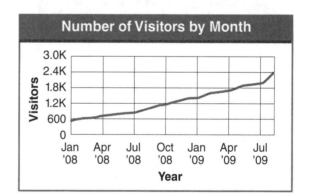

Number of Visitors by Month

2 The Northern Hemisphere experiences winter from December until March. During these months, the Southern Hemisphere is experiencing summer. Looking at the graph shown, is the area represented located in the Northern Hemisphere or Southern Hemisphere?

_____

_____

_____

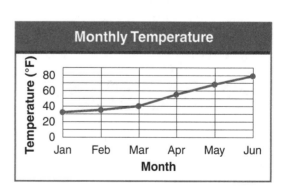

Monthly Temperature

Name _____

3 If you are planning a family vacation, what would be the best 2 months to avoid earthquakes, according to the graph below?

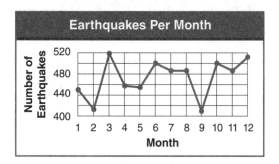

_____

4 Would the graph below support the claim that New Zealand had cut down on its overall greenhouse emissions during the period of 1990 to 2004?

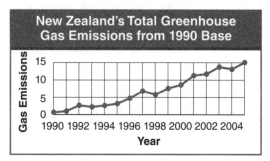

_____

5 Look at the population graph below. Which years represent a steep interval?

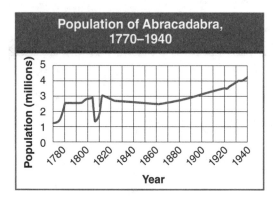

_____

6 Approximately how many people lived in the Southern Region of the U.S. in 1966, according to the line graph below?

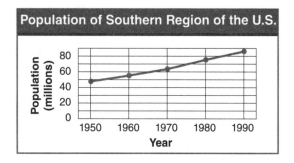

_____

7 The weather reporter forecasted a warming trend for the six-day period shown in the graph below. How accurate was the forecast?

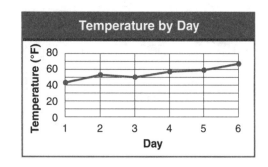

_____

8 The red line in the graph below shows the price of a stock during the period of April to December. What was the approximate high price during the period of April to November?

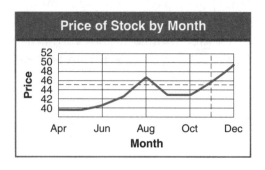

_____

Double-Line Graphs

Is there a way to show how information changes over time for *two or more* people, places, or things? Yes, you could show this information in a **Double-Line Graph**, which compares data for two or more people, places, or things as time passes.

With this graph, you can compare the distances driven by both Mr. and Mrs. Jones at different times during the month.

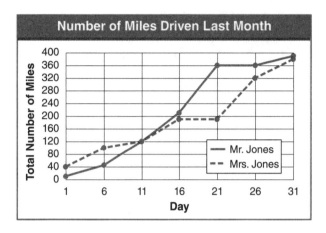

Exercises   INTERPRET

1 What sort of relationship can you see in the graph below between sales and profits?

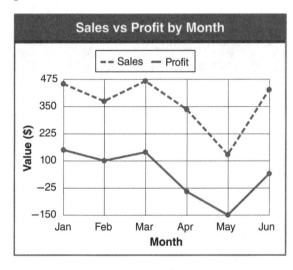

2 There is an old saying that "money does not buy happiness." Does the double-line graph below support that? Why or why not?

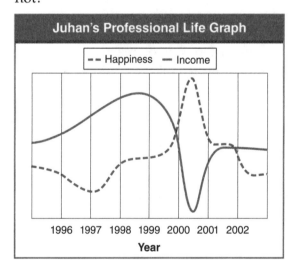

_____

_____

_____

_____

_____

_____

_____

_____

_____

_____

_____

_____

Name _____

3 In this double-line graph, the life expectancy of males and females appears to stay at a constant difference of about 4 years. What is the good news for males in spite of this? Explain your answer.

_____

_____

_____

_____

_____

_____

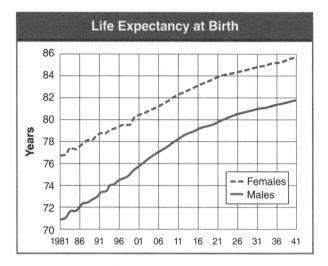

Life Expectancy at Birth

4 Utilizing this triple-line graph. what conclusion can you reach about expenditures for the Criminal Justice system during the period 1982–2006?

_____

_____

_____

_____

_____

_____

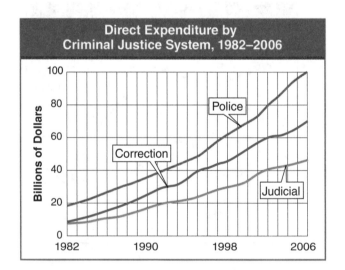

Direct Expenditure by Criminal Justice System, 1982–2006

Circle Graphs

Is there a way to compare parts to a whole using a graph? Yes, a **Circle Graph**, or pie chart, compares parts to a whole. However, it does not necessarily compare in hundredths, it compares amounts visually, like slices of a pie. *Sometimes*, you can calculate how big a part is exactly, but not always.

The whole circle graph shows the total number of shows that LaWanda watches on TV. It does not *really* show the total number of shows, because the graph compares the types of shows she watches without using numbers. However, if you know that LaWanda regularly spends 16 hours watching TV each week, you *can* calculate some information.

Types of TV Shows LaWanda Watches

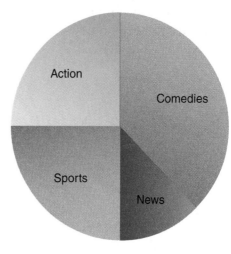

Exercises   INTERPRET

1 Does the circle graph below support the idea that a large percentage of money spent on education is applied to non-instructional purposes? Explain your answer.

The Cost of an Education: Breakdown of Average Cost per Student Expenditures (in Dollars) for Public Education

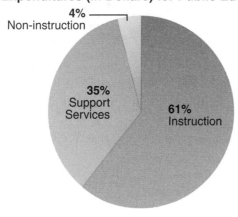

_____

_____

_____

_____

2 The graph below represents the distribution of colors in a bag of candies. Should Patrick expect to pick an orange piece of candy if he only gets one pick? Explain your answer.

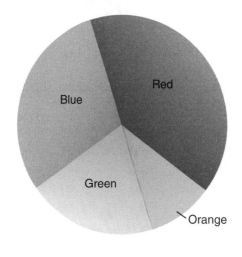

_____

_____

_____

_____

3 The circle graph below shows sales for the prior year at a popular shoe store in Dallas. According to the chart, during what month would the manager need the most employees working in the store? During what month would she need the fewest? Explain your answer.

Sales

_____

4 The circle graph below represents Maria's favorite types of movies. What 2 genres, when added together, make up half of the movies Maria watches?

Favorite Type of Movie

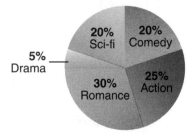

_____

5 Below is a circle graph showing a breakdown of some of the common toppings on a pizza. The crust and the cheese make up what percent of the pizza? How did you reach this answer?

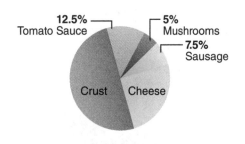

_____

6 Below is a graph showing the costs for a manufacturer in New York City. Does it make sense that she wants to cut over 20% of her costs by focusing largely on reducing the budget for tools? Explain your answer.

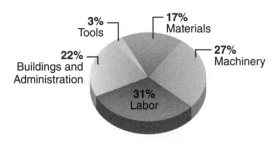

_____

7 If you eliminate the two smallest sections of the circle graph below, what percentage of the total would you have left?

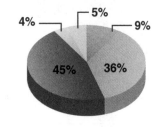

_____

8 According to the information in the circle graph below, is there one type of pie that is preferred by a majority of people? Explain your answer.

Pie Preferences

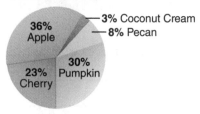

_____

Measures of Central Tendency

What other kinds of comparisons can you make with numbers? You can compare numbers to other numbers using **statistics**, the branch of mathematics that studies data expressed in numbers. Using statistics, you can answer some common questions like: How big, how long, how many, how far, and so on.

There are a number of things you can say about any collection of numbers. The greatest number minus the smallest number is called the **range**. The number that appears most *often* in the collection is called the **mode**. The number that is right in the middle is the **median**. If your collection has an even number of addends, you find the median by adding the two numbers in the middle and dividing by 2. The total of the whole collection divided by the number of addends is called the **mean**, or the average. The range, the mode, the median, and the mean may all be different. Or two or more of them may be the same.

> **Example:** 39, 15, 11, 13, 25, 30, 43, 13, 18
>
> **Step 1:** Order 11, 13, 13, 15, 18, 25, 30, 39, 43
>
> Range = 43 − 11 = 32
>
> Mode = 13   Median = 18
>
> Mean = (11 + 13 + 13 + 15 + 18 +
>   25 + 30 + 39 + 43) ÷ 9
>   = 207 ÷ 9 = 23

Exercises   CALCULATE

1 Calculate the mean of
[3.2, 2.5, 2.1, 3.7, 2.8, 2.0]

_____

2 Find the median of
[7, 4, 5, 5, 6, 8, 2]

_____

3 Calculate the range of
[43, −22, 5, 10, 31, 4]

_____

4 Find the mode of
[2, 3, 5, 6, 4, 3, 3, 1]

_____

5 Find the mode of
[7, 4, 5, 5, 6, 8, 2]

_____

6 Calculate the range of
[1, −1, 0, 2, −2, −7]

_____

7 Calculate the mean of
[10, 11, −9, 14, 22, 61, −2]

_____

8 Find the median of
[4, 12, 7, 5, 9, 22, 23, 19, 21]

_____

9 Calculate the mean of
[−22, −21, 44, 37, 100, 2.75]

_____

10 Find the mode of
[13, 12, 14, 15, 13, 12, 12, 11, 13, 15, 16]

_____

22.2

Name _____

Stem-and-Leaf Plots

Can you use charts to show statistics? Yes, there are many ways to show statistics in charts. For example, a **Stem-and-Leaf Plot** organizes data by the place-value of digits. It is named because it reminded some people of a plant with stems, each of which had a different number of leaves.

Example:

Data = 93, 62, 75, 88, 93, 91, 72, 61, 86, 79, 93, 75, 68, 77

Stems	Leaves
6	1 2 8
7	2 5 5 7 9
8	8 6
9	1 3 3 3

Each leaf is attached to the stem to its left. Therefore, the top line represents the numbers 61, 62, and 68. If a number is repeated in the data, you must include *each* repeat in your plot.

Exercises   INTERPRET

1 What is the range of the numbers represented in the stem-and-leaf plot below?

_____

Stem	Leaf
9	0 6
8	3 5 7
7	1 6 6 7 8
6	0 2 2 4 4 5 6 8 8
5	1 1 2 2 4 5 7
4	3 4 7 8
3	5 7
2	
1	6

2 Generate the number set represented by the stem-and-leaf plot below.

_____

Stem	Leaf
1	0 7 9
2	1 1 3 4 6 7 8
3	0 1 3 5 6 7 7
4	0 1 1 1 2
5	
6	9

3 Generate the number set represented by the stem-and-leaf plot below.

_____

Stem	Leaf
8	0 5
7	1 5 6
6	
5	1 6 8
4	0 6

4 What is the range of the numbers represented by the stem-and-leaf plot below?

_____

Stem	Leaf
2	2 6 7
3	1 3 5
4	2 4 6
5	7 8 9
6	1 3 4 5 7

Box-and-Whisker Plots

You may have heard of a **Box-and-Whisker Plot,** which allows you to quickly look at data to tell where most of the numbers lie.

Example

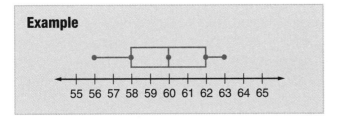

The lowest number in your set of data is called the **lower extreme**. The greatest number is called the **upper extreme**. The median of all the data, as you have learned, is the number in the exact middle of the collection. The median of the numbers from the lower extreme to the median is called the **lower quartile**. The median of the numbers from the median to the upper extreme is called the **upper quartile**.

The word "quartile" is related to "quarter," or fourth. Each outer section of the plot, from the extreme to the nearest quartile, contains one quarter of the data. The box in the middle, extending from the lower quartile to the upper quartile, contains two quarters—or *half*—of the data.

Exercises INTERPRET

1 Which of the three classes has the widest range of scores? The smallest range?

Widest Range _____

Smallest Range _____

2 Which class has the highest median score?

_____

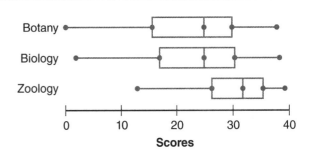

Make a box-and-whisker plot with the following data:

    Minimum – 15
    Q1 – 25
    Q2 – 35
    Q3 – 45
    Maximum – 55

3 What is the range of this plot? The median?

Range _____

Median _____

4 What is the lower quartile? The upper quartile?

Lower Quartile _____

Upper Quartile _____

Tree Diagrams

Are there other mathematical visual aids named after things we might see every day? Yes, there is a **Tree Diagram**, which looks like a tree with branches. A tree diagram can be used to show possible combinations of people, places, or things.

Example:

If you roll a six-sided number cube, you have an equal chance of getting an odd number (O = 1, 3, 5) or an even number (E = 2, 4, 6). If you roll two number cubes, there are four different combinations you could have: OO; EO; OE; EE. How many possible combinations are there of odd and even if you roll three number cubes?

Count the number of branches on the right of the diagram to find out how many possible combinations there are.

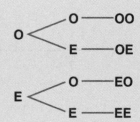

Exercises INTERPRET AND CREATE

1. The tree diagram at the right illustrates the outcomes when you choose two balls from a bag that contains a large number of red, white, and green balls. How many of these outcomes result in you not choosing at least 1 white ball? How many of these outcomes result in you choosing both a red ball and a green ball?

_____

_____

_____

First Stage   Second Stage   Outcome

red — RR
red — RW
red — RG
white — WR
white — WW
white — WG
green — GR
green — GW
green — GG

2. Draw a tree diagram to describe the following situation: You go to the ice cream store and you have a choice of vanilla, chocolate, or strawberry ice cream. On your ice cream, you can get either nuts or sprinkles.

Name _____

Venn Diagrams

What other kinds of diagrams can be used to show data? Have you seen a **Venn Diagram**? A Venn Diagram is used to show groups of data when some data can be placed in *more than one group*.

Example:

Animals Larger than People

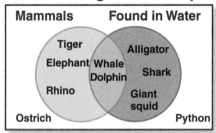

This Venn Diagram shows two groupings for animals that are larger than people. A few large animals can be placed in both groups, while some large animals cannot be placed in either group. What animals are placed in both groups?

Exercises DIAGRAM

1 This Venn Diagram represents numbers that are even and numbers that are divisible by the variable *b*. What does their intersection represent?

_____

_____

_____

_____

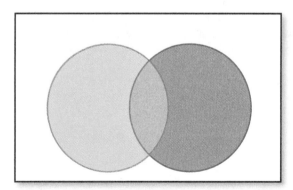

2 Make a Venn Diagram of people who are kickball fans, and people who are baseball fans. The only person that is a fan of both is your friend Kelsey.

22.6

Sampling

A population is a group of people. Examples could be all the students at your school, Canadians, women over the age of 40, and so on. A common technique for generating statistics about a population is sampling. A sample is a smaller group within the larger population. Surveys or polls are done on just a sample of the population and the results are projected onto the larger population as a whole. For the conclusions drawn to be valid, the sample must be representative of the population. This means that the sample is not biased. The best way to eliminate the possibility of bias is to do a completely random sample. For example, if you wanted to use a representative sample of the students at your school, you might let a computer select 100 students' names at random.

Once you have taken a representative sample of a population, you may be able to draw conclusions about certain characteristics of the population based on the data gathered. Be careful, however, not to draw conclusions that are not well supported by the data.

Example:

A random survey of Lakeville Academy students about their favorite flavor of ice cream produced the following results.

Chocolate	31
Vanilla	29
Strawberry	11

The survey concluded that chocolate is the most popular flavor of ice cream at Lakeville Academy.

Is this conclusion valid?

No. While it is true that chocolate got the most votes (31), that is not a lot more than the 29 votes vanilla got. If every student at the school were asked, vanilla is as likely to win as chocolate. A better conclusion would be that chocolate and vanilla are equally popular and that both are more popular than strawberry. In fact, you could also conclude that chocolate and vanilla are about 3 times as popular as strawberry.

Example:

Is the following sample representative?

In a survey of 23 people at an ice cream shop, 98% said they like ice cream. The survey concluded that most people like ice cream.

This survey is flawed. The sample is not representative of the population "most people." Only surveying people who are at an ice cream shop makes it very likely that those people are biased toward liking ice cream. A better survey would be a random sampling of people walking down the street. In addition, a survey of only 23 people is too small a sample to draw a conclusion about all people everywhere.

Exercises EVALUATE

1 To predict who will become the next president of the United States, a news organization asked people leaving voting sites around the country who they had just voted for. Who is the population in this situation? _____

What is the sample group in this situation? _____

2 The high school principle wants to find out which elective class the 200 students at her school prefer. Which sampling method should she use?

(a) ask all the students in the chess club

(b) ask all the seniors

(c) ask the first 25 students in an alphabetical list of all the students

3 Kai has a giant bag of red, yellow, and blue marbles. He wants to find out approximately what percent are blue, but doesn't want to count every marble in the bag. Which sampling method should he use?

(a) Shake up the bag, pull out 30 marbles, and see how many are blue.

(b) Reach into the bag and grab the biggest marbles he can feel.

(c) Pull out three marbles from the top of the bag and see how many are blue.

4 Mrs. Webster is the coordinator for the school field trip and is trying to decide between a trip to the museum or a trip to the zoo. She decides to do a survey of some of the students about their preference. Who should she survey?

(a) 30 students chosen at random by the office computer

(b) all the girls in the school

(c) the first 30 students to arrive at school

5 In a random sampling of 100 fish caught in a fishing net in a river, there were 39 trout, 19 flounder, and 42 perch. Which of the following is the most valid conclusion?

(a) Perch is the most common fish in the river.

(b) The river has about twice as many perch and trout as it does flounder.

(c) There are only three kinds of fish in the river.

22.7

Mean Absolute Deviation

Whenever you gather data about a population, there will be variance in the data. Not everyone likes the same kind of music or makes the same score on a test. **Mean absolute deviation** (MAD) is a measurement of how spread out the data set is. To calculate mean absolute deviation, first find the average (mean) of the data set. Then find how far from the average each data point is and average those distances. That is the mean absolute deviation.

Example:

Find the mean absolute deviation.

Six students took a math test. Their scores were 90, 85, 73, 92, 87, and 79.

Step 1: Find the average (mean) of the scores.

$$\frac{90 + 85 + 77 + 92 + 87 + 79}{6} = \frac{510}{6} = 85$$

Step 2: Find how far from the average each score is.

$$|90 - 85| = 5$$
$$|85 - 85| = 0$$

$$|77 - 85| = |-8| = 8$$
$$|92 - 85| = 7$$
$$|87 - 85| = 2$$
$$|79 - 85| = |-6| = 6$$

Step 3: Average those distances.

$$\frac{5 + 0 + 8 + 7 + 2 + 6}{6} = \frac{28}{6} = 4.67$$

The mean absolute deviation (MAD) is 4.76. This means that the data points are an average of 4.76 points away from the mean score of 85.

Exercises **CALCULATE**

Sarah and Sadie recorded the numbers of points they scored in each of 5 basketball games.

	Sarah	Sadie
GAME 1	4	3
GAME 2	6	7
GAME 3	5	2
GAME 4	4	6
GAME 5	4	2

1 What is Sarah's average?

_____

2 What is Sadie's average?

_____

3 What is the mean absolute deviation for Sarah's scores?

_____

4 What is the mean absolute deviation for Sadie's scores?

_____

5 How many times greater is the mean absolute deviation of Sadie's scores than for Sarah's scores?

_____

Calculating Probabilities

Imagine that you want to play a game with a spinner that has the numbers from 1 to 8. You need a 6 or higher to win. Can you figure out how likely you are to spin a good number?

Yes, you can calculate the **probability**, or the likelihood of something occurring. When you figure probability, you are making a prediction using mathematics. Calculating probability will tell you what will *probably* happen, but it cannot tell you what will *definitely* happen.

There is a formula to figure out probability (P). It is the number of favorable outcomes (f) divided by the total number of *all* possible outcomes (o). In mathematical terms: $P = \frac{f}{o}$.

Example:

There are 3 favorable outcomes. You could spin a 6, a 7, or an 8.

There are 8 possible numbers to spin.

So $P = \frac{3}{8}$

Exercises **CALCULATE**

1 If there are 4 girls and 8 boys in a gym class, what is the probability of picking a girl as the person to lead the exercises?

_____

2 In a deck of 52 cards, what is the probability of drawing a king from the deck?

_____

3 There are 4 pizzas: 2 cheese, 1 vegetable and 1 everything. What is the probability that if you open a box it will be a cheese pizza?

_____

4 George is 1 of 5 white horses that is in a group of 15 horses in total. If you see a white horse, what is the probability that it is George?

_____

5 You have change in your pocket: 5 quarters, 3 dimes, 2 nickels, and 4 pennies. If you pull a coin out of your pocket, what is the probability that it will be a dime?

_____

6 There are 3 different prizes at the fair: 1 first prize of $100, 3 second prizes of $50, and 5 third prizes of $10. If there are 35 participants in the contest, what is the probability that you will win a prize?

_____

Name _____

Probability Models

A **probability model** is a chart or table that shows the different outcomes possible for an event and their relative probabilities.

Take a set of data, such as a list of how many marbles of several different colors are in a bag of 100 marbles: 26 red, 43 blue, and 31 green. A probability model shows you the probability of choosing each of those colors in a random draw.

Color	Number	Probability
Red	$\frac{26}{100}$	0.26
Blue	$\frac{43}{100}$	0.43
Green	$\frac{31}{100}$	0.31

Example:

Alex does an experiment by randomly choosing a sock from a drawer and writing down the color. He added up the totals and found that he had drawn 7 white socks, 2 orange socks, 3 black socks, and 5 blue socks.

Construct a probability model to show the results.

Color	Number	Probability
White	$\frac{7}{17}$	0.41
Orange	$\frac{2}{17}$	0.12
Black	$\frac{3}{17}$	0.18
Blue	$\frac{5}{17}$	0.29

Exercises SOLVE

Lynda played in a tic-tac-toe tournament and recorded the outcomes. She won 23 games, she lost 14 games, and 53 games ended in a draw.

1 Complete the probability model.

Outcome	Number	Probability
Win		
Lose		
Draw		

2 If Lynda plays one more game, what is the approximate probability that the game will end in a draw?

_____

_____

3 If Lynda plays 7 more games and wins them all, how does that change her probability model?

Outcome	Number	Probability
Win		
Lose		
Draw		

4 What is the probability that a game will end in a draw now?

_____

_____

5 Based on the new model, how many times more likely is Lynda to win than to lose?

_____

_____

Probability of Compound Events

A compound event is a set of two or more different events in a series. You have learned to find the probability of one event occurring, such as flipping a coin and getting heads. A compound event would be two or more events, such as flipping a coin twice and getting heads both times. We can find the probability of multiple events occurring in several different ways.

You could find this probability by doing a tree diagram:

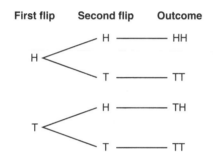

First flip   Second flip   Outcome

H — H ——— HH
H — T ——— TT
T — H ——— TH
T — T ——— TT

Out of the four possible outcomes, only one has heads twice, so the probability is $\frac{1}{4}$.

You could find this probability by constructing a table:

	Heads	Tails
Heads	H H	H T
Tails	H T	T H

Out of the four possible outcomes, only one has heads twice, so the probability is $\frac{1}{4}$.

You could find this probability by finding the probability for each event and then multiplying those probabilities together:

Find the probability for each event. On the first flip, the probability of getting heads is $\frac{1}{2}$. On the second flip, the probability of getting heads is also $\frac{1}{2}$. Multiply the probabilities together:
$\frac{1}{2} \times \frac{1}{2} = \frac{1}{4}$.

This third method is especially useful if you are working with a situation in which there are a large number of potential outcomes.

Example:

Sydney draws a card from a deck of 52 playing cards. Without replacing it, he draws a second card. What is the probability that he first draws a king and then a queen?

Since there are 52 possible outcomes when a card is drawn, let's use the multiplication method.

Step 1: Find the probability for each event. For the first card, there are 52 cards total and 4 kings, so the probability is $\frac{4}{52}$ or $\frac{1}{13}$. Be careful with the second card. The question says he does not replace the first card, so there are no longer 52 cards in the deck. Now there are only 51. There are 4 queens, so the probability for the second card is $\frac{4}{51}$

Step 2: Multiply the probabilities together:
$\frac{1}{13} \times \frac{4}{51} = \frac{4}{663}$.

23.3

Exercises   CALCULATE

1 Zane rolls a six-sided die twice. What is the probability that he will roll a 3 and then a 4?

_____

_____

2 Marisa draws a coin from a box that contains 7 quarters, 5 dimes, 10 nickels, and 8 pennies. After looking at the coin, she puts it back and draws another. What is the probability that the coins she drew were a dime and then a penny?

_____

_____

3 Mrs. Castanon chose two students' names from a hat (she chose the second name without replacing the first name). There are 30 students in her class. What is the probability that she chose John and then Nicholle?

_____

_____

4 Lori and Sergio love lollipops. At the same time, they each take one lollipop from a bag containing 8 cherry, 4 orange, and 7 grape lollipops. What is the probability that they both got an orange one?

_____

_____

5 Kalee and Nick are choosing two different movies to watch. In their collection, they have 10 sci-fi movies, 12 comedies, and 5 dramas. If Kalee chooses the first movie at random and then Nick chooses the second movie at random, what is the probability that they both choose sci-fi movies?

_____

_____

6 Amee wants to make a simulation to help her find the probability that there will be one girl and one boy from her class chosen for student council, if two students in the class are chosen at random. How can she design her simulation?

_____

_____

Challenge Questions

Let's see if you can apply your skills to a couple of really challenging questions. Ready?

1) The probability of drawing a red marble out of a bag of 36 marbles is 1/9. How many marbles in the bag are NOT red?

2) If Rhonda rolls a pair of six-sided dice, what is the probability that she will not roll a 4?

Answers and Explanations are on p. 220.

Name _____

Lessons 21–23

Review the graph and answer the following questions.

1 Is there more trash on the beach due to plastic or paper? _____

2 Which material accounts for more than twice as much trash on the beach as Styrofoam? _____

3 What material accounts for the least amount of trash on the beach? _____

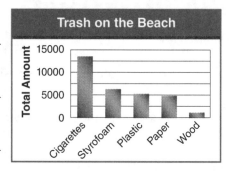

Trash on the Beach

Use data from the graphs to answer the following questions.

4 Which city has the highest average temperature in the summer? _____

The lowest? _____

5 The average temperature of Chicago is 4 degrees warmer than Cleveland, true or false? _____

6 Which city is cooler during the summertime, San Francisco or Milwaukee? _____

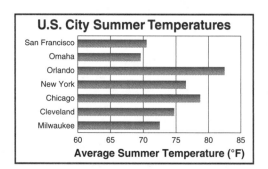

U.S. City Summer Temperatures

7 On what day did Jason practice his guitar the most? _____

The least? _____

8 Jason practices 2.5 hours more on Thursday than on what other day? _____

9 What is the total number of hours that Jason practices from Monday to Saturday? _____

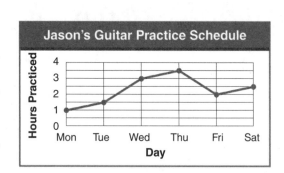

Jason's Guitar Practice Schedule

10 In what year did Rocco hit more home runs than doubles? _____

11 One year, Rocco injured his leg sliding into second base and missed some games while he recovered. What year do you think that was?

_____

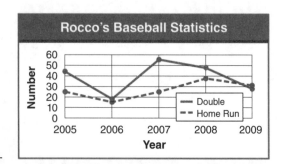

Rocco's Baseball Statistics

Lessons 21–23

12 Fredo is planning the menu for his restaurant. He conducted a survey of restaurant guests and converted that information into a circle graph. Based on the data, what is the most popular type of entree that Fredo's restaurant serves?

_____

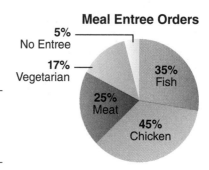

Meal Entree Orders

5% No Entree
17% Vegetarian
35% Fish
25% Meat
45% Chicken

13 Based on the data, which is more popular as an entree, fish or meat? _____

14 Fredo would like to add more vegetarian entrees, but he won't until at least 10% of the patrons want them. Should Fredo add more vegetarian entrees, and why? _____

_____

15 Look at the following data group: 2, 3, 5, 8, 8, 9, 16, 24, 28, 40, 44

What is the median of the data group? _____

What is the mean? _____

What is the range? _____

16 Put the following data into a stem-and-leaf plot:
19, 22, 22, 25, 26, 27, 28, 30, 34, 36, 37, 44, 44, 44, 45, 48, 48, 49, 50, 53, 55, 57, 58, 64, 67

What is the mode of the set of data? _____

What is the median? _____

What is the mean? _____

17 What is the approximate range of the third quartile? _____

What is the median of the data? _____

What is the range of the data? _____

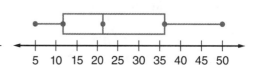

5 10 15 20 25 30 35 40 45 50

Lessons 21-23

18 How many of the outcomes in this tree diagram result in having less than two tails?

_____

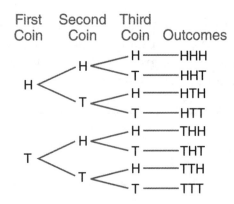

First Coin   Second Coin   Third Coin   Outcomes

H — HHH
H — HHT
H — HTH
T — HTT
H — THH
T — THT
H — TTH
T — TTT

19 James conducted a survey of students in his class. He found that out of the 50 people he surveyed, 35 used a backpack to carry their books and 28 carried calculators. If 13 students carried a calculator and a backpack, how many students carry only a backpack?

_____

Fill in the Venn Diagram to model the problem.

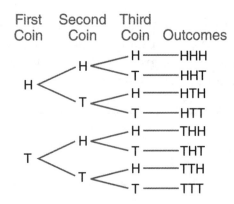

Venn Diagram

20 What does this Venn Diagram tell you?

_____

_____

_____

_____

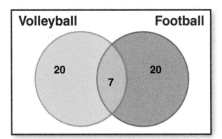

Volleyball   **Football**

20   7   20

21 You have a bag of 20 markers, 5 of which are green, 3 of which are red, 7 of which are yellow, 3 of which are blue, and 2 of which are orange. What is the chance of reaching into the bag and pulling out a yellow marker?

_____

Anything but a green marker? _____

Unit Test

Lessons 21-23

22 A grocery store did a taste test of 3 brands of cookies. In a random survey of 50 people walking down the street in front of the store, 20 people said they preferred Brand A, 14 people preferred Brand B, and 16 people preferred Brand C. Which of the following is the most valid conclusion?

(a) The grocery store should stop selling Brand B.

(b) Brands B and C have roughly the same popularity.

(c) Brand A is twice as popular as Brand B.

23 Find the mean absolute deviation for the values below.

_____

Student	Score
Kathy	84
Carolyn	68
Preston	92
Britt	76

24 Andy did a random survey to find out what type of pet is most popular in his town. 17 people chose dogs, 18 people chose cats, and 6 people chose fish. Complete the probability model.

Outcome	Number	Probability
Dog		
Cat		
Fish		

25 Alex rolls a pair of six-sided dice. What is the probability that he will roll a 2 and a 6?

_____

_____

_____

Unit Test

Name _____

Answers and Explanations

1. Plastic

2. Cigarettes

3. Wood

4. Orlando; Omaha

5. True

6. San Francisco

7. Thursday; Monday

8. Monday

9. $13\frac{1}{2}$ hours

10. 2009

11. 2006

12. Chicken

13. Fish

14. Yes. 17% order vegetarian meals

15. Median 9, Mean 17, Range 42   There are 11 numbers; the median is #6, which is 9. The mean is

$$\frac{2 + 3 + 5 + 8 + 8 + 9 + 16 + 24 + 28 + 40 + 44}{11}$$

$$= \frac{187}{11} = 17.$$

The range is 44 − 2 = 42.

16.
1	9
2	2, 2, 5, 6, 7, 8
3	0, 4, 6, 7
4	4, 4, 4, 5, 8, 8, 9
5	0, 3, 5, 7, 8
6	4, 7

Mode 44, Median 44, Mean 41.3

17. Third quartile range 14; median 22; range of data 45

18. 4

19. 22

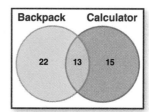

20. 7 people liked both volleyball and football; 47 people in total were surveyed, 20 people liked only volleyball and 20 people liked only football.

21. Yellow marker $\frac{7}{20}$; anything but a green marker $\frac{15}{20}$ or $\frac{3}{4}$

22. B

23. 8   Mean: $\frac{84 + 68 + 92 + 76}{4} = \frac{320}{4} = 80$;

$84 − 80 = 4$, $80 − 68 = 12$,

$92 − 80 = 12$, $80 − 76 = 4$;

$\frac{4 + 12 + 12 + 4}{4} = \frac{32}{4} = 8$

24.

Outcome	Number	Probability
Dog	$\frac{17}{41}$	0.41
Cat	$\frac{18}{41}$	0.44
Fish	$\frac{6}{41}$	0.15

25. $\frac{1}{36}$ Each is $\frac{1}{6}$, so both $= \frac{1}{6} \times \frac{1}{6} = \frac{1}{36}$

Points and Lines

You have probably used the words "point" and "line" before, but do those terms have mathematical meanings?

You probably think of a point as a dot, which is what we mean when we use "point" in everyday use. However, a **point** in mathematics is a specific location in space. It has no dimensions at all. Each point is usually labeled with a capital letter.

A **line** is a perfectly straight path of points. It goes in both directions, and it never ends. When we draw a line, we use a pencil so we can see it. However, a line in mathematics has only one dimension, length.

Since a line is a path of points, it can be named by *any* two points located *anywhere* on it, and you can use those points in either order. So in the previous illustration, Line YZ = Line ZY, and Line WX = Line XW.

Intersecting lines cross each other at a specific point. In this example, Lines YZ and WX cross at Point U.

Exercises   IDENTIFY

1 List the points located in the figure below.

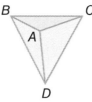

_____

2 How many different points are located in the figure below?

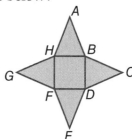

_____

3 Do the figures for exercises 1 and 2 contain any lines? Why or why not?

_____
_____
_____

4 List all possible names for the line pictured below.

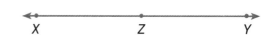

_____

Line Segments and Rays

If lines go on forever in both directions, can you talk about a line that ends at one or both sides? Yes, and you may have guessed that there are some mathematical terms for these.

S_____T

A **line segment** is a specific part of a line that has ends at two points. It is named by its two endpoints. So segment ST = segment TS. We can write it this way:

$$\overline{ST} = \overline{TS}$$

Q_____R→

A **ray** is a part of a line that begins at a specific point, called a **vertex**, or endpoint. The line then extends from there in one direction without coming to an end. To define a ray, you must use one other letter along the line's path—but remember that the second letter is *not* the line's end. The *first* point in the name of a ray is its vertex. So ray QR *does not* equal ray RQ. Ray QR has a different vertex from ray RQ, and goes in the opposite direction!

$$\overrightarrow{QR} \neq \overleftarrow{RQ}$$

Exercises   IDENTIFY

1 How many line segments are there if you connect all the vertexes in this figure? Some, but not all, have been connected for you.

_____

2 Let A stand for the town Augusta, and B stand for the town Bar Harbor. Using these two letters, what would be the ray if you were traveling from Bar Harbor through Augusta?

_____

3 Name all the possible line segments in this figure.

_____

_____

4 At the right is a drawing of an airport runway. Name all the possible rays that could be used to describe the different ways a plane could take off. For points, use the numbers at the end of the runways: 15, 24, 8 and 33. An example of one is ray 15–33. Name the other three.

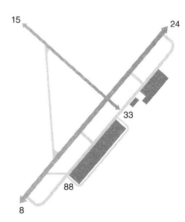

_____

Measuring Angles

Rays from two intersecting lines can meet at the same vertex. When they do, they form an **angle**, which is named by both its lines. The vertex is in the middle of the name.

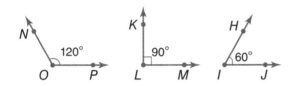

Rays NO and OP intersect at point O, the vertex of each line, to form angle NOP.

You measure angles in degrees. A straight line is 180°, so angles are always smaller than 180°. If an angle is greater than 90°, it is an **obtuse angle**. If it is less than 90°, it is an **acute angle**. If it is *exactly* 90°, it is a **right angle**, which is often shown with a small square inside the angle.

∠NOP is an obtuse angle. ∠KLM is a right angle. ∠HIJ is an acute angle.

Exercises IDENTIFY

Label the angles as acute, obtuse, or right.

1 63° _____

2 123° _____

3 90° _____

4 23° _____

5 93° _____

6 80° _____

7 90° ∠DEF = _____

8 130° ∠RST = _____

9 105° ∠LMN = _____

10 50° ∠QRS = _____

11 35° ∠ABC = _____

12 155° ∠GHI = _____

Name _____

Types of Angles

Angles always measure fewer degrees than a straight line. Two angles can be added together to form 180°, or a straight line.

Two angles that form a line are called **supplementary angles**. Their sum will equal 180°. So if you know the measurement of one angle, you can figure out the measurement of the other angle. Notice that a single letter placed near the vertex can sometimes be used to identify angles.

Angles have other kinds of relationships, too. Two acute angles that form a right angle are called **complementary angles**. The sum of these two angles equals 90°.

Example:

If ∠E = 35°, you subtract 35 from 90 to find angle D. Angle D = 55°.

Example:

If ∠F = 75°, you subtract this value from 180°.
180 − 75 equals angle G.
Angle G = 105°.

Two intersecting lines will always form four angles. The angles opposite each other are called **vertical angles**, and they are equal. ∠A = ∠C. ∠B = ∠D.

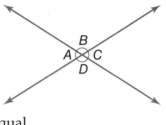

Exercises   IDENTIFY

1 What is the measure of angle Q?

_____

2 What is the measure of angle Z?

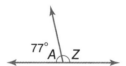

_____

3 Identify the supplementary angles in the figure below.

_____

4 The measure of ∠G is given. Determine the measure of the remaining angles.

_____

Types of Angles (cont.)

There is a simple way to prove that vertical angles are equal.

∠A and ∠B form a straight line.
So ∠B = 180° − ∠A.

∠B and ∠C also form a straight line.
∠B = 180° − ∠C.

Therefore ∠A = ∠C.

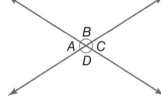

Exercises SOLVE

1 From this figure, give examples of two complementary, two supplementary, and two vertical angles.

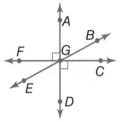

Complementary _____

_____

Supplementary _____

_____

Vertical _____

_____

2 For the figure below, list all complementary and supplementary angles.

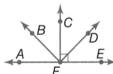

Complementary _____

_____

Supplementary _____

_____

3

Are angle DOB and angle DOC complementary? _____

Explain. _____

_____

_____

4 Identify the measure of the angles in this figure.

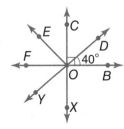

COD _____

COF _____

FOY _____

YOX _____

FOX _____

26.1

Name _____

Triangles

You know that a 2-dimensional figure with three sides is called a **triangle**. The three angles in a triangle add up to 180°.

acute triangle   right triangle   obtuse triangle

All triangles have at least two angles that are acute. In an **acute triangle**, *all* three angles are acute. In a **right triangle**, one of the angles is a right angle. In an **obtuse triangle**, one of the angles is obtuse. Because all three of its angles add up to 180°, a triangle can have only one angle that measures 90° or more.

equilateral triangle isosceles triangle   scalene triangle

Another way of looking at triangles is to look at the length of their sides. In an **equilateral triangle**, all three sides are the same length. They are **congruent**, or equal. In an **isosceles triangle**, two sides are congruent, but the third side is not. In a **scalene triangle**, none of the sides are congruent.

Look at the red marks on some of the triangles. Sides marked the same way are congruent.

Remember...

Right angles are usually marked with a special symbol: 90°

Exercises   IDENTIFY

Label the triangle as acute, right, or obtuse.

1  55° 80° 45°

_____

2 10° 20° 150°

_____

3 x° 40°

_____

4 A b H c a B

_____

5 60° 60° 60°

_____

6 120° 30° 30°

_____

Label the triangle as equilateral, isosceles, or scalene.

7

_____

8 60° 60°

_____

9

_____

Quadrilaterals

Can you name a 2-dimensional figure with 4 angles? A 2-dimensional figure with four angles—and four sides—is called a **quadrilateral**.

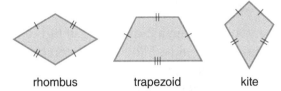

rhombus   trapezoid   kite

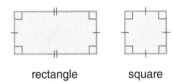

rectangle   square

You probably already recognize a **rectangle**, which has four right angles. A rectangle's opposite sides are parallel and the same length. If *all* four sides of a rectangle are the same length, it is a **square**.

Like a rectangle, the opposite sides of a **rhombus** are parallel and have the same length. Unlike a rectangle, a rhombus does *not* have four right angles.

A **trapezoid** has two opposite sides that are parallel, but they are *not* the same length. The other two sides of a trapezoid are *not* parallel.

If a quadrilateral looks like a typical toy kite, it's called a **kite**. Two of its angles are equal. Its longer two *touching* sides are equal in length, and so are its shorter two *touching* sides.

Exercises   IDENTIFY

Label the shape as: square, rectangle, rhombus, trapezoid, or kite.

1 2.5 m / 2.5 m / 2.5 m / 2.5 m

_____

2 45° 45°

_____

3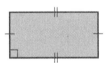

_____

4

_____

5

_____

6

_____

7

_____

8

_____

9 6 in. / 6 in. / 6 in.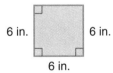

_____

Name _____

Polygons

Have you ever seen a 2-dimensional figure that has more than 4 sides? You have if you have ever seen a stop sign. A stop sign is an octagon, an 8-sided **polygon**. A polygon is a closed 2-dimensional figure made up of line segments. In fact, triangles and quadrilaterals are polygons, too. However, mathematicians usually don't call a figure a polygon unless it has more than 3 sides. The most common polygons are named for the number of their sides.

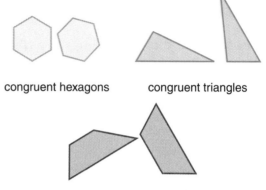

congruent hexagons   congruent triangles

not congruent trapezoids

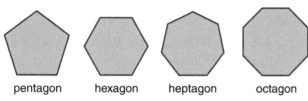

pentagon   hexagon   heptagon   octagon

penta = 5, **hexa** = 6, **hepta** = 7, **octa** = 8

If two polygons have exactly the same shape, size, and angles, then they are congruent. Congruent polygons do *not* have to face in the same direction. So do *not* trust your eyes. The best way to tell if two polygons are congruent is to measure the sides and angles of both.

To find the perimeter of a polygon, add the lengths of its sides.

Exercises   IDENTIFY

Label the polygons.

1

_____

2

_____

3

_____

4

_____

5

_____

6

_____

7

_____

8

_____

9 Are these two figures congruent? Why or why not?

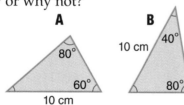

_____

_____

10 Are these two figures congruent? Why or why not?

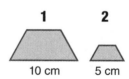

1   2

10 cm   5 cm

_____

_____

Circles

There are some special terms you need to know when describing circles. The distance around a circle is called its **circumference**. Every point on a circle's circumference is an equal distance from the circle's center point, or **origin**.

A **radius** is a line segment that begins at a circle's origin and extends to its circumference. In a circle, all radii (plural of "radius") are equal in length.

A line segment that has both its endpoints on the circumference is called a **chord**. If a chord passes through the origin, it is called a **diameter**. The length of a circle's diameter is two times the length of the circle's radius.

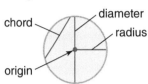

Exercises   IDENTIFY

1 What is the radius of the circle?

_____

2 What is the radius of the circle?

_____

3 Identify the 2 radii and the one chord below.

_____

4 Identify the radius and chord in the figure below.

_____

5 What are the 5 chords formed by inscribing the pentagon inside of the circle below?

_____

_____

6 Using the letters provided, can the diameter in the figure below be named? Explain your answer.

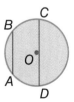

_____

_____

Circles (cont.)

Pi (π) is the Greek letter that stands for a very long decimal used to calculate a circle's circumference and area. Pi is the ratio of a circle's diameter to its circumference. Pi is exactly the same ratio for every circle. Sometimes the decimal is rounded to 3.14, but most mathematicians just use π to stand for it.

The circumference of a circle = pi times its diameter (πd).

The area of a circle = pi times the square of its radius = πr^2.

Remember to express area in square units. For example, square inches, square feet, square yards, and so on.

Exercises   IDENTIFY

7 How many ways can you describe the radius in this circle?

_____

8 Which two lines in the circle below are chords?

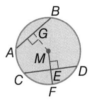

_____

9 Identify the chord and the diameter below.

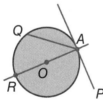

_____

10 Calculate the area of the circle below. Leave your answer in the form of pi.

10 in.

_____

Calculate the circumference and the area.

10

11 Circumference = _____

Area = _____

7

12 Circumference = _____

Area = _____

Surface Area of Solid Figures

Not all figures are 2-dimensional. Can you name some common 3-dimensional—or **solid**—figures?

You need to learn some new terms:

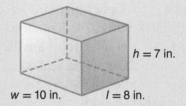

cube

Face: A flat surface of a solid figure. Each face looks like a 2-dimensional figure.

Edge: The line at which two faces meet.

Vertex (of a Solid): A specific point at which *more than* 2 faces meet or where a curve originates.

Base: The face on the bottom of a solid figure.

Example:

$h = 7$ in.
$w = 10$ in. $l = 8$ in.

rectangular solid

To find the surface area of a rectangular, square, or triangular solid figure, you *could* add up the areas of all its faces. There is an easier way to find the surface area of a rectangular solid. The formula is: $2lw + 2lh + 2wh$

The surface area of the solid above is $(2 \times 8 \times 7) + (2 \times 8 \times 10) + (2 \times 7 \times 10) = 112 + 160 + 140 = 412$ **square inches**

Exercises   CALCULATE SURFACE AREA

1

3 in.
3 in.
3 in.

_____

2

2 m
6 m   5 m

_____

3

8.85 in.
10 in.
7.25 in.

_____

4

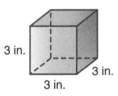

9.9 ft
1.5 ft
4.2 ft

_____

5

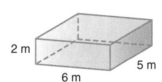

14 cm
10 cm
12 cm

_____

6

13 m
11 m
12 m

_____

7

11 m
7 m
9 m

_____

8

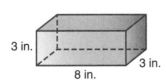

3 in.
3 in.
8 in.

_____

9

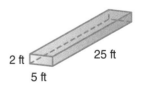

2 ft   25 ft
5 ft

_____

26.5

Name _____

Surface Area of Solid Figures (cont.)

A **cylinder** is the only other kind of solid figure you will work with. To calculate the surface area of a cylinder, you *could* measure the area of each of its circular bases. Then you could unfold the rest of the cylinder to make a rectangle and find the area of that. Finally, you could add the three surface areas you calculated.

Example:

There is an easier way to find the surface area of a cylinder. Use the formula: $2\pi r^2 + 2\pi rh$.

So the surface area of this cylinder
$= 2 \times \pi \times 3^2 + 2 \times \pi \times 3 \times 3$
$= 18\pi + 18\pi = 36\pi$ square centimeters.

Exercises   CALCULATE SURFACE AREA

Keep your answer in a form of pi.

10

3 cm
7 cm

_____

11

5 in.
12 in.

_____

12
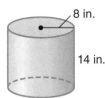
9 m
5 m

_____

13

11 m
1.5 m

_____

14

4.5 ft
6.2 ft

_____

15

8 in.
14 in.

_____

16

6 cm
1 cm

_____

17

4.25 in.
12 in.

_____

18
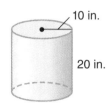
10 in.
20 in.

_____

Volume of Solid Figures

You can calculate the volume of solid figures. The ones you will need to work with right now are rectangular solids, triangular solids, and cylinders.

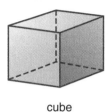
cube

You have already learned how to calculate the volume (V) of a rectangular solid.

$V = l \times w \times h$

The volume of a cylinder is the area of the circular base (B) × the height of the solid (h). The formula is $V = B \times h$.

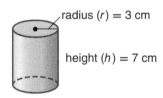
radius (r) = 3 cm
height (h) = 7 cm

$V = \pi r^2 \times h$
$\quad = \pi \times 3^2 \times 7$
$\quad = 63\pi$ cu cm

The volume of a triangular prism is the area of a triangular base (B) × the height of the solid (H). Remember that the area of the triangular base is $\frac{1}{2} \times l \times h$. The small letter h represents the height of a 2-dimensional *triangle*. The capital letter H represents the height of the 3-dimensional *solid*. Be careful, because they are usually different numbers. The formula for volume is $V = B \times H$.

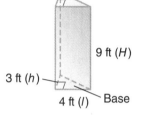
9 ft (H)
3 ft (h)
4 ft (l)
Base

$V = \frac{1}{2} l \times h \times H$
$\quad = \frac{1}{2} \times 4 \times 3 \times 9$
$\quad = 54$ cu ft

Exercises CALCULATE VOLUME

1
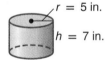
r = 5 in.
h = 7 in.

_____

2

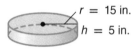
r = 15 in.
h = 5 in.

_____

3
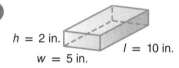
h = 2 in.
l = 10 in.
w = 5 in.

_____

4
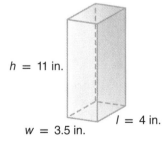
h = 11 in.
l = 4 in.
w = 3.5 in.

_____

5
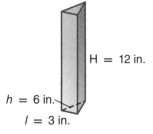
H = 12 in.
h = 6 in.
l = 3 in.

_____

6
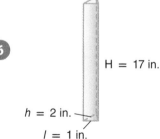
H = 17 in.
h = 2 in.
l = 1 in.

_____

Challenge Questions

Let's see if you can apply your skills to a couple of really challenging questions. Ready?

1) Which of the following shows the volume of a cylinder with a diameter of 5 centimeters and a height of x centimeters? (Use $\pi = 3.14$.)

A) $V = 7.85x$ cubic cm

B) $V = 15.7x$ cubic cm

C) $V = 19.625x$ cubic cm

D) $V = 78.5x$ cubic cm

2) There is a $3\frac{1}{2}$-foot-wide walkway around a circular pond. The diameter of the pond is 7 feet. Which of the following shows the area of the walkway?

A) $A = 12.25$ square feet

B) $A = 24.5\pi$ square feet

C) $A = 36.75\pi$ square feet

D) $A = 49\pi$ square feet

Answers and Explanations are on p. 220.

Unit Test

Lessons 24–26

Identify each angle as obtuse, acute, or right.

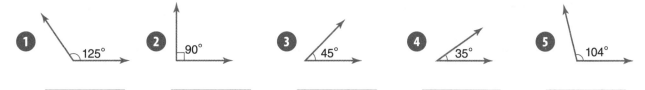

1 125° _____

2 90° _____

3 45° _____

4 35° _____

5 104° _____

Identify each pair of angles as supplementary, complementary, vertical, or not any of these. Explain why.

6
B C 52° 38° A D _____

7
C 66° 114° B A D _____

8
B C 66° 24° A D _____

9
E F 44° 45° D G _____

10
H 144° G 25° I J _____

Identify the following triangles as scalene, equilateral, or isosceles.

11 _____

12 _____

13 _____

Lessons 24–26

  **14** _____

15 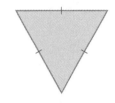 _____

16 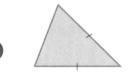 _____

Identify the following triangles as obtuse, right, or acute.

17 _____

18 _____

19 _____

20  _____

21 _____

22 _____

Answer the following questions by looking at the figure on the right.

23 Name the center point _____

24 Which segments are chords? _____

25 Which segment is the diameter? _____

26 Which segments are radii? _____

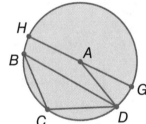

Identify the figures and fill in the missing information.

27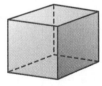

Figure _____

Base is _____

Number of faces _____

Number of edges _____

Number of vertices _____

28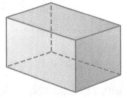

Figure _____

Base is _____

Number of faces _____

Number of edges _____

Number of vertices _____

29

Figure _____

Base is _____

Number of faces _____

Number of edges _____

Number of vertices _____

Lessons 24–26

30

Figure _____

Base is _____

Number of faces _____

Number of edges _____

Number of vertices _____

31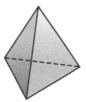

Figure _____

Base is _____

Number of faces _____

Number of edges _____

Number of vertices _____

32

Figure _____

Base is _____

Number of faces _____

Number of edges _____

Number of vertices _____

Identify the figures.

33

_____

34

_____

35

_____

36

_____

37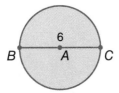

What is the circumference of the circle? (Use 3.14 for π.)

_____

What is the area of the circle?

_____

38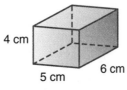

4 cm   5 cm   6 cm

Jerome bought a present that came in a box that looked like the figure above. If he wants to wrap the present before he gives it to his sister, how much wrapping paper will he need to wrap the present?

_____

39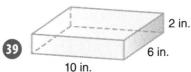

2 in.   6 in.   10 in.

How many 1-inch cube wooden blocks can fit in the box shown in the figure?

_____

Unit Test

Name _____

Answers and Explanations

1. Obtuse

2. Right

3. Acute

4. Acute

5. Obtuse

6. Complementary; angle measures sum to 90°

7. Supplementary; angle measures sum to 180°

8. Complementary; angle measures sum to 90°

9. Neither; angle measures sum to 89°

10. Neither; angle measures sum to 169°

11. Equilateral

12. Scalene

13. Isosceles

14. Scalene

15. Equilateral

16. Isosceles

17. Right

18. Acute

19. Acute

20. Acute

21. Obtuse

22. Right

23. Point A

24. $\overline{HG}$, $\overline{BD}$, $\overline{BC}$, $\overline{CD}$

25. $\overline{HG}$

26. $\overline{AG}$, $\overline{AD}$, $\overline{AH}$

27. Cube; square; 6 faces; 12 edges; 8 vertices

28. Rectangular solid; rectangle; 6 faces; 12 edges; 8 vertices

29. Rectangular Pyramid; rectangle; 5; 8; 5

30. Cone; circle; 1 face; no edges; 1 vertex

31. Triangular Pyramid; Triangle; 4 faces; 6 edges; 4 vertices

32. Triangular Prism; Triangle; 5 faces; 9 edges; 6 vertices

33. Pentagon

34. Hexagon

35. Heptagon

36. Octagon

37. Circumference 18.84; Area 28.26 sq units

   $C = \pi d = (3.14)(6) = 18.84$;
   $A = \pi r^2 = \pi(3^2) = 9\pi = 28.26$

38. 148 sq cm

   $SA = 2(4 \times 5) + 2(4 \times 6)$
   $+2(5 \times 6) = 2(20) + 2(24)$
   $+2(30) = 40 + 48 + 60$
   $= 148$ sq cm

39. 120 wooden blocks

   $V = lwh = (10)(6)(2)$
   $= 120$ cu in.

Posttest

Complete the following test items on pages 156–160.

1 Restate the number 5,176,802.4539.

Expanded form: _____

Written form: _____

2 Brian's Bakery is having a sale on cakes. They have 95 cakes and will be baking 23 more before the start of the sale. If at the end of the sale they still have 7 cakes, how many cakes did they sell? _____

3 Stuart pedals 19 miles a day on his bicycle. How many miles does he pedal in the month of February? (Remember, February has 28 days.) _____

4
$$\begin{array}{r} 134 \\ \times\ -15 \\ \hline \end{array}$$

5 $\dfrac{3}{4} \div \dfrac{27}{32} =$ ___

6 $\$133.25 + \$68.98$
= _____

7 $238.62 - 7.438$
= _____

8 $\left|-\dfrac{1}{2}\right| + \left|\dfrac{1}{3}\right| =$ ___

9 $-12\overline{)252}$

10 $4.8\overline{)932}$

11 $-27 + 9 - (-5)$
= ___

12 Danetta bought $19\dfrac{3}{8}$ kilograms of gerbil food. On the way home, she spilled $3\dfrac{4}{5}$ kilograms. How much gerbil food does she still have?

_____

13 To make his favorite fruit punch, Ezekiel mixes 1950 centiliters of juice with $1\dfrac{3}{4}$ liters of seltzer and $\dfrac{3}{8}$ liters of orange juice. How many liters of punch will this make?

_____

14 What is the volume of a cube with sides of 3.2 inches? _____

15 $-5 + |-17| - (-6) + 7(-5) - \dfrac{9}{3} =$ ___

16 Solve for x: $x - 91 \geq 13$ _____

17 Solve for x: $4x + 11 = 15$ _____

18 What property is represented by the following equation?
$2(6 + 9) = 2 \times 6 + 2 \times 9$

_____

19 What property is represented by the following equation?
$(4 + 8) + 8 = 4 + (8 + 8)$

_____

20 $|-7| + (1 + 3)^2 - (9 \div 3) + 5(8 \times 3) + 2(10 - 7) =$

_____

Posttest

21 Give the coordinates for the points.

A _____

B _____

C _____

D _____

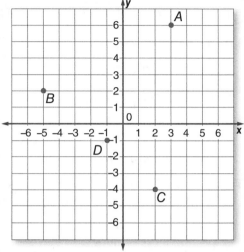

22 Restate in exponent form, then solve:

$5 \times 5 \times 5 + 3 \times 3 =$

_____

23 What is the area of the rectangle?

_____

What is the perimeter of the rectangle?

_____

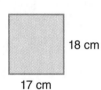

18 cm

17 cm

24 What is the area of the circle? (Use 3.14 for π.)

_____

What is the circumference of the circle?

_____

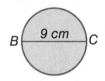

B   9 cm   C

25 Identify the following angles as obtuse, acute, or right.

        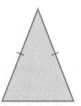

95°   90°   45°

_____   _____   _____

26 Identify the triangles as scalene, isosceles, or equilateral.

    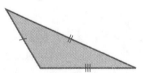

_____   _____   _____

27 Jackie spends $37.95 a month on art supplies. She is working on a project that will take 19 months to finish. How much should she plan to spend on art supplies for the project? _____

28 Restate 7.6 as an improper fraction and a mixed number. _____

29 $\sqrt{21}$ is between _____ and _____.

30 Is the following true or false? $\frac{4}{11} = \frac{68}{187}$ _____

31 Put the following numbers in order from least to greatest:
1.141, 1.014, 1.044, 1.004, 1.9, 1.996, 1.89, 0.9

_____

32 Juliette deposits $295 in a bank account that earns 6% simple interest. How much money will she have in the account after 1 year?

_____ After 2 years? _____

33 What is the mode of the data distribution?

_____

What is the median?

_____

Stems	Leaves
1	4 6
2	2 7 5
3	1 6 6 6
4	3 3 5 7 7
5	2 5 6

34 $\frac{2}{7} \times 2\frac{5}{22} =$ _____

35 What is $\frac{5}{8}$ of 75%? _____

36 What is 25% of 0.525? _____

37 $0.24\overline{)564}$

38 $\frac{5}{4} + \frac{7}{4} + \frac{15}{4} - \frac{9}{4} - \frac{17}{4} =$ _____

39 Identify each quadrilateral as a square, rectangle, kite, rhombus, or trapezoid.

_____   _____   _____   _____   _____

40 Identify the following figures.

_____   _____   _____

41 Restate $9\frac{11}{13}$ as an improper fraction.

_____

42 Restate $\frac{72}{13}$ as a mixed number.

_____

Posttest

43 What are the chances of choosing a blue marble out of a bag containing 7 red marbles, 6 green marbles, 11 yellow marbles, and 4 blue marbles? _____

What is the probability of choosing a blue marble, not replacing it, and then choosing a green marble? _____

44 According to the graph, how many miles did Janice swim in September?

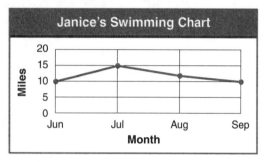

_____

45 During which week did Brian and Ray run the same distance?

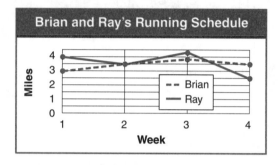

_____

46 Which vegetable is most preferred by the students?

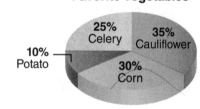

_____

47 Dean's score was about 20 points higher than whose score?

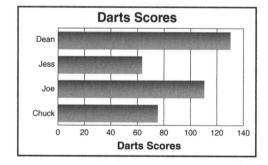

_____

48 What is the range of the data in the box-and-whisker plot below?

_____

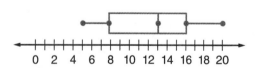

What is the range of the upper quartile _____

49 How much plastic wrap would you need to cover this rectangular solid?

_____

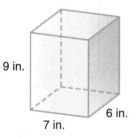

9 in.

6 in.

7 in.

50 Name two line segments. _____

Name 4 rays. _____

Name a line. _____

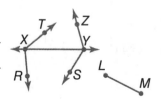

51 Fill in a Venn Diagram that displays the following data:

There are two groups of students, 25 who are in the drama club and 15 who enjoy math. There are 8 students who are in the drama club who also enjoy math.

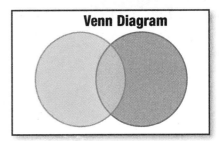

Venn Diagram

52 Are the rates in the table below proportional?

Vegetable	Price	Quantity
Artichoke	$5.00	2 pounds
Asparagus	$1.25	0.5 pound

53 What is the unit rate for the speed of the car shown on the graph below?

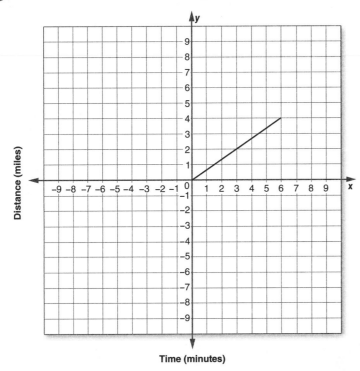

Distance (miles)

Time (minutes)

54 Ebony asked four of her female friends if they liked wearing sandals better than wearing boots. All four said yes. Ebony concluded that none of the girls her age like boots. Is her conclusion valid? Did she use a representative sample for her survey?

_____

_____

55 Create a probability table for choosing a marble out of a bag of 14 white, 18 black, and 6 red marbles.

Outcome	Number	Probability
White		
Black		
Red		

Posttest

Name _____

Answers and Explanations for Posttest

1. $(5 \times 1,000,000) + (1 \times 100,000) + (7 \times 10,000) + (6 \times 1000) + (8 \times 100) + (2 \times 1) + (4 \times 0.01) + (5 \times 0.01) + (3 \times 0.001) + (9 \times 0.0001)$; five million one hundred seventy-six thousand eight hundred two and four thousand five hundred thirty-nine ten-thousandths

2. 111 cakes $95 + 23 - 7 = 111$

3. 532 miles

$$
\begin{array}{r}
\overset{7}{19} \\
\times\ 28 \\
\hline
1^{1}52 \\
380 \\
\hline
532
\end{array}
$$

4. -2010

$$
\begin{array}{r}
\overset{1\ 2}{134} \\
\times -15 \\
\hline
6^{1}70 \\
1^{1}340 \\
\hline
-2010
\end{array}
$$

5. 8/9 $\dfrac{3}{4} \div \dfrac{27}{32} = \dfrac{\cancel{3}^{1}}{\cancel{4}^{1}} \times \dfrac{\cancel{32}^{8}}{\cancel{27}^{9}} = \dfrac{8}{9}$

6. $202.23

$$
\begin{array}{r}
\overset{1\ 1\ 1\ 1}{\$133.25} \\
+\ 68.98 \\
\hline
\$\ 202.23
\end{array}
$$

7. 231.182

$$
\begin{array}{r}
238.\overset{5}{\cancel{6}}\overset{1}{\cancel{2}}\overset{1}{0} \\
-\ 7.4\ 3\ 8 \\
\hline
231.1\ 8\ 2
\end{array}
$$

8. 5/6 $\left|-\dfrac{1}{2}\right| + \left|\dfrac{1}{3}\right| = \dfrac{1}{2} + \dfrac{1}{3} = \dfrac{3}{6} + \dfrac{2}{6} = \dfrac{5}{6}$

9. -21

$$
\begin{array}{r}
-21 \\
-12\overline{)252} \\
24 \\
\hline
12 \\
12 \\
\hline
0
\end{array}
$$

10. 194.167

$$
\begin{array}{r}
194.166\ldots \\
4.8.\overline{)932.0.000} \\
48 \\
\hline
452 \\
432 \\
\hline
200 \\
192 \\
\hline
80 \\
48 \\
\hline
320 \\
288 \\
\hline
320 \\
288 \\
\hline
32\ldots
\end{array}
$$

11. −13 $-27 + 9 - (-5) = -27 + 9 + 5 = -13$

12. $15\frac{23}{40}$ kg $19 - 3 = 16; \frac{3}{8} - \frac{4}{5} = \frac{15}{40} - \frac{32}{40} = -\frac{17}{40}; 16 - \frac{17}{40} = 15\frac{23}{40}$

13. $21\frac{5}{8}$ $1950\,\text{cL} = 19.5\,\text{L}; 19\frac{1}{2} + 1\frac{3}{4} + \frac{3}{8} = 20 + \left(\frac{4}{8} + \frac{6}{8} + \frac{3}{8}\right) = 20 + \frac{13}{8} = 21\frac{5}{8}$

14. 32.768 square inches $3.2 \times 3.2 \times 3.2 = 32.768$

15. −20 $-5 + 17 + 6 + 7(-5) - \frac{9}{3} = -5 + 17 + 6 - 35 - 3 = -20$

16. $x \geq 104$
$$\begin{array}{r} x - 91 \geq 13 \\ +91 \quad +91 \\ \hline x \geq 104 \end{array}$$

17. $x = 1$
$$\begin{array}{r} 4x + 11 = 15 \\ -11 \quad -11 \\ \hline 4x \quad\ = 4 \\ \div 4 \quad\ \div 4 \\ \hline x = 1 \end{array}$$

18. Distributive Property of Multiplication over Addition

19. Associative Property of Addition

20. 146 $7 + 4^2 - 3 + 5(24) + 2(3) = 7 + 16 - 3 + 5(24) + 2(3) = 7 + 16 - 3 + 120 + 6 = 146$

21. A(3,6), B(−5,2), C(2,−4), D(−1,−1)

22. $5^3 + 3^2 = 125 + 9 = 134$

23. Area = 306 sq cm; Perimeter = 70 cm $17 \times 18 = 306; 17 + 17 + 18 + 18 = 70$

24. Area = 63.585 sq cm; Circumference = 28.26 cm $A = \pi r^2; A = \pi(4.5^2) = (3.14)(20.25) = 63.585; C = \pi d;$
$C = 3.14 \times 9 = 28.26$

25. Obtuse; right; acute $95° > 90°; 90° = 90°; 45° < 90°$

26. Equilateral; scalene; isosceles   all 3 sides equal; all 3 sides different; 2 sides equal

27. $721.05
$$\begin{array}{r} {}^7 3 {}^8 7.{}^4 95 \\ \times \quad\quad 19 \\ \hline 3{}^1 4{}^1 1{}^1 55 \\ 3\ 7\ 9\ 50 \\ \hline 7\ 21.05 \end{array}$$

28. $\frac{38}{5}; 7\frac{3}{5}$ $7.6 = 7\frac{6}{10} = 7\frac{3}{5} = \frac{38}{5}$

29. 4 and 5 $\sqrt{16} = 4$ and $\sqrt{25} = 5$, so $\sqrt{21} \cong 4.5$

30. True $\frac{68}{182} \div \frac{17}{17} = \frac{4}{11}$

31. 0.9, 1.004, 1.014, 1.044, 1.141, 1.89, 1.9, 1.996

32. $312.70; $330.40 $295 \times 0.06 = 17.70, so $312.70; $312.70 \times 0.06 = 18.76, so $330.40 in 2 years

33. Mode = 36; median = 36   36 appears 3 times; there are 17 values, so the median is value #9, which is 36

34. $\frac{7}{11}$ $\frac{2}{7} \times \frac{49}{22} = \frac{1}{1} \times \frac{7}{11} = \frac{7}{11}$

35. 46.875% $\frac{5}{8} \times 75 = \frac{375}{8} = 46.875\%$

36. 0.13125 $0.25 \times 0.525 = 0.13125$

37. 2350

$$\begin{array}{r} 2350. \\ .24\overline{)564.00.} \\ \underline{48} \\ 84 \\ \underline{72} \\ 120 \\ \underline{120} \\ 0 \end{array}$$

38. $\dfrac{1}{4}$ $\dfrac{5+7+15-9-17}{4} = \dfrac{1}{4}$

39. Trapezoid; square; rhombus; rectangle; kite

40. Hexagon; pentagon; heptagon

41. $\dfrac{128}{13}$ $\dfrac{(9 \times 13) + 11}{13} = \dfrac{128}{13}$

42. $5\dfrac{7}{13}$ $72 \div 13 = 5$ R7, so $5\dfrac{7}{13}$

43. $\dfrac{1}{7}$; $\dfrac{6}{189}$ There are 4 blue out of 28 total, so $\dfrac{4}{28} = \dfrac{1}{7}$. Blue, then green: $\dfrac{1}{7} \times \dfrac{6}{27} = \dfrac{6}{189}$

44. 10 miles

45. Week 2

46. Cauliflower   35% is the largest, so cauliflower

47. Joe's   Dean is about 130; 130−20 = 110; Joe is about 110.

48. 15; 4   20−5 = 15; upper quartile: 20−16 = 4

49. 318 sq in.   surface area = 2(9 × 7) + 2(7 × 6) + 2(9 × 6) = 2(63) + 2(42) + 2(54) = 126 + 84 + 108 = 318

50. Line segments: $\overline{YS}$, $\overline{XT}$, $\overline{XR}$, $\overline{YZ}$, $\overline{LM}$, $\overline{ML}$, $\overline{XY}$, $\overline{TX}$, $\overline{RX}$, $\overline{SY}$, $\overline{ZY}$; Rays: $\overrightarrow{XR}$, $\overrightarrow{XT}$, $\overrightarrow{YS}$, $\overrightarrow{YZ}$, $\overrightarrow{XY}$, $\overrightarrow{YX}$; Line $\overleftrightarrow{XY}$

51.

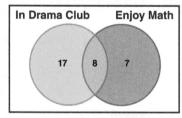

52. Yes. Both are $2.50 per pound.   Artichoke: $\dfrac{\$5}{2 \text{ pounds}} = \dfrac{\$2.50}{1 \text{ pounds}}$; asparagus $\dfrac{\$1.25}{\frac{1}{2} \text{ pounds}} = \dfrac{\$2.50}{1 \text{ pounds}}$

53. $\dfrac{1}{2}$ When $x = 1$, $y = 0.5$

54. No. The conclusion is based on too small a sample and the sample is not representative since she only asked her friends.

55.

Outcome	Number	Probability
White	$\dfrac{14}{38}$	0.37
Black	$\dfrac{18}{38}$	0.47
Red	$\dfrac{6}{38}$	0.16

Posttest

Evaluation Chart

As you review your Posttest, check the chart below to see which lessons relate to the questions you missed. Review those lessons!

1. Lesson 1.1
2. Lesson 1.2
3. Lessons 2.1 and 18.1
4. Lesson 2.1 and 4.5
5. Lesson 8.3
6. Lesson 10.3
7. Lesson 10.2
8. Lesson 5.2
9. Lesson 5.4
10. Lesson 12.2
11. Lesson 5.3
12. Lesson 6.6
13. Lesson 6.6 and 19.2
14. Lesson 18.6
15. Lesson 4.1
16. Lesson 17.4
17. Lesson 17.3
18. Lesson 4.3
19. Lesson 4.2

20. Lesson 4.1
21. Lesson 14.1
22. Lesson 16.1
23. Lesson 18.4 and 18.5
24. Lesson 26.4
25. Lesson 25.2
26. Lesson 26.1
27. Lesson 11.2
28. Lesson 9.3
29. Lesson 16.2
30. Lesson 13.2
31. Lesson 9.1
32. Lesson 15.5 and 15.6
33. Lesson 22.1 and 22.2
34. Lesson 7.3
35. Lesson 15.2
36. Lesson 15.3
37. Lesson 12.2
38. Lesson 6.3

39. Lesson 26.2
40. Lesson 26.3
41. Lesson 6.2
42. Lesson 6.1
43. Lesson 23.1 and 23.3
44. Lesson 21.2
45. Lesson 21.3
46. Lesson 21.4
47. Lesson 21.1
48. Lesson 22.3 and 22.1
49. Lesson 26.5
50. Lesson 24.2
51. Lesson 22.5
52. Lesson 13.3 and 13.2
53. Lesson 14.3
54. Lesson 22.6
55. Lesson 23.2

Glossary

Absolute Value: A number without its sign; it represents the distance between the number and 0 on the number line. *(p. 25)*

Acute Angle: An angle with a measure of less than 90°. *(p. 163)*

Acute Triangle: A triangle with only acute angles, angles less than 90°. *(p. 166)*

Addend: Any number that is added to another number. *(p. 13)*

Algebra: A branch of math used to find the value of unknown variables. *(p. 108)*

Algebraic Expression: A group of letters, numbers, and symbols used in a series of operations. *(p. 108)*

Angle: Two rays that share an endpoint. *(p. 163)*

Area: The measure of a 2-dimensional figure's interior, in square units. *(p. 119)*

Associative Property of Addition: States that addends may be grouped in any order without changing the sum. *(p. 20)*

Associative Property of Multiplication: States that numbers may be grouped in any way without changing the product. *(p. 20)*

Bar Graph: A graph that uses numbers to compare two or more people, places, or things. Each bar represents a number and may be represented horizontally or vertically. *(p. 135)*

Base: The bottom face of a solid figure. *(p. 171)*

Base of an Exponent: The number used as the factor when writing in exponential form. In 10^3, the base is 10. *(p. 104)*

Box-and-Whisker Plot: Organizes data to show where the most data points lie and also shows the median of the data. *(p. 145)*

Carry: To place an extra digit—when adding or multiplying—in the next place-value column on the left. *(p. 13)*

Celsius: Used in the metric system to measure temperature and expressed as °C, also expressed as Centigrade. *(p. 127)*

Chord: A line segment with both endpoints on a circle's circumference. *(p. 169)*

Circle: A 2-dimensional figure with every point on its circumference an equal distance from its center point. *(p. 141)*

Circle Graph: Shows parts of a whole as a percentage to the whole and is also known as a pie chart. *(p. 141)*

Circumference: The length of distance around a circle's perimeter. *(p. 160)*

Coefficient: The number that replaces the symbol × and multiplies the variable in a multiplication expression. The statement $9m$ shows 9 as the coefficient and m as the variable. *(p. 108)*

Common Denominator: A number that can be divided evenly by all the denominators in a group of fractions. *(p. 38)*

Commutative Property of Additions: States that numbers may be added in any order without changing the sum. *(p. 20)*

Commutative Property of Multiplication: States that multiplication may be done in any order without changing the product. *(p. 20)*

Compatible Numbers: Numbers that are easy to work with in your head. *(p. 18)*

Complementary Angles: Two angles that form a right angle. Their sum is 90°. *(p. 164)*

Congruent: A term used to describe something that is equal. *(p. 166)*

Cross-multiplying: A method for finding a missing numerator or denominator. *(p. 81)*

Cylinder: A three-dimensional figure with two parallel and congruent circular bases and one curved surface. *(p. 172)*

Data: Information gathered and sometimes displayed in graphs and charts. *(p. 135)*

Denominator: The number below the line in a fraction. *(p. 34)*

Diameter: A chord that passes through a circle's center point. *(p. 169)*

Distributive Property of Multiplication: States that each number may be multiplied separately and added together. *(p. 21)*

Dividend: The number to be divided in a division problem. *(p. 17)*

Divisor: The number by which the dividend will be divided. *(p. 17)*

Double-Line Graph: Compares how information changes as time passes between two or more people, places, or things. *(p. 139)*

Edge: The line on a solid figure where two faces meet. *(p. 171)*

Equality Property of Addition: States that when adding a number on one side of an equation, you must add the same number on the other side of an equation. Both sides will then still be equal. *(p. 23)*

Equality Property of Division: States that when dividing a number on one side of an equation, you must divide by the *same* number on the other side of the equation. Both sides will then still be equal. *(p. 22)*

Equality Property of Multiplication: States that when multiplying a number on one side of an equation, you must multiply by the *same* number on the other side of the equation. Both sides will then still be equal. *(p. 22)*

Equality Property of Subtraction: States that when subtracting a number on one side of an equation, you must subtract the *same* number on the other side of the equation. Both sides will then still be equal. *(p. 22)*

Equation: A mathematical statement used to show that two amounts are equal. *(p. 81)*

Equilateral Triangle: A triangle with all three sides being the same length. *(p. 166)*

Exponent: The number that tells how many times the base number is multiplied by itself. The exponent ^{3} in 10^3 shows 10 × 10 × 10. *(p. 104)*

Face: The flat surface of a solid figure. On a solid figure each face looks two-dimensional. *(p. 171)*

Fahrenheit: Temperature scale in customary degrees. *(p. 127)*

First Power: In an exponent, a base raised to the first power equals the base. *(p. 104)*

Identity Elements: Numbers in a problem that do not affect the answer. Addition and multiplication have identity elements. *(p. 21)*

Improper Fraction: A fraction greater than 1 because its numerator is greater than its denominator. *(p. 34)*

Intersecting Lines: Lines that meet or cross each other at a specific point. *(p. 161)*

Interval: The distance between each measurement on a line graph. *(p. 137)*

Inverse: A number's exact opposite on the other side of the number line. The inverse of −9 is 9. *(p. 23)*

Isosceles Triangle: A triangle with two sides the same length, but the third side being a different length. *(p. 166)*

Kite: A quadrilateral with two angles that are equal, two touching sides that are equal in length, and the other two touching sides are equal in length. *(p. 167)*

Like Denominators: Fractions that have the same denominator. *(p. 36)*

Line: A straight path that goes in both directions and does not end. A line is measured in length. *(p. 161)*

Line Graph: A type of graph used to show a change in information as time passes. *(p. 137)*

Line Segment: A specific part of a line that ends at two identified points. *(p. 162)*

Liquid Volume: Units of liquid a container can hold and expressed in cups (c), pints (pt), quarts (qt), and gallons (gal). *(p. 116)*

Lower Extreme: The lowest number in the data used in a box-and-whisker plot. *(p. 145)*

Lower Quartile: The median of numbers from the lower extreme to the median on a box-and-whisker plot. *(p. 145)*

Mean: The total number of the whole collection divided by the number of addends. *(p. 143)*

Mean Absolute Deviation: A measurement of how spread out a data set is. *(p. 150)*

Median: The middle number in a set of numbers when the numbers are arranged from least to greatest. *(p. 143)*

Mixed Number: A number with a whole number part and a fraction part. *(p. 34)*

Mode: The number that appears most often in a set of numbers. *(p. 143)*

Negative Exponent: A negative exponent creates a fraction. *(p. 105)*

Negative Number: A number less than 0 and identified with the minus sign. *(p. 23)*

Numerator: The number above the line in a fraction. *(p. 34)*

Obtuse Angle: An angle with a measure of more than 90°. *(p. 163)*

Obtuse Triangle: A triangle with one obtuse angle. *(p. 166)*

Order of Operations: The steps to follow when doing a computation. *(p. 19)*

Origin of a Circle: The circle's center point. *(p. 169)*

PEMDAS: An acronym that helps you remember the Order of Operations. It stands for Parentheses, Exponents, Multiplication and Division, Addition and Subtraction. *(p. 19)*

Percent: A special ratio that compares a number to 100 using the % symbol. *(p. 91)*

Perfect Square: The result of squaring an integer. *(p. 106)*

Perimeter: The distance around a figure. *(p. 118)*

Periods: Organization of numbers in groups of three in a place-value chart. *(p. 12)*

Pi: The ratio of a circle's diameter to its circumference—a ratio that is exactly the same for every circle. *Pi* is often rounded to 3.14. *(p. 170)*

Place Value: The value of a position of a digit in a number. *(p. 12)*

Point: An exact location in space that has no dimensions and cannot be measured usually represented by a dot. *(p. 161)*

Polygon: Any closed two-dimensional figure that is made up of line segments. Triangles and quadrilaterals are two types of polygons. *(p. 168)*

Power of 10: In a place-value chart, each place value is 10 times the place value of the number to its right. *(p. 64)*

Principal: The amount borrowed or deposited into a bank. *(p. 95)*

Probability: The likelihood of an event happening in the future. *(p. 151)*

Probability Model: A chart or table that shows the different outcomes possible for an event and their relative probabilities. *(p. 152)*

Product: The result, or answer, of a multiplication problem. *(p. 15)*

Property of Additive Inverse: States that when adding a negative number to its inverse the sum will be 0. −8 + 8 = 0. *(p. 23)*

Proportion: An equation that shows two ratios are equal. *(p. 81)*

Quadrilateral: A two-dimensional figure with four sides and four angles. *(p. 167)*

Quotient: The result of dividing one number by another. *(p. 17)*

Radius: A line segment from a circle's center point to its perimeter. *(p. 169)*

Range: The greatest number minus the smallest number in a set of numbers. *(p. 143)*

Ratio: A comparison of two numbers using division. *(p. 79)*

Ray: A part of a line that extends from a specific point in only one direction. *(p. 162)*

Reciprocals: Two fractions that look like upside-down reflections of one another. *(p. 43)*

Rectangle: A quadrilateral with four right angles. A rectangle's opposite sides are parallel and the same length. *(p. 167)*

Reducing: The act of changing a fraction to its simplest form. *(p. 44)*

Regroup: In place value, to use part of the value from one place in another place to make adding or subtracting easier. *(p. 13)*

Rhombus: A quadrilateral having four equal sides with opposite sides parallel. *(p. 167)*

Right Angle: An angle that measures exactly 90°. *(p. 163)*

Right Triangle: A triangle with one right angle of exactly 90°. *(p. 166)*

Rounding: To drop or zero-out digits in a number to a higher or lower value. *(p. 14)*

Rounding Place: The highest place value used in rounding. *(p. 14)*

Scalene Triangle: A triangle with all three sides being of different lengths. *(p. 166)*

Scientific Notation: A way of writing numbers as the product of a power of 10 and a decimal that is greater than 1 but less than 10. *(p. 107)*

Solid Figure: A three-dimensional figure such as a cube or pyramid. *(p. 171)*

Square: A quadrilateral with four right angles and four equal sides. *(p. 167)*

Square Root: A value that, when multiplied by itself, gives the number. The square root of 16 is 4 because $4 \times 4 = 16$. *(p. 106)*

Statistics: A branch of math that answers questions about how many, how long, how often, how far, or how big. *(p. 143)*

Stem-and-Leaf Plot: Used to organize data and compare it. A stem-and-leaf plot organizes data from least to greatest using the digits or the greatest place value to group data. *(p. 144)*

Supplementary Angles: Any two angles that add up to a sum of 180°. *(p. 164)*

Tree Diagram: Used to show possible combinations of data including people, places, or things in a diagram that looks like a tree with branches. *(p. 146)*

Trapezoid: A quadrilateral that has two sides that are parallel to each other and two sides that are not parallel. *(p. 167)*

Triangle: A two-dimensional figure with three sides. *(p. 166)*

Unit Rate: A comparison of two measurements in which one of the terms has a value of 1. *(p. 90)*

Upper Extreme: The highest number in the data used in a box-and-whisker plot. *(p. 145)*

Upper Quartile: The median of the numbers from the median to the upper extreme on a box-and-whisker plot. *(p. 145)*

Variable: An unknown number usually expressed as a letter. In the statement $n - 18$, n is the variable. *(p. 108)*

Venn Diagram: A diagram used to show how different sets of data can overlap. *(p. 147)*

Vertex: The specific point of a ray, also called an endpoint. *(p. 162)*

Vertex of a Solid: A specific point at which more than two faces meet, or a point where a curve begins. *(p. 171)*

Vertical Angles: The angles opposite each other when two lines intersect. *(p. 164)*

Volume: The number of units a solid figure contains, expressed in cubic inches, feet, yards, or miles. *(p. 120)*

Whole Number: A number that does not include a fraction or decimal. *(p. 13)*

Zero Power: In an exponent, a base raised to the zero power equals 1. *(p. 104)*

Zero Property of Multiplication: States that any number times zero equals zero. *(p. 22)*

Answers and Explanations

Lesson 1.1

1. Hundred thousands
2. Tenths
3. Thousands
4. Ones
5. Hundreds
6. 5
7. Tens
8. Ones
9. Hundredths

Lesson 1.2

1. 12
$$\begin{array}{r} 7 \\ +5 \\ \hline 12 \end{array}$$

2. 110
$$\begin{array}{r} \overset{1}{3}3 \\ +77 \\ \hline 110 \end{array}$$

3. 2121
$$\begin{array}{r} 21 \\ +2100 \\ \hline 2121 \end{array}$$

4. 78
$$\begin{array}{r} \overset{9\,1}{10}0 \\ -22 \\ \hline 78 \end{array}$$

5. 5098
$$\begin{array}{r} 5\overset{7\,1}{8}88 \\ -790 \\ \hline 5098 \end{array}$$

6. 1889
$$\begin{array}{r} 544 \\ 322 \\ +1023 \\ \hline 1889 \end{array}$$

7. 1112
$$\begin{array}{r} \overset{9\,9\,9\,1}{10}000 \\ -8888 \\ \hline 1112 \end{array}$$

8. 1332
$$\begin{array}{r} 1010 \\ 11 \\ +311 \\ \hline 1332 \end{array}$$

9. 589
$$\begin{array}{r} 212 \\ 355 \\ +22 \\ \hline 589 \end{array}$$

10. 13
$$\begin{array}{r} \overset{9\,9\,1}{10}01 \\ -988 \\ \hline 13 \end{array}$$

11. 1514
$$\begin{array}{r} \overset{1\,1}{10}\overset{5}{5}5 \\ +454 \\ \hline 1514 \end{array}$$

12. 2876
$$\begin{array}{r} \overset{6\,13\,13\,1}{74}43 \\ -4567 \\ \hline 2876 \end{array}$$

Lesson 1.3

1. 180 $100 + 80 = 180$
2. 600 $200 + 400 = 600$
3. 110 $30 + 80 = 110$
4. 800 $200 + 600 = 800$
5. 160 $30 + 130 = 160$
6. 70 $50 + 20 = 70$
7. 200 $100 + 100 = 200$
8. 100 $300 - 200 = 100$
9. 1100 $2000 - 900 = 1100$
10. 1200 $600 + 600 = 1200$
11. 500 $700 - 200 = 500$
12. 30 $20 + 10 = 30$
13. 55,000 $60,000 - 5000 = 55,000$
14. 5200 $5000 + 200 = 5200$
15. 730 $50 + 600 + 80 = 730$
16. 500 $300 + 200 = 500$
17. 80,000 $100,000 - 20,000 = 80,000$
18. 4300 $3000 + 500 + 800 = 4300$
19. 4000 $10,000 - 6000 = 4000$

Lesson 2.1

1. 60
$$\begin{array}{r} \overset{1}{5} \\ \times 12 \\ \hline 10 \\ 50 \\ \hline 60 \end{array}$$

2. 352
$$\begin{array}{r} 32 \\ \times 11 \\ \hline 32 \\ 320 \\ \hline 352 \end{array}$$

3. 133
$$\begin{array}{r} 7 \\ \times 19 \\ \hline 63 \\ 70 \\ \hline 133 \end{array}$$

4. 572
$$\begin{array}{r} \overset{1}{4}4 \\ \times 13 \\ \hline 132 \\ 440 \\ \hline 572 \end{array}$$

5. 861
$$\begin{array}{r} 41 \\ \times 21 \\ \hline 41 \\ 820 \\ \hline 861 \end{array}$$

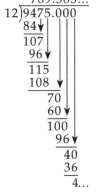

Answers and Explanations

6. 2860

$$\begin{array}{r}{\scriptstyle2}\\{\scriptstyle1}\\55\\\times52\\\hline110\\2750\\\hline2860\end{array}$$

7. 1641

$$\begin{array}{r}{\scriptstyle3}\\\times547\\\hline21\\120\\1500\\\hline1641\end{array}$$

8. 40,848

$$\begin{array}{r}{\scriptstyle3\ 3}\\444\\\times92\\\hline8^{1}88\\3^{1}9^{1}9\ 60\\\hline4\ 0\ 8\ 48\end{array}$$

9. 2376

$$\begin{array}{r}72\\\times33\\\hline216\\2160\\\hline2376\end{array}$$

10. 89,082

$$\begin{array}{r}{\scriptstyle2\ 1\ 2\ 1}\\1414\\\times63\\\hline4^{1}242\\84\ 840\\\hline89\ 082\end{array}$$

11. 3599

$$\begin{array}{r}{\scriptstyle5}\\59\\\times61\\\hline59\\3540\\\hline3599\end{array}$$

12. 1083

$$\begin{array}{r}{\scriptstyle6}\\57\\\times19\\\hline513\\570\\\hline1083\end{array}$$

13. 2250 potatoes

$$\begin{array}{r}{\scriptstyle1}\\75\\\times30\\\hline2250\end{array}$$

14. 1320 stamps

$$\begin{array}{r}{\scriptstyle1}\\22\\\times60\\\hline1320\end{array}$$

Lesson 2.2

1. 2100 $30 \times 70 = 2100$

2. 15,000 $500 \times 30 = 15,000$

3. 3500 $50 \times 70 = 3500$

4. 42,000 $700 \times 60 = 42,000$

5. 32,000 $80 \times 400 = 32,000$

6. 20,000 $100 \times 200 = 20,000$

7. 150,000 $300 \times 500 = 150,000$

8. 16,000 $400 \times 40 = 16,000$

9. 2500 $50 \times 50 = 2500$

10. 40,000 $500 \times 80 = 40,000$

11. 560,000 $700 \times 800 = 560,000$

12. 35,000 $500 \times 70 = 35,000$

13. 60,000 $3,000 \times 20 = 60,000$

14. 5600 $80 \times 70 = 5600$

15. 300,000 $500 \times 600 = 300,000$

16. 90,000 $300 \times 300 = 90,000$

17. 350,000 $700 \times 500 = 350,000$

18. 18,000 $90 \times 200 = 18,000$

19. 16,000 $40 \times 400 = 16,000$

20. 30,000 $500 \times 60 = 30,000$

Lesson 3.1

1. 56.43

$$\begin{array}{r}56.428\\7\overline{)395.000}\\35\\\hline45\\42\\\hline30\\28\\\hline20\\14\\\hline60\\56\\\hline4\ldots\end{array}$$

round to 56.43

2. 45.24

$$\begin{array}{r}45.238\\21\overline{)950.000}\\84\\\hline110\\105\\\hline50\\42\\\hline80\\63\\\hline170\\168\\\hline2\ldots\end{array}$$

round to 45.24

3. 789.58

$$\begin{array}{r}789.583\ldots\\12\overline{)9475.000}\\84\\\hline107\\96\\\hline115\\108\\\hline70\\60\\\hline100\\96\\\hline40\\36\\\hline4\ldots\end{array}$$

4. 527.22

$$\begin{array}{r}527.22\ldots\\36\overline{)18980.00}\\180\\\hline98\\72\\\hline260\\252\\\hline80\\72\\\hline80\ldots\end{array}$$

5. 639

$$\begin{array}{r}639\\13\overline{)8307}\\78\\\hline50\\39\\\hline117\\117\\\hline0\end{array}$$

6. 45.45

$$\begin{array}{r}45.45\ldots\\44\overline{)2000.00}\\176\\\hline240\\220\\\hline200\\176\\\hline240\\220\\\hline20\ldots\end{array}$$

7. 85.33

$$\begin{array}{r}85.33\ldots\\3\overline{)256.00}\\24\\\hline16\\15\\\hline10\\9\\\hline10\\9\\\hline1\ldots\end{array}$$

8. 36.5.

$$\begin{array}{r}36.5\\22\overline{)803.0}\\66\\\hline143\\132\\\hline110\\110\\\hline0\end{array}$$

9. 15 days

$$\begin{array}{r}15\\20\overline{)300}\\20\\\hline100\\100\\\hline0\end{array}$$

10. 50 people

$$\begin{array}{r}50\\28\overline{)1400}\\140\\\hline0\end{array}$$

Answers and Explanations

Lesson 3.2

1. 60 $480 \div 8 = 60$
2. 200 $2200 \div 11 = 200$
3. 80 $640 \div 8 = 80$
4. 300 $4500 \div 15 = 300$
5. 3000 $36,000 \div 12 = 3000$
6. 500 $4500 \div 9 = 500$
7. 4000 $64,000 \div 16 = 4000$
8. 20 $380 \div 19 = 20$
9. 20 $700 \div 35 = 20$
10. 3000 $90,000 \div 30 = 3000$
11. 30 $660 \div 22 = 30$
12. 200 $7000 \div 35 = 200$
13. 30 $840 \div 28 = 30$
14. 300 $5100 \div 17 = 300$
15. 200 $8800 \div 44 = 200$
16. 70 $490 \div 7 = 70$
17. 3000 $90,000 \div 30 = 3000$
18. 2000 $90,000 \div 45 = 2000$
19. 2000 $80,000 \div 40 = 2000$
20. 1000 $11,000 \div 11 = 1000$

Lesson 4.1

1. 10 $6 \times 2 - 6 + 2^{4-2} = 6 \times 2 - 6 + 2^2 = 6 \times 2 - 6 + 4 = 12 - 6 + 4 = 10$
2. 4 $1 \times 4 - 2^2 + 4 = 1 \times 4 - 4 + 4 = 4 - 4 + 4 = 4$
3. 15 $2^3 + 2^2 + 1 - 2 + 2^2 = 8 + 4 + 1 - 2 + 4 = 15$
4. 12 $6 \times 2 + 3^2 - 3^2 = 6 \times 2 + 0 = 12$
5. 1 $2^3 - 2^3 + 2 - 1 = 0 + 2 - 1 = 1$
6. 6 $2^2 - (8 - 2) + (4 + 4) = 2^2 - 6 + 8 = 4 - 6 + 8 = 6$
7. 3 $3 + 2 - 2 = 3$
8. 21 $7 \times 3 \times 1^2 = 7 \times 3 \times 1 = 21$
9. 62 $2 + 10^2 - 2 \times 12 - 4^2 = 2 + 100 - 2 \times 12 - 16 = 2 + 100 - 24 - 16 = 62$
10. 12 $4 \times 7 - 4^2 = 4 \times 7 - 16 = 28 - 16 = 12$
11. 4 $11 - 3^2 + 10 - 8 = 11 - 9 + 10 - 8 = 4$
12. 48 $7^2 + 3 \times 5 - 2 \times 2^3 = 49 + 3 \times 5 - 2 \times 8 = 49 + 15 - 16 = 48$

Lesson 4.2

1. Commutative Property of Multiplication
2. Commutative Property of Addition
3. Associative Property of Multiplication
4. Commutative Property of Multiplication
5. Commutative Property of Multiplication
6. Associative Property of Multiplication
7. Commutative Property of Addition
8. Commutative Property of Multiplication
9. Associative Property of Addition
10. Commutative Property of Multiplication
11. Associative Property of Addition
12. Commutative Property of Multiplication

Lesson 4.3

1. 6 $0 + 6 = 6$
2. 28 $4(7) = 28$
3. 7 $7 + 0 = 7$
4. 36 $4(9) = 36$
5. 150 $15(10) = 150$
6. 30 $6(5) = 30$
7. 30 $12 + 18 = 30$
8. 48 $12(4) = 48$
9. 41 $34 + 7 = 41$
10. 175 $35(5) = 175$
11. 14 $7 + 7 = 14$
12. 110 $5(2) = 110$
13. 72 $36(2) = 72$
14. 0 $7 + {-7} = 7 - 7 = 0$
15. 16 $8(2) = 16$

Lesson 4.4

1. 0
2. 0
3. 0
4. 35
5. 0
6. 0
7. 0
8. 2
9. 0
10. Yes. Equality Property of Multiplication
11. Yes. Equality Property of Addition
12. Yes. Equality Property of Subtraction
13. Yes. Equality Property of Division

Lesson 5.1

1. 0   These are inverses.
2. 100 $210 - 110 = 100$

Answers and Explanations

3. 0   These are inverses.

4. 20 $145 - 125 = 20$

5. 10 $48 - 38 = 10$

6. 0 $(732 - 712) + (55 - 75) = 20 + -20 = 0$

7. 0   These are inverses.

8. -200 $641 - 641 = 0$ and $541 - 741 = -200$

9. -33 $44 - 77 = -33$

10. 6 $16 - 10 = 6$

Lesson 5.2

1. 9

2. 567

3. 48

4. 0.24

5. $\frac{7}{8}$

6. $\frac{1}{3}$

7. <

8. =

9. >

10. <

11. <

12. <

13. $112.48

14. April

15. –$1.10

Lesson 5.3

1. 14 $17 - 3 = 14$

2. -9 $6 - 15 = -9$

3. -11 $1 - 12 = -11$

4. 39 $75 - 36 = 39$

5. 68 $110 + (-56) + 14 = 110 + 14 - 56 = 124 - 56 = 68$

6. 29 $95 - 65 - 1 = 30 - 1 = 29$

7. -33 $-40 + 7 = -33$

8. 38 $51 - 33 + 20 = 71 - 33 = 38$

9. 8 $30 - 22 = 8$

10. 18 $18 + 0 = 18$

11. -11 $14 - 25 = -11$

12. 22 $80 + 13 + 29 - 100 = 122 - 100 = 22$

13. 28 $57 - 39 + 10 = 67 - 39 = 28$

14. 31 $-23 + 63 - 9 = 63 - 32 = 31$

15. -2 $4 + 2 - 7 - 1 = 6 - 8 = -2$

16. 1 $1 + 0 = 1$

Lesson 5.4

1. -15 $5 \times 3 = 15$ and the signs are different, so -15

2. -130 $13 \times 10 = 130$ and the signs are different, so -130

3. -100 $100 \times 1 = 100$ and the signs are different, so -100

4. -69 $23 \times 3 = 69$ and the signs are different, so -69

5. -225 $15 \times 15 = 225$ and the signs are different, so -225

6. -240 $12 \times 20 = 240$ and the signs are different, so -240

7. 8 $2 \times 4 = 8$ and the signs are the same, so $+8$

8. -1 $1 \times 1 = 1$ and the signs are different, so -1

9. 125 $125 \times 1 = 125$ and the signs are the same, so $+125$

10. -309 $3 \times 103 = 309$ and the signs are different, so -309

11. -1 $20 \div 20 = 1$ and the signs are different, so -1

12. 0 $22 \times 0 = 0$

13. 3 $3 \times 1 = 3$ and the signs are the same, so $+3$

14. -3 $12 \div 4 = 3$ and the signs are different, so -3

15. -5 $15 \div 3 = 5$ and the signs are different, so -5

16. $\frac{1}{3}$ $-9 \div \frac{1}{9} = -9 \times \frac{9}{1} = \frac{-81}{1} = -81;$

$-27 \div -81 = \frac{-27}{-81} = \frac{1}{3}$

Lesson 6.1

1. $14\frac{2}{3}$ $44 \div 3 = 14$ R2, so $14\frac{2}{3}$

2. $22\frac{3}{4}$ $91 \div 4 = 22$ R3, so $22\frac{3}{4}$

3. $2\frac{1}{2}$ $5 \div 2 = 2$ R1, so $2\frac{1}{2}$

4. $7\frac{1}{3}$ $22 \div 3 = 7$ R1, so $7\frac{1}{3}$

5. $4\frac{7}{12}$ $55 \div 12 = 4$ R7, so $4\frac{7}{12}$

6. $-9\frac{8}{11}$ $-107 \div 11 = -9$ R8, so $-9\frac{8}{11}$

7. $9\frac{3}{4}$ $156 \div 16 = 9$ R12, so $9\frac{12}{16} = 9\frac{3}{4}$

8. $3\frac{7}{8}$ $31 \div 8 = 3$ R7, so $3\frac{7}{8}$

9. $4\frac{17}{21}$ $101 \div 21 = 4$ R17, so $4\frac{17}{21}$

10. $16\frac{1}{2}$ $33 \div 2 = 16$ R1, so $16\frac{1}{2}$

11. $4\frac{3}{11}$ $47 \div 11 = 4$ R3, so $4\frac{3}{11}$

Answers and Explanations

12. $-10\frac{12}{19}$ $-202 \div 19 = -10$ R12, so $-10\frac{12}{19}$

13. $9\frac{3}{4}$ $78 \div 8 = 9$ R6, so $9\frac{6}{8} = 9\frac{3}{4}$

14. $6\frac{5}{7}$ $47 \div 7 = 6$ R5, so $6\frac{5}{7}$

15. $-12\frac{1}{4}$ $-147 \div 12 = -12$ R3, so $-12\frac{3}{12} = -12\frac{1}{4}$

16. $16\frac{1}{4}$ $260 \div 16 = 16$ R4, so $16\frac{4}{16} = 16\frac{1}{4}$

17. $19\frac{1}{3}$ $58 \div 3 = 19$ R1, so $19\frac{1}{3}$

18. $-19\frac{1}{4}$ $-77 \div 4 = -19$ R1, so $-19\frac{1}{4}$

19. $11\frac{1}{12}$ $133 \div 12 = 11$ R1, so $11\frac{1}{12}$

20. $49\frac{2}{7}$ $345 \div 7 = 49$ R2, so $49\frac{2}{7}$

Lesson 6.2

1. $\frac{13}{4}$ $\frac{3 \times 4 + 1}{4} = \frac{12 + 1}{4} = \frac{13}{4}$

2. $-\frac{38}{7}$ $-\frac{5 \times 7 + 3}{7} = -\frac{35 + 3}{7} = -\frac{38}{7}$

3. $\frac{135}{11}$ $\frac{12 \times 11 + 3}{11} = \frac{132 + 3}{11} = \frac{135}{11}$

4. $\frac{73}{5}$ $\frac{14 \times 5 + 3}{5} = \frac{70 + 3}{5} = \frac{73}{5}$

5. $\frac{15}{13}$ $\frac{1 \times 13 + 2}{13} = \frac{13 + 2}{13} = \frac{15}{13}$

6. $\frac{297}{14}$ $\frac{21 \times 14 + 3}{14} = \frac{294 + 3}{14} = \frac{297}{14}$

7. $\frac{298}{9}$ $\frac{33 \times 9 + 1}{9} = \frac{297 + 1}{9} = \frac{298}{9}$

8. $-\frac{69}{17}$ $-\frac{4 \times 17 + 1}{17} = -\frac{68 + 1}{17} = -\frac{69}{17}$

9. $\frac{715}{7}$ $\frac{102 \times 7 + 1}{7} = \frac{714 + 1}{7} = \frac{715}{7}$

10. $-\frac{65}{2}$ $-\frac{32 \times 2 + 1}{2} = -\frac{64 + 1}{2} = -\frac{65}{2}$

11. $\frac{842}{29}$ $\frac{29 \times 29 + 1}{29} = \frac{841 + 1}{29} = \frac{842}{29}$

12. $\frac{299}{8}$ $\frac{37 \times 8 + 3}{8} = \frac{296 + 3}{8} = \frac{299}{8}$

13. $\frac{47}{3}$ $\frac{15 \times 3 + 2}{3} = \frac{45 + 2}{3} = \frac{47}{3}$

14. $\frac{859}{14}$ $\frac{61 \times 14 + 5}{14} = \frac{854 + 5}{14} = \frac{859}{14}$

15. $\frac{121}{17}$ $\frac{7 \times 17 + 2}{17} = \frac{119 + 2}{17} = \frac{121}{17}$

16. $-\frac{135}{22}$ $-\frac{6 \times 22 + 3}{22} = -\frac{132 + 3}{22} = -\frac{135}{22}$

17. $\frac{71}{3}$ $\frac{23 \times 3 + 2}{3} = \frac{69 + 2}{3} = \frac{71}{3}$

18. $\frac{109}{7}$ $\frac{15 \times 7 + 4}{7} = \frac{105 + 4}{7} = \frac{109}{7}$

19. $-\frac{170}{13}$ $-\frac{13 \times 13 + 1}{13} = -\frac{169 + 1}{13} = -\frac{170}{13}$

20. $\frac{180}{44}$ or $\frac{45}{11}$ $\frac{4 \times 44 + 4}{44} = \frac{176 + 4}{44} = \frac{180}{44} = \frac{45}{11}$

Lesson 6.3

1. 1 $\frac{1 + 1}{2} = \frac{2}{2} = 1$

2. $\frac{7}{5}$ $\frac{4 + 3}{5} = \frac{7}{5}$

3. $\frac{10}{8} = \frac{5}{4}$ $\frac{7 + 3}{8} = \frac{10}{8} = \frac{5}{4}$

4. $\frac{8}{7}$ $\frac{6 + 2}{7} = \frac{8}{7}$

5. $\frac{24}{11}$ $\frac{10 + 14}{11} = \frac{24}{11}$

6. $\frac{74}{17}$ $\frac{71 + 3}{17} = \frac{74}{17}$

7. $\frac{38}{9}$ $\frac{4 + 34}{9} = \frac{38}{9}$

8. $\frac{9}{3} = 3$ $\frac{2 + 7}{3} = \frac{9}{3} = 3$

9. $\frac{58}{23}$ $\frac{4 + 54}{23} = \frac{58}{23}$

10. $\frac{57}{37}$ $\frac{3 + 54}{37} = \frac{57}{37}$

11. $\frac{8}{4} = 2$ $\frac{3 + 5}{4} = \frac{8}{4} = 2$

12. $\frac{12}{11}$ $\frac{7 + 5}{11} = \frac{12}{11}$

13. $\frac{15}{27} = \frac{5}{9}$ $\frac{5 + 10}{27} = \frac{15}{27} = \frac{5}{9}$

14. $\frac{16}{4} = 4$ $\frac{3 + 13}{4} = \frac{16}{4} = 4$

15. $\frac{42}{24} = \frac{7}{4}$ $\frac{23 + 19}{24} = \frac{42}{24} = \frac{7}{4}$

16. $\frac{13}{37}$ $\frac{3 + 10}{37} = \frac{13}{37}$

Lesson 6.4

1. $\frac{2}{4} = \frac{1}{2}$ $\frac{3 - 1}{4} = \frac{2}{4} = \frac{1}{2}$

2. $\frac{2}{8} = \frac{1}{4}$ $\frac{7 - 5}{8} = \frac{2}{8} = \frac{1}{4}$

3. $\frac{6}{4} = \frac{3}{2}$ $\frac{7 - 1}{4} = \frac{6}{4} = \frac{3}{2}$

4. $\frac{6}{5}$ $\frac{14 - 8}{5} = \frac{6}{5}$

Answers and Explanations

5. $\frac{4}{7}$ $\frac{33-29}{7}=\frac{4}{7}$

6. $\frac{2}{11}$ $\frac{9-7}{11}=\frac{2}{11}$

7. $\frac{7}{3}$ $\frac{14-7}{3}=\frac{7}{3}$

8. $\frac{8}{19}$ $\frac{21-13}{19}=\frac{8}{19}$

9. 2 $\frac{12-2}{5}=\frac{10}{5}=2$

10. $\frac{6}{7}$ $\frac{23-17}{7}=\frac{6}{7}$

11. $\frac{8}{8}=1$ $\frac{45-37}{8}=\frac{8}{8}=1$

12. $\frac{8}{51}$ $\frac{12-4}{51}=\frac{8}{51}$

13. $\frac{29}{13}$ $\frac{43-14}{13}=\frac{29}{13}$

14. $\frac{21}{17}$ $\frac{56-35}{17}=\frac{21}{17}$

15. $\frac{4}{4}=1$ $\frac{7-3}{4}=\frac{4}{4}=1$

16. $\frac{18}{37}$ $\frac{32-14}{37}=\frac{18}{37}$

Lesson 6.5

1. $\frac{9}{20}$ $\frac{1}{4}+\frac{1}{5}=\frac{5}{20}+\frac{4}{20}=\frac{9}{20}$

2. $\frac{20}{21}$ $\frac{2}{7}+\frac{2}{3}=\frac{6}{21}+\frac{14}{21}=\frac{20}{21}$

3. $\frac{83}{60}$ $\frac{21}{20}+\frac{1}{3}=\frac{63}{60}+\frac{20}{60}=\frac{83}{60}$

4. $\frac{11}{26}$ $\frac{12}{13}-\frac{1}{2}=\frac{24}{26}-\frac{13}{26}=\frac{11}{26}$

5. $\frac{17}{28}$ $\frac{3}{4}-\frac{1}{7}=\frac{21}{28}-\frac{4}{28}=\frac{17}{28}$

6. $\frac{136}{105}$ $\frac{23}{21}+\frac{1}{5}=\frac{115}{105}+\frac{21}{105}=\frac{136}{105}$

7. $\frac{74}{33}$ $\frac{32}{11}-\frac{2}{3}=\frac{96}{33}-\frac{22}{33}=\frac{74}{33}$

8. $\frac{50}{21}$ $\frac{12}{7}+\frac{2}{3}=\frac{36}{21}+\frac{14}{21}=\frac{50}{21}$

9. $\frac{3}{15}=\frac{1}{5}$ $\frac{8}{15}-\frac{1}{3}=\frac{8}{15}-\frac{5}{15}=\frac{3}{15}=\frac{1}{5}$

10. $\frac{19}{40}$ $\frac{7}{8}-\frac{2}{5}=\frac{35}{40}-\frac{16}{40}=\frac{19}{40}$

11. $\frac{400}{77}$ $\frac{54}{11}+\frac{2}{7}=\frac{378}{77}+\frac{22}{77}=\frac{400}{77}$

12. $\frac{17}{60}$ $\frac{13}{12}-\frac{4}{5}=\frac{65}{60}-\frac{48}{60}=\frac{17}{60}$

13. $\frac{142}{39}$ $\frac{56}{13}-\frac{2}{3}=\frac{168}{39}-\frac{26}{39}=\frac{142}{39}$

14. $\frac{7}{20}$ $\frac{3}{4}-\frac{2}{5}=\frac{15}{20}-\frac{8}{20}=\frac{7}{20}$

15. $\frac{11}{4}$ $\frac{21}{4}-\frac{5}{2}=\frac{42}{8}-\frac{20}{8}=\frac{22}{8}=\frac{11}{4}$

Lesson 6.6

1. $5\frac{3}{4}$ $2+3=5;\frac{1}{2}+\frac{1}{4}=\frac{2}{4}+\frac{1}{4}=\frac{3}{4};5+\frac{3}{4}=5\frac{3}{4}$

2. $8\frac{2}{21}$ $3+4=7;\frac{2}{3}+\frac{3}{7}=\frac{14}{21}+\frac{9}{21}=\frac{23}{21};7+\frac{23}{21}=8\frac{2}{21}$

3. $12\frac{7}{12}$ $4+7=11;\frac{5}{6}+\frac{3}{4}=\frac{10}{12}+\frac{9}{12}=\frac{19}{12};11+\frac{19}{12}=12\frac{7}{12}$

4. $6\frac{1}{12}$ $3+2=5;\frac{3}{4}+\frac{1}{3}=\frac{9}{12}+\frac{4}{12}=\frac{13}{12};5+\frac{13}{12}=6\frac{1}{12}$

5. $13\frac{7}{10}$ $9+4=13;\frac{1}{2}+\frac{1}{5}=\frac{5}{10}+\frac{2}{10}=\frac{7}{10};13\frac{7}{10}$

6. $69\frac{1}{6}$ $54+14=68;\frac{1}{2}+\frac{2}{3}=\frac{3}{6}+\frac{4}{6}=\frac{7}{6};68+\frac{7}{6}=69\frac{1}{6}$

7. $23\frac{8}{21}$ $10+12=22;\frac{5}{7}+\frac{2}{3}=\frac{15}{21}+\frac{14}{21}=\frac{29}{21};22+\frac{29}{21}=23\frac{8}{21}$

8. $7\frac{32}{63}$ $4+3=7;\frac{2}{9}+\frac{2}{7}=\frac{14}{63}+\frac{18}{63}=\frac{32}{63};7\frac{32}{63}$

9. $18\frac{4}{55}$ $13+4=17;\frac{4}{5}+\frac{3}{11}=\frac{44}{55}+\frac{15}{55}=\frac{59}{55};17+\frac{59}{55}=18\frac{4}{55}$

10. $80\frac{31}{78}$ $23+57=80;\frac{1}{6}+\frac{3}{13}=\frac{13}{78}+\frac{18}{78}=\frac{31}{78};80\frac{31}{78}$

11. $36\frac{37}{55}$ $22+14=36;\frac{3}{11}+\frac{2}{5}=\frac{15}{55}+\frac{22}{55}=\frac{37}{55};36\frac{37}{55}$

12. $8\frac{1}{21}$ $4+3=7;\frac{5}{7}+\frac{1}{3}=\frac{15}{21}+\frac{7}{21}=\frac{22}{21};7+\frac{22}{21}=8\frac{1}{21}$

13. $12\frac{23}{60}$ $5+7=12;\frac{1}{4}+\frac{2}{15}=\frac{15}{60}+\frac{8}{60}=\frac{23}{60};12\frac{23}{60}$

14. $457\frac{61}{66}$ $102+355=457;\frac{5}{6}+\frac{1}{11}=\frac{55}{66}+\frac{6}{66}=\frac{61}{66};457\frac{61}{66}$

15. $145\frac{29}{42}$ $56+89=145;\frac{1}{3}+\frac{5}{14}=\frac{14}{42}+\frac{15}{42}=\frac{29}{42};145\frac{29}{42}$

16. $143\frac{7}{8}$ $21+122=143;\frac{1}{2}+\frac{3}{8}=\frac{4}{8}+\frac{3}{8}=\frac{7}{8};143\frac{7}{8}$

Lesson 6.7

1. $3\frac{1}{4}$ $5-2=3;\frac{1}{2}-\frac{1}{4}=\frac{2}{4}-\frac{1}{4}=\frac{1}{4};3\frac{1}{4}$

2. $6\frac{19}{77}$ $10-4=6;\frac{3}{7}-\frac{2}{11}=\frac{33}{77}-\frac{14}{77}=\frac{19}{77};6\frac{19}{77}$

3. $17\frac{7}{45}$ $21-4=17;\frac{5}{9}-\frac{2}{5}=\frac{25}{45}-\frac{18}{45}=\frac{7}{45};17\frac{7}{45}$

4. $3\frac{11}{18}$ $13-10=3;\frac{5}{6}-\frac{2}{9}=\frac{15}{18}-\frac{4}{18}=\frac{11}{18};3\frac{11}{18}$

5. $9\frac{1}{2}$ $14-5=9;\frac{2}{3}-\frac{1}{6}=\frac{4}{6}-\frac{1}{6}=\frac{3}{6}=\frac{1}{2};9\frac{1}{2}$

6. $10\frac{7}{36}$ $21-11=10;\frac{3}{4}-\frac{5}{9}=\frac{27}{36}-\frac{20}{36}=\frac{7}{36};10\frac{7}{36}$

Answers and Explanations

7. $10\frac{29}{42}$ $\qquad$ $13 - 3 = 10; \frac{5}{6} - \frac{1}{7} = \frac{35}{42} - \frac{6}{42} = \frac{29}{42}; 10\frac{29}{42}$

8. $14\frac{29}{55}$ $\qquad$ $43 - 29 = 14; \frac{4}{5} - \frac{3}{11} = \frac{44}{55} - \frac{15}{55} = \frac{29}{55}; 14\frac{29}{55}$

9. $6\frac{1}{22}$ $\qquad$ $10 - 4 = 6; \frac{6}{11} - \frac{1}{2} = \frac{12}{22} - \frac{11}{22} = \frac{1}{22}; 6\frac{1}{22}$

10. $2\frac{1}{9}$ $\qquad$ $13 - 11 = 2; \frac{2}{3} - \frac{5}{9} = \frac{6}{9} - \frac{5}{9} = \frac{1}{9}; 2\frac{1}{9}$

11. $36\frac{28}{51}$ $\qquad$ $77 - 41 = 36; \frac{2}{3} - \frac{2}{17} = \frac{34}{51} - \frac{6}{51} = \frac{28}{51}; 36\frac{28}{51}$

12. $16\frac{9}{14}$ $\qquad$ $19 - 3 = 16; \frac{5}{7} - \frac{1}{14} = \frac{10}{14} - \frac{1}{14} = \frac{9}{14}; 16\frac{9}{14}$

13. $\frac{3}{4}$ hours $\qquad$ $3 - 2 = 1; \frac{1}{4} - \frac{1}{2} = \frac{1}{4} - \frac{2}{4} = -\frac{1}{4}; 1 - \frac{1}{4} = \frac{3}{4}$

14. No $\frac{7}{12} < \frac{2}{3}$ $\qquad$ $1 - 0 = 1; \frac{1}{4} - \frac{2}{3} = \frac{3}{12} - \frac{8}{12} = -\frac{5}{12};$
$$1 - \frac{5}{12} = \frac{12}{12} - \frac{5}{12} = \frac{7}{12}$$

Lessons 6.8

1. $36\frac{1}{2}$ $\qquad$ $12\frac{1}{2} + 24 = 36\frac{1}{2}$

2. 92 $\qquad$ $57\frac{1}{2} + 34\frac{1}{2} = 92$

3. 111 $\qquad$ $81 + 30 = 111$

4. 168 $\qquad$ $202 - 34 = 168$

5. 5045 $\qquad$ $5501 - 456 = 5045; \frac{3}{4} - \frac{3}{5} \approx 0;$
$$5045 + 0 = 5045$$

6. 359 $\qquad$ $457 - 98 = 359; \frac{8}{13} - \frac{8}{13} = 0; 359 + 0 = 359$

7. $120\frac{1}{2}$ $\qquad$ $67 + 53\frac{1}{2} = 120\frac{1}{2}$

8. 512 $\qquad$ $190 + 322 = 512$

9. 504 $\qquad$ $547 - 44 = 503; 1 - 0 = 1; 503 + 1 = 504$

10. 101 $\qquad$ $50 + 51 = 101$

11. 114 $\qquad$ $67\frac{1}{2} + 46\frac{1}{2} = 114$

12. 312 $\qquad$ $456 - 145 = 311; 1 - 0 = 1; 311 + 1 = 312$

13. 11 ounces $\qquad$ $3\,(7\text{ oz}) = 21\text{ oz}; 32 - 21 = 11\text{ oz}$

14. About $8\frac{1}{2}$ dozen cookies $\qquad$ $5 + 3\frac{1}{2} = 8\frac{1}{2}$

Lesson 7.1

1. $\frac{3}{4}$ $\qquad$ $\frac{3 \times 1}{4} = \frac{3}{4}$

2. $\frac{30}{7} = 4\frac{2}{7}$ $\qquad$ $\frac{15 \times 2}{7} = \frac{30}{7} = 4\frac{2}{7}$

3. $-4\frac{1}{2}$ $\qquad$ $\frac{12 \times -3}{8} = \frac{-36}{8} = -4\frac{4}{8} = -4\frac{1}{2}$

4. 6 $\qquad$ $\frac{22 \times 3}{11} = \frac{66}{11} = 6$

5. $-2\frac{1}{4}$ $\qquad$ $\frac{15 \times -3}{20} = \frac{-45}{20} = -2\frac{5}{20} = -2\frac{1}{4}$

6. $3\frac{11}{17}$ $\qquad$ $\frac{31 \times 2}{17} = \frac{62}{17} = 3\frac{11}{17}$

7. $1\frac{3}{4}$ $\qquad$ $\frac{6 \times 7}{24} = \frac{42}{24} = 1\frac{18}{24} = 1\frac{3}{4}$

8. $12\frac{8}{11}$ $\qquad$ $\frac{14 \times 10}{11} = \frac{140}{11} = 12\frac{8}{11}$

9. $2\frac{2}{9}$ $\qquad$ $\frac{16 \times 5}{36} = \frac{80}{36} = 2\frac{8}{36} = 2\frac{2}{9}$

10. $4\frac{2}{3}$ $\qquad$ $\frac{7 \times 2}{3} = \frac{14}{3} = 4\frac{2}{3}$

11. $-9\frac{3}{5}$ $\qquad$ $\frac{16 \times -3}{5} = \frac{-48}{5} = -9\frac{3}{5}$

12. $10\frac{1}{12}$ $\qquad$ $\frac{11 \times 11}{12} = \frac{121}{12} = 10\frac{1}{12}$

13. 30 $\qquad$ $\frac{42 \times 5}{7} = \frac{210}{7} = 30$

14. $1\frac{1}{2}$ $\qquad$ $\frac{20 \times 3}{40} = \frac{60}{40} = 1\frac{20}{40} = 1\frac{1}{2}$

15. 20 $\qquad$ $\frac{32 \times 5}{8} = \frac{160}{8} = 20$

16. -1 $\qquad$ $\frac{15 \times -1}{15} = \frac{-15}{15} = -1$

17. -3 $\qquad$ $\frac{16 \times -3}{16} = \frac{16}{16} \times \frac{-3}{1} = 1 \times -3 = -3$

18. 1 $\qquad$ $\frac{3 \times 1}{3} = \frac{3}{3} = 1$

19. 39 $\qquad$ $\frac{45 \times 13}{15} = \frac{45}{15} \times \frac{13}{1} = \frac{3}{1} \times \frac{13}{1} = 3 \times 13 = 39$

20. 4 $\qquad$ $\frac{7 \times 4}{7} = \frac{7}{7} \times \frac{4}{1} = 1 \times 4 = 4$

Lesson 7.2

1. $\frac{1}{3}$ $\qquad$ $\frac{1}{\cancel{2}_1} \times \frac{\cancel{2}^1}{3} = \frac{1}{3}$

2. $\frac{15}{56}$ $\qquad$ $\frac{5}{7} \times \frac{3}{8} = \frac{15}{56}$

3. $\frac{8}{21}$ $\qquad$ $\frac{\cancel{20}^4}{21} \times \frac{2}{\cancel{5}_1} = \frac{8}{21}$

4. $-\frac{9}{4}$ or $-2\frac{1}{4}$ $\qquad$ $-\frac{3}{2} \times \frac{3}{2} = -\frac{9}{4}$ or $-2\frac{1}{4}$

5. 1 $\qquad$ $\frac{\cancel{2}^1}{\cancel{3}_1} \times \frac{\cancel{3}^1}{\cancel{2}_1} = 1$

6. $-\frac{28}{3}$ or $-9\frac{1}{3}$ $\qquad$ $-\frac{7}{\cancel{4}_1} \times \frac{\cancel{16}^4}{3} = -\frac{28}{3}$ or $-9\frac{1}{3}$

7. 5 $\qquad$ $\frac{\cancel{5}^1}{\cancel{9}_1} \times \frac{\cancel{90}^{10}}{\cancel{10}^2} = \frac{10}{2} = 5$

8. $\frac{3}{49}$ $\qquad$ $\frac{\cancel{4}^1}{7} \times \frac{3}{\cancel{28}_7} = \frac{3}{49}$

Answers and Explanations

9. 1 $\dfrac{\cancel{3}^{1}}{\cancel{11}_{1}} \times \dfrac{\cancel{11}^{1}}{\cancel{3}_{1}} = 1$

10. 18 $\dfrac{\cancel{12}^{6}}{\cancel{13}_{1}} \times \dfrac{\cancel{39}^{3}}{\cancel{2}_{1}} = 18$

11. $\dfrac{3}{52}$ $-\dfrac{3}{\cancel{8}_{4}} \times -\dfrac{\cancel{2}^{1}}{13} = \dfrac{3}{52}$

12. $\dfrac{14}{3}$ or $4\dfrac{2}{3}$ $\dfrac{7}{\cancel{8}_{1}} \times \dfrac{\cancel{16}^{2}}{3} = \dfrac{14}{3}$ or $4\dfrac{2}{3}$

13. $\dfrac{9}{7}$ or $1\dfrac{2}{7}$ $-\dfrac{\cancel{81}^{9}}{7} \times -\dfrac{1}{\cancel{9}_{1}} = \dfrac{9}{7}$ or $1\dfrac{2}{7}$

14. $\dfrac{1}{2}$ $\dfrac{\cancel{7}^{1}}{\cancel{3}_{1}} \times \dfrac{\cancel{3}^{1}}{\cancel{14}_{2}} = \dfrac{1}{2}$

15. $\dfrac{9}{16}$ $\dfrac{\cancel{15}^{3}}{16} \times \dfrac{3}{\cancel{5}_{1}} = \dfrac{9}{16}$

16. $\dfrac{40}{7}$ or $5\dfrac{5}{7}$ $\dfrac{10}{\cancel{13}_{1}} \times \dfrac{\cancel{52}^{4}}{7} = \dfrac{40}{7}$ or $5\dfrac{5}{7}$

Lesson 7.3

1. $2\dfrac{5}{8}$ $5\dfrac{1}{4} = \dfrac{21}{4}$; $\dfrac{21}{4} \times \dfrac{1}{2} = \dfrac{21}{8}$ or $2\dfrac{5}{8}$

2. $1\dfrac{7}{9}$ $5\dfrac{1}{3} = \dfrac{16}{3}$; $\dfrac{1}{3} \times \dfrac{16}{3} = \dfrac{16}{9}$ or $1\dfrac{7}{9}$

3. $-18\dfrac{3}{8}$ $-12\dfrac{1}{4} = -\dfrac{49}{4}$; $-\dfrac{49}{4} \times \dfrac{3}{2} = -\dfrac{147}{8}$ or $-18\dfrac{3}{8}$

4. $14\dfrac{2}{3}$ $3\dfrac{1}{7} = \dfrac{22}{7}$; $\dfrac{22}{\cancel{7}_{1}} \times \dfrac{\cancel{14}^{2}}{3} = \dfrac{44}{3}$ or $14\dfrac{2}{3}$

5. $-\dfrac{7}{20}$ $1\dfrac{3}{4} = \dfrac{7}{4}$; $-\dfrac{1}{5} \times \dfrac{7}{4} = -\dfrac{7}{20}$

6. $4\dfrac{10}{21}$ $6\dfrac{5}{7} = \dfrac{47}{7}$; $\dfrac{47}{7} \times \dfrac{2}{3} = \dfrac{94}{21}$ or $4\dfrac{10}{21}$

7. $1\dfrac{13}{20}$ $4\dfrac{2}{5} = \dfrac{22}{5}$; $\dfrac{\cancel{22}^{11}}{5} \times \dfrac{3}{\cancel{8}_{4}} = \dfrac{33}{20}$ or $1\dfrac{13}{20}$

8. $2\dfrac{1}{32}$ $3\dfrac{1}{4} = \dfrac{13}{4}$; $\dfrac{13}{4} \times \dfrac{5}{8} = \dfrac{65}{32}$ or $2\dfrac{1}{32}$

9. $1\dfrac{8}{9}$ $3\dfrac{2}{5} = \dfrac{17}{5}$; $\dfrac{17}{\cancel{5}_{1}} \times \dfrac{\cancel{5}^{1}}{9} = \dfrac{17}{9}$ or $1\dfrac{8}{9}$

10. $1\dfrac{1}{12}$ $4\dfrac{1}{3} = \dfrac{13}{3}$; $\dfrac{1}{4} \times \dfrac{13}{3} = \dfrac{13}{12}$ or $1\dfrac{1}{12}$

11. $4\dfrac{5}{7}$ $3\dfrac{2}{3} = \dfrac{11}{3}$; $1\dfrac{2}{7} = \dfrac{9}{7}$; $\dfrac{11}{\cancel{3}_{1}} \times \dfrac{\cancel{9}^{3}}{7} = \dfrac{33}{7}$ or $4\dfrac{5}{7}$

12. $9\dfrac{3}{10}$ $-4\dfrac{1}{5} = -\dfrac{21}{5}$; $-2\dfrac{3}{14} = -\dfrac{31}{14}$; $-\dfrac{\cancel{21}^{3}}{5} \times \dfrac{-31}{\cancel{14}_{2}} = \dfrac{93}{10}$ or $9\dfrac{3}{10}$

13. $17\dfrac{1}{2}$ $5\dfrac{1}{4} = \dfrac{21}{4}$; $3\dfrac{1}{3} = \dfrac{10}{3}$; $\dfrac{\cancel{21}^{7}}{\cancel{4}_{2}} \times \dfrac{\cancel{10}^{5}}{\cancel{3}_{1}} = \dfrac{35}{2}$ or $17\dfrac{1}{2}$

14. 12 $-2\dfrac{4}{5} = \dfrac{-14}{5}$; $-4\dfrac{2}{7} = -\dfrac{30}{7}$; $-\dfrac{\cancel{14}^{2}}{\cancel{5}_{1}} \times -\dfrac{\cancel{30}^{6}}{\cancel{7}_{1}} = \dfrac{12}{1} = 12$

15. $12\dfrac{3}{8}$ $3\dfrac{3}{4} = \dfrac{15}{4}$; $3\dfrac{3}{10} = \dfrac{33}{10}$; $\dfrac{\cancel{15}^{3}}{4} \times \dfrac{33}{\cancel{10}_{2}} = \dfrac{99}{8}$ or $12\dfrac{3}{8}$

16. 12 $3\dfrac{1}{3} = \dfrac{10}{3}$; $3\dfrac{3}{5} = \dfrac{18}{5}$; $\dfrac{\cancel{10}^{2}}{\cancel{3}_{1}} \times \dfrac{\cancel{18}^{6}}{\cancel{5}_{1}} = \dfrac{12}{1} = 12$

Lesson 8.1

1. $-\dfrac{1}{8}$ $2 \times 4 = 8$; $\dfrac{-1}{8}$

2. $\dfrac{3}{20}$ $5 \times 4 = 20$; $\dfrac{3}{20}$

3. $\dfrac{2}{7}$ $7 \times 3 = 21$; $\dfrac{6}{21} = \dfrac{2}{7}$

4. $\dfrac{1}{55}$ $5 \times 11 = 55$; $\dfrac{1}{55}$

5. $\dfrac{5}{38}$ $19 \times 2 = 38$; $\dfrac{5}{38}$

6. $-\dfrac{4}{35}$ $5 \times 7 = 35$; $\dfrac{-4}{35}$

7. $\dfrac{1}{81}$ $9 \times 9 = 81$; $\dfrac{1}{81}$

8. $\dfrac{1}{44}$ $11 \times 12 = 132$; $\dfrac{3}{132} = \dfrac{1}{44}$

9. $\dfrac{17}{72}$ $18 \times 4 = 72$; $\dfrac{17}{72}$

10. $\dfrac{4}{13}$ $13 \times 3 = 39$; $\dfrac{12}{39} = \dfrac{4}{13}$

11. $\dfrac{1}{9}$ $3 \times 6 = 18$; $\dfrac{2}{18} = \dfrac{1}{9}$

12. $-\dfrac{1}{44}$ $11 \times 20 = 220$; $\dfrac{-5}{220} = -\dfrac{1}{44}$

13. $\dfrac{3}{77}$ $7 \times 11 = 77$; $\dfrac{3}{77}$

14. $-\dfrac{1}{27}$ $3 \times 9 = 27$; $\dfrac{-1}{27}$

15. $\dfrac{2}{11}$ $11 \times 5 = 55$; $\dfrac{10}{55} = \dfrac{2}{11}$

16. $\dfrac{5}{26}$ $13 \times 4 = 52$; $\dfrac{10}{52} = \dfrac{5}{26}$

17. $\dfrac{1}{5}$ $5 \times 4 = 20$; $\dfrac{4}{20} = \dfrac{1}{5}$

18. $\dfrac{12}{65}$ $13 \times 5 = 65$; $\dfrac{12}{65}$

19. $-\dfrac{1}{22}$ $11 \times 4 = 44$; $\dfrac{-2}{44} = -\dfrac{1}{22}$

20. $\dfrac{3}{28}$ $4 \times 7 = 28$; $\dfrac{3}{28}$

Lesson 8.2

1. 20 $5 \times \dfrac{4}{1} = \dfrac{20}{1} = 20$

2. $-3\dfrac{3}{4}$ $3 \times -\dfrac{5}{4} = -\dfrac{15}{4} = -3\dfrac{3}{4}$

3. 49 $7 \times \dfrac{7}{1} = \dfrac{49}{1} = 49$

4. $15\dfrac{3}{4}$ $9 \times \dfrac{7}{4} = \dfrac{63}{4} = 15\dfrac{3}{4}$

5. 4 $2 \times \dfrac{2}{1} = \dfrac{4}{1} = 4$

Answers and Explanations

6. 14 $\qquad$ $4 \times \dfrac{7}{2} = \dfrac{28}{2} = 14$

7. 21 $\qquad$ $15 \times \dfrac{7}{5} = 3 \times \dfrac{7}{1} = 21$

8. -18 $\qquad$ $4 \times -\dfrac{9}{2} = -\dfrac{36}{2} = -18$

9. $-25\dfrac{1}{2}$ $\qquad$ $17 \times -\dfrac{3}{2} = -\dfrac{51}{2} = -25\dfrac{1}{2}$

10. $8\dfrac{1}{3}$ $\qquad$ $5 \times \dfrac{5}{3} = \dfrac{25}{3} = 8\dfrac{1}{3}$

11. 9 $\qquad$ $6 \times \dfrac{3}{2} = \dfrac{18}{2} = 9$

12. $13\dfrac{1}{2}$ $\qquad$ $9 \times \dfrac{3}{2} = \dfrac{27}{2} = 13\dfrac{1}{2}$

13. 55 $\qquad$ $5 \times \dfrac{11}{1} = \dfrac{55}{1} = 55$

14. 4 $\qquad$ $14 \times \dfrac{2}{7} = \dfrac{28}{7} = 4$

15. -27 $\qquad$ $3 \times -\dfrac{9}{1} = -\dfrac{27}{1} = -27$

16. $\dfrac{6}{7}$ $\qquad$ $3 \times \dfrac{2}{7} = \dfrac{6}{7}$

Lesson 8.3

1. $\dfrac{20}{21}$ $\qquad$ $\dfrac{5}{7} \times \dfrac{4}{3} = \dfrac{20}{21}$

2. $2\dfrac{1}{3}$ $\qquad$ $\dfrac{\cancel{2}^{1}}{3} \times \dfrac{7}{\cancel{2}^{1}} = \dfrac{7}{3}$ or $2\dfrac{1}{3}$

3. $-\dfrac{7}{27}$ $\qquad$ $\dfrac{1}{9} \times -\dfrac{7}{3} = -\dfrac{7}{27}$

4. $6\dfrac{3}{4}$ $\qquad$ $\dfrac{3}{4} \times \dfrac{9}{1} = \dfrac{27}{4}$ or $6\dfrac{3}{4}$

5. $1\dfrac{1}{26}$ $\qquad$ $-\dfrac{3}{13} \times -\dfrac{9}{2} = \dfrac{27}{26}$ or $1\dfrac{1}{26}$

6. $\dfrac{1}{3}$ $\qquad$ $\dfrac{1}{\cancel{9}_{3}} \times \dfrac{\cancel{3}^{1}}{1} = \dfrac{1}{3}$

7. $\dfrac{10}{13}$ $\qquad$ $\dfrac{2}{13} \times \dfrac{5}{1} = \dfrac{10}{13}$

8. $1\dfrac{1}{2}$ $\qquad$ $\dfrac{3}{\cancel{13}_{1}} \times \dfrac{\cancel{13}^{1}}{2} = \dfrac{3}{2}$ or $1\dfrac{1}{2}$

9. $5\dfrac{1}{3}$ $\qquad$ $\dfrac{4}{3} \times \dfrac{4}{1} = \dfrac{16}{3}$ or $5\dfrac{1}{3}$

10. $2\dfrac{13}{16}$ $\qquad$ $\dfrac{15}{4} \times \dfrac{3}{4} = \dfrac{45}{16}$ or $2\dfrac{13}{16}$

11. 6 $\qquad$ $\dfrac{6}{\cancel{7}_{1}} \times \dfrac{\cancel{7}^{1}}{1} = \dfrac{6}{1} = 6$

12. $-\dfrac{3}{4}$ $\qquad$ $\dfrac{3}{\cancel{17}_{1}} \times -\dfrac{\cancel{17}^{1}}{4} = -\dfrac{3}{4}$

13. $\dfrac{3}{242}$ $\qquad$ $\dfrac{1}{11} \times \dfrac{3}{22} = \dfrac{3}{242}$

14. 9 $\qquad$ $-\dfrac{3}{\cancel{7}_{1}} \times -\dfrac{\cancel{21}^{3}}{1} = \dfrac{9}{1} = 9$

15. $2\dfrac{1}{2}$ $\qquad$ $\dfrac{5}{\cancel{14}_{2}} \times \dfrac{\cancel{7}^{1}}{1} = \dfrac{5}{2}$ or $2\dfrac{1}{2}$

16. $\dfrac{9}{32}$ $\qquad$ $\dfrac{3}{4} \times \dfrac{3}{8} = \dfrac{9}{32}$

Lesson 8.4

1. $-\dfrac{8}{15}$ $\qquad$ $1\dfrac{1}{3} = \dfrac{4}{3}$; $-2\dfrac{1}{2} = -\dfrac{5}{2}$

$\dfrac{4}{3} \div -\dfrac{5}{2} = \dfrac{4}{3} \times -\dfrac{2}{5} = -\dfrac{8}{15}$

2. $3\dfrac{1}{5}$ $\qquad$ $3\dfrac{3}{5} = \dfrac{18}{5}$; $1\dfrac{1}{8} = \dfrac{9}{8}$

$\dfrac{18}{5} \div \dfrac{9}{8} = \dfrac{\cancel{18}^{2}}{5} \times \dfrac{8}{\cancel{9}_{1}} = \dfrac{16}{5} = 3\dfrac{1}{5}$

3. $2\dfrac{1}{7}$ $\qquad$ $7\dfrac{1}{7} = \dfrac{50}{7}$; $3\dfrac{1}{3} = \dfrac{10}{3}$

$\dfrac{50}{7} \div \dfrac{10}{3} = \dfrac{\cancel{50}^{5}}{7} \times \dfrac{3}{\cancel{10}_{1}} = \dfrac{15}{7} = 2\dfrac{1}{7}$

4. $1\dfrac{41}{84}$ $\qquad$ $3\dfrac{4}{7} = \dfrac{25}{7}$; $2\dfrac{2}{5} = \dfrac{12}{5}$

$\dfrac{25}{7} \div \dfrac{12}{5} = \dfrac{25}{7} \times \dfrac{5}{12} = \dfrac{125}{84} = 1\dfrac{41}{84}$

5. 2 $\qquad$ $6\dfrac{4}{5} = \dfrac{34}{5}$; $3\dfrac{2}{5} = \dfrac{17}{5}$

$\dfrac{34}{5} \div \dfrac{17}{5} = \dfrac{\cancel{34}^{2}}{\cancel{5}_{1}} \times \dfrac{\cancel{5}^{1}}{\cancel{17}_{1}} = \dfrac{2}{1} = 2$

6. $1\dfrac{7}{15}$ $\qquad$ $5\dfrac{1}{2} = \dfrac{11}{2}$; $3\dfrac{3}{4} = \dfrac{15}{4}$

$\dfrac{11}{2} \div \dfrac{15}{4} = \dfrac{11}{\cancel{2}_{1}} \times \dfrac{\cancel{4}^{2}}{15} = \dfrac{22}{15} = 1\dfrac{7}{15}$

7. $1\dfrac{8}{11}$ $\qquad$ $4\dfrac{2}{9} = \dfrac{38}{9}$; $2\dfrac{4}{9} = \dfrac{22}{9}$

$\dfrac{38}{9} \div \dfrac{22}{9} = \dfrac{\cancel{38}^{19}}{\cancel{9}_{1}} \times \dfrac{\cancel{9}^{1}}{\cancel{22}_{11}} = \dfrac{19}{11} = 1\dfrac{8}{11}$

8. $3\dfrac{5}{7}$ $\qquad$ $-9\dfrac{2}{7} = -\dfrac{65}{7}$; $-2\dfrac{1}{2} = \dfrac{-5}{2}$

$\dfrac{-65}{7} \div \dfrac{-5}{2} = -\dfrac{\cancel{65}^{13}}{7} \times -\dfrac{2}{\cancel{5}_{1}} = \dfrac{26}{7} = 3\dfrac{5}{7}$

9. $2\dfrac{1}{136}$ $\qquad$ $5\dfrac{6}{17} = \dfrac{91}{17}$; $2\dfrac{2}{3} = \dfrac{8}{3}$

$\dfrac{91}{17} \div \dfrac{8}{3} = \dfrac{91}{17} \times \dfrac{3}{8} = \dfrac{273}{136} = 2\dfrac{1}{136}$

10. $1\dfrac{129}{143}$ $\qquad$ $5\dfrac{3}{13} = \dfrac{68}{13}$; $2\dfrac{3}{4} = \dfrac{11}{4}$

$\dfrac{68}{13} \div \dfrac{11}{4} = \dfrac{68}{13} \times \dfrac{4}{11} = \dfrac{272}{143} = 1\dfrac{129}{143}$

11. $-\dfrac{35}{92}$ $\qquad$ $1\dfrac{3}{4} = \dfrac{7}{4}$; $-4\dfrac{3}{5} = -\dfrac{22}{5}$

$\dfrac{7}{4} \div -\dfrac{23}{5} = \dfrac{7}{4} \times -\dfrac{5}{23} = -\dfrac{35}{92}$

Answers and Explanations

12. $7\frac{1}{2}$ $\quad 9\frac{3}{8} = \frac{75}{8}; \; 1\frac{1}{4} = \frac{5}{4}$

$\frac{75}{8} \div \frac{5}{4} = \frac{\cancel{75}^{15}}{\cancel{8}_2} \times \frac{\cancel{4}^1}{\cancel{5}_1} = \frac{15}{2} = 7\frac{1}{2}$

13. $9\frac{43}{45}$ $\quad -44\frac{4}{5} = -\frac{224}{5}; \; -4\frac{1}{2} = -\frac{9}{2}$

$-\frac{224}{5} \div -\frac{9}{2} = -\frac{224}{5} \times -\frac{2}{9} = \frac{448}{45} = 9\frac{43}{45}$

14. $\frac{3}{7}$ $\quad 1\frac{1}{2} = \frac{3}{2}; \; 3\frac{1}{2} = \frac{7}{2}$

$\frac{3}{2} \div \frac{7}{2} = \frac{3}{\cancel{2}_1} \times \frac{\cancel{2}^1}{7} = \frac{3}{7}$

15. $4\frac{1}{5}$ $\quad 5\frac{3}{5} = \frac{28}{5}; \; 1\frac{1}{3} = \frac{4}{3}$

$\frac{28}{5} \div \frac{4}{3} = \frac{\cancel{28}^7}{5} \times \frac{3}{\cancel{4}_1} = \frac{21}{5} = 4\frac{1}{5}$

16. $\frac{39}{110}$ $\quad 1\frac{2}{11} = \frac{13}{11}; \; 3\frac{1}{3} = \frac{10}{3}$

$\frac{13}{11} \div \frac{10}{3} = \frac{13}{11} \times \frac{3}{10} = \frac{39}{110}$

Lesson 9.1

1. 46
2. 77
3. 146
4. 1001
5. 89
6. 1501
7. 14.4
8. 125.5
9. 149.5
10. 33.4
11. 275.8
12. 213
13. 1435.34
14. 3.56
15. 111.12
16. 32.76
17. 999.99
18. 954.38
19. 3.238
20. 329.330
21. 109.109
22. 8256.784
23. 49.495
24. 0.114

Lesson 9.2

1. 0.3125

$$
\begin{array}{r}
0.3125 \\
16\overline{)5.0000} \\
48 \\
\hline
20 \\
16 \\
\hline
40 \\
32 \\
\hline
80 \\
80 \\
\hline
0
\end{array}
$$

2. 0.5714

$$
\begin{array}{r}
0.57142\ldots \\
7\overline{)4.00000} \\
35 \\
\hline
50 \\
49 \\
\hline
10 \\
7 \\
\hline
30 \\
28 \\
\hline
20 \\
14 \\
\hline
6\ldots
\end{array}
$$

3. 0.4839

$$
\begin{array}{r}
0.48387\ldots \\
31\overline{)15.00000} \\
124 \\
\hline
260 \\
248 \\
\hline
120 \\
93 \\
\hline
270 \\
248 \\
\hline
220 \\
217 \\
\hline
3\ldots
\end{array}
$$

4. 0.6000

$$
\begin{array}{r}
0.6 \\
5\overline{)3.0} \\
30 \\
\hline
0
\end{array}
$$

5. 0.0005

$$
\begin{array}{r}
0.00049\ldots \\
2001\overline{)1.00000} \\
8004 \\
\hline
19960 \\
18009 \\
\hline
1951\ldots
\end{array}
$$

6. 0.9200

$$
\begin{array}{r}
0.92 \\
25\overline{)23.00} \\
225 \\
\hline
50 \\
50 \\
\hline
0
\end{array}
$$

Answers and Explanations

7. 0.7500

$$\begin{array}{r} 0.75 \\ 4\overline{)3.00} \\ \underline{28}\downarrow \\ 20 \\ \underline{20} \\ 0 \end{array}$$

8. 0.8333

$$\begin{array}{r} 0.8333... \\ 66\overline{)55.0000} \\ \underline{528}\downarrow \\ 220 \\ \underline{198}\downarrow \\ 220 \\ \underline{198} \\ 22... \end{array}$$

Lesson 9.3

1. $\dfrac{17}{20}$ $\quad \dfrac{85}{100} = \dfrac{17}{20}$

2. $\dfrac{77}{100}$

3. $\dfrac{111}{125}$ $\quad \dfrac{888}{1000} = \dfrac{111}{125}$

4. $\dfrac{1}{80}$ $\quad \dfrac{125}{10,000} = \dfrac{1}{80}$

5. $\dfrac{339}{500}$ $\quad \dfrac{678}{1000} = \dfrac{339}{500}$

6. $\dfrac{1251}{2000}$ $\quad \dfrac{6255}{10,000} = \dfrac{1251}{2000}$

7. $\dfrac{331}{1000}$

8. $\dfrac{909}{2000}$ $\quad \dfrac{4545}{10,000} = \dfrac{909}{2000}$

9. $\dfrac{219}{250}$ $\quad \dfrac{876}{1000} = \dfrac{219}{250}$

10. $\dfrac{5}{16}$ $\quad \dfrac{3125}{10,000} = \dfrac{5}{16}$

11. $\dfrac{687}{2000}$ $\quad \dfrac{3435}{10,000} = \dfrac{687}{2000}$

12. $\dfrac{7007}{10,000}$

13. $\dfrac{42}{125}$ $\quad \dfrac{336}{1000} = \dfrac{42}{125}$

14. $\dfrac{2141}{10,000}$

15. $\dfrac{14}{25}$ $\quad \dfrac{56}{100} = \dfrac{14}{25}$

16. $\dfrac{11}{2000}$ $\quad \dfrac{55}{10,000} = \dfrac{11}{2000}$

Lesson 9.4

1. 4

2. 10.10

---

3. 0.5677

4. 45.449

5. 14.00126

6. 21.21

7. 11.111

8. 12.1023

9. 166.66

10. 144.32

11. 25.205

12. 156.12

Lesson 10.1

1. 47.55

$$\begin{array}{r} 45.45 \\ + \ 2.10 \\ \hline 47.55 \end{array}$$

2. 74.92

$$\begin{array}{r} 33.70 \\ + \ 41.22 \\ \hline 74.92 \end{array}$$

3. 13.94

$$\begin{array}{r} 5.40 \\ + \ 8.54 \\ \hline 13.94 \end{array}$$

4. 5.221

$$\begin{array}{r} 2.220 \\ + \ 3.001 \\ \hline 5.221 \end{array}$$

5. 33.056

$$\begin{array}{r} 33.045 \\ + \ \ .011 \\ \hline 33.056 \end{array}$$

6. 22.3351

$$\begin{array}{r} \overset{1}{0}9.\overset{1}{0}901 \\ + \ 13.2450 \\ \hline 22.3351 \end{array}$$

7. 6.382

$$\begin{array}{r} \overset{1}{0}.782 \\ + \ 5.600 \\ \hline 6.382 \end{array}$$

8. 456.431

$$\begin{array}{r} 454.320 \\ + \ \ 2.111 \\ \hline 456.431 \end{array}$$

9. 14.0001

$$\begin{array}{r} \overset{1}{4}.5000 \\ + \ 9.5001 \\ \hline 14.0001 \end{array}$$

10. 68.56

$$\begin{array}{r} 63.10 \\ + \ 5.46 \\ \hline 68.56 \end{array}$$

11. 9.60201

$$\begin{array}{r} \overset{1}{2}.22201 \\ + \ 7.38000 \\ \hline 9.60201 \end{array}$$

---

12. 26.7041

$$\begin{array}{r} \overset{1}{0}8.7040 \\ + \ 18.0001 \\ \hline 26.7041 \end{array}$$

13. 10.11

$$\begin{array}{r} \overset{1}{4}.\overset{1\ 1}{147} \\ + \ 5.963 \\ \hline 10.110 \end{array}$$

14. 65.1822

$$\begin{array}{r} \overset{1\ 1}{0}9.4600 \\ + \ 55.7222 \\ \hline 65.1822 \end{array}$$

15. 152.15372

$$\begin{array}{r} 000.00152 \\ + \ 152.15220 \\ \hline 152.15372 \end{array}$$

16. 5.5051

$$\begin{array}{r} 3.2020 \\ + \ 2.3031 \\ \hline 5.5051 \end{array}$$

17. 11.613

$$\begin{array}{r} \overset{1\ 1}{9}.781 \\ + \ 1.832 \\ \hline 11.613 \end{array}$$

18. 11.1102

$$\begin{array}{r} \overset{1\ 1\ 1}{2}.2222 \\ + \ 8.8880 \\ \hline 11.1102 \end{array}$$

19. 482.6242

$$\begin{array}{r} 47\overset{1\ 1\ 1}{8}.6540 \\ + \ \ \ 3.9702 \\ \hline 482.6242 \end{array}$$

20. 22.3801

$$\begin{array}{r} \overset{1\ \ 1}{0}3.3030 \\ + \ 19.0771 \\ \hline 22.3801 \end{array}$$

Lesson 10.2

1. 7.63

$$\begin{array}{r} \overset{14\ 1}{1}5.45 \\ - \ 7.82 \\ \hline 7.63 \end{array}$$

2. 42.381

$$\begin{array}{r} 4\overset{7\ 9\ 1}{8}.001 \\ - \ 5.620 \\ \hline 42.381 \end{array}$$

3. 85.91

$$\begin{array}{r} 8\overset{7\ 1}{8}.88 \\ - \ 2.97 \\ \hline 85.91 \end{array}$$

4. 47.7015

$$\begin{array}{r} 5\overset{4\ 9\ 1\ 1\ 1}{0}.2020 \\ - \ 2.5005 \\ \hline 47.7015 \end{array}$$

5. 5.523

$$\begin{array}{r} 1\overset{9\ 12\ 9\ 1}{0}.300 \\ - \ 4.777 \\ \hline 5.523 \end{array}$$

6. 94.737

$$\begin{array}{r}{\scriptstyle 9\ 9\ 10\ 10\ 1}\\ \cancel{100.111}\\ -\ \ \ 5.374\\ \hline 94.737\end{array}$$

7. 552.657

$$\begin{array}{r}{\scriptstyle 4\ 9\ 9\ 1}\\ \cancel{565.002}\\ -\ 12.345\\ \hline 552.657\end{array}$$

8. 0.707

$$\begin{array}{r}{\scriptstyle 6\ 16\ 9\ 1}\\ \cancel{7.701}\\ -\ 6.994\\ \hline 0.707\end{array}$$

9. 0.9414

$$\begin{array}{r}{\scriptstyle 4\ 15}\\ \cancel{5.5514}\\ -\ 4.6100\\ \hline 0.9414\end{array}$$

10. 6.957

$$\begin{array}{r}{\scriptstyle 11\ 11}\\ \cancel{12.157}\\ -\ 5.200\\ \hline 6.957\end{array}$$

11. 26.07

$$\begin{array}{r}{\scriptstyle 6\ 1}\\ 89.70\\ -63.63\\ \hline 26.07\end{array}$$

12. 0.5738

$$\begin{array}{r}{\scriptstyle 2\ 14\ 15\ 10\ 1}\\ \cancel{3.5610}\\ -2.9872\\ \hline 0.5738\end{array}$$

13. 4233.77

$$\begin{array}{r}{\scriptstyle 8\ 12\ 1}\\ \cancel{4789.32}\\ -\ 555.55\\ \hline 4233.77\end{array}$$

14. 1.671

$$\begin{array}{r}{\scriptstyle 7\ 15\ 1}\\ \cancel{8.651}\\ -\ 6.980\\ \hline 1.671\end{array}$$

15. 11.871

$$\begin{array}{r}{\scriptstyle 4\ 17\ 16\ 1}\\ \cancel{45.870}\\ -\ 33.999\\ \hline 11.871\end{array}$$

16. 954.951

$$\begin{array}{r}{\scriptstyle 5\ 12\ 1}\\ \cancel{963.751}\\ -\ \ \ 8.800\\ \hline 954.951\end{array}$$

17. 6.999

$$\begin{array}{r}{\scriptstyle 7\ 16\ 1}\\ \cancel{8.789}\\ -\ 1.790\\ \hline 6.999\end{array}$$

18. 1.629

$$\begin{array}{r}{\scriptstyle 4\ 11\ 9\ 1}\\ \cancel{5.200}\\ -\ 3.571\\ \hline 1.629\end{array}$$

19. 4.07

$$\begin{array}{r}{\scriptstyle 8\ 1}\\ 6.91\\ -\ 2.84\\ \hline 4.07\end{array}$$

20. 5.975

$$\begin{array}{r}{\scriptstyle 7\ 1}\\ \cancel{8}.888\\ -\ 2.913\\ \hline 5.975\end{array}$$

Lesson 10.3

1. $88.00

$$\begin{array}{r}56\\ +\ 32\\ \hline 88\end{array}$$

2. $27.91

$$\begin{array}{r}22.71\\ +\ 5.20\\ \hline 27.91\end{array}$$

3. $2.60

$$\begin{array}{r}{\scriptstyle 4\ 1}\\ \cancel{15.00}\\ -\ 12.40\\ \hline 2.60\end{array}$$

4. $11.38

$$\begin{array}{r}11.06\\ +\ 0.32\\ \hline 11.38\end{array}$$

5. $2.79

$$\begin{array}{r}{\scriptstyle 9\ 9\ 1}\\ \cancel{10.00}\\ -\ 7.21\\ \hline 2.79\end{array}$$

6. $17.71

$$\begin{array}{r}{\scriptstyle 2\ 10\ 14\ 1}\\ \cancel{315.32}\\ -\ 297.61\\ \hline 17.71\end{array}$$

7. $85.95

$$\begin{array}{r}{\scriptstyle 8\ 1}\\ 89.45\\ -\ 3.50\\ \hline 85.95\end{array}$$

8. $29.23

$$\begin{array}{r}{\scriptstyle 2\ 13\ 9\ 1}\\ \cancel{34.00}\\ -\ 4.77\\ \hline 29.23\end{array}$$

9. $911.61

$$\begin{array}{r}{\scriptstyle 9\ 9\ 9\ 1}\\ \cancel{1000.03}\\ -\ 88.42\\ \hline 911.61\end{array}$$

10. $47.30

$$\begin{array}{r}45.00\\ +\ 2.30\\ \hline 47.30\end{array}$$

11. $32.19

$$\begin{array}{r}{\scriptstyle 8\ 9\ 1}\\ \cancel{89.00}\\ -\ 56.81\\ \hline 32.19\end{array}$$

12. $805.29

$$\begin{array}{r}{\scriptstyle 0\ 12\ 9\ 1}\\ \cancel{813.00}\\ -\ 7.71\\ \hline 805.29\end{array}$$

13. $2.07

$$\begin{array}{r}{\scriptstyle 4\ 9\ 1}\\ \cancel{5.00}\\ -\ 2.93\\ \hline 2.07\end{array}$$

14. $67.89

$$\begin{array}{r}{\scriptstyle 6\ 10\ 13\ 1}\\ \cancel{71.45}\\ -\ 3.56\\ \hline 67.89\end{array}$$

15. $5.94

$$\begin{array}{r}{\scriptstyle 7\ 1}\\ \cancel{8}.55\\ -\ 2.61\\ \hline 5.94\end{array}$$

16. $1.21

$$\begin{array}{r}3.21\\ -\ 2.00\\ \hline 1.21\end{array}$$

17. $1473.13

$$\begin{array}{r}{\scriptstyle 4\ 15\ 10\ 9\ 1}\\ \cancel{1561.00}\\ -\ \ \ 87.87\\ \hline 1473.13\end{array}$$

18. $1510.93

$$\begin{array}{r}{\scriptstyle 6\ 1}\\ 1987.23\\ -\ 476.30\\ \hline 1510.93\end{array}$$

19. $58.43

$$\begin{array}{r}{\scriptstyle 7\ 10\ 9\ 1}\\ \cancel{81.00}\\ -\ 22.57\\ \hline 58.43\end{array}$$

20. $38.60

$$\begin{array}{r}{\scriptstyle 3\ 1}\\ \cancel{45.60}\\ -\ 7.00\\ \hline 38.60\end{array}$$

Lesson 10.4

1. $57 $34.50 + $22.50 = $57.00
2. $78 $55.00 + $23.00 = $78.00
3. $79 $77.00 + $2.00 = $79.00
4. $870.50 $908.00 − $37.50 = $870.50
5. $11 $33.00 − $22.00 = $11.00
6. $559 $561.00 − $2.00 = $559.00
7. $21.50 $77.50 − $56.00 = $21.50
8. $11.50 $234.50 − $223.00 = $11.50
9. $144.50 $45.50 + $99.00 = $144.50
10. $9 $10.00 − $1.00 = $9.00
11. $15.50 $13.00 + $2.50 = $15.50
12. $232 $14.50 + $217.50 = $232.00

Answers and Explanations

13. $3 $21.50 − $18.50 = $3.00
14. $0.50 $2.50 − $2.00 = $0.50
15. $512 $444.50 + $67.50 = $512.00
16. $1234 $232.50 + $1001.50 = $1,234.00
17. $322 $68.00 + $254.00 = $322.00
18. $82.50 $7.50 + $75.00 = $82.50
19. $2527 $2303.50 + $223.50 = $2,527.00
20. $10.50 $32.50 − $22.00 = $10.50

Lesson 11.1

1. 16.25   2 decimal places
2. 15.048   3 decimal places
3. −28.5212   4 decimal places
4. 5367.24   2 decimal places
5. 0.90012   5 decimal places
6. 10.1101   4 decimal places
7. −2088.1447   4 decimal places
8. 425.606   3 decimal places
9. −0.147852   6 decimal places
10. 427.68   3 decimal places
11. 2223.144   3 decimal places
12. 2314.1   2 decimal places
13. 61.84937   5 decimal places
14. 199.4882   4 decimal places
15. 0.00001274   8 decimal places
16. −19.55   2 decimal places

Lesson 11.1 (cont.)

1. 0.46731   the decimal moves left 1 place
2. 7135   the decimal moves right 2 places
3. 580   the decimal moves right 3 places
4. 1.645   the decimal moves left 1 place
5. 0.10005   the decimal moves left 2 places
6. 1112   the decimal moves right 3 places
7. 5.93   the decimal moves right 1 place
8. 0.00322   the decimal moves left 2 places
9. 105.632   the decimal moves left 1 place
10. 28.90   the decimal stays in the same place
11. 0.156   the decimal moves left 1 place
12. 21000   the decimal moves right 4 places
13. 583.1   the decimal moves right 1 place
14. 8181   the decimal moves right 2 places
15. 9.73   the decimal moves right 1 place
16. 0.000002   the decimal moves left 3 places

Lesson 11.2

1. $18.08 $565 \times 32 = 18,080$; 3 decimal places, so 18.080 = $18.08
2. $808.50 $84 \times 9625 = 80,8500$; 3 decimal places, so 808.500 = $808.50
3. $76.95 $342 \times 225 = 76,950$; 3 decimal places, so 76.950 = $76.95
4. $16.86 $301 \times 56 = 16,856$; 3 decimal places, so 16.856 = $16.86
5. $15.44 $63 \times 245 = 15,435$; 3 decimal places, so 15.435 = $15.44
6. $0.84 $557 \times 15 = 8355$; 4 decimal places, so 0.8355 = $0.84
7. $506.68 $643 \times 788 = 506,684$; 3 decimal places, so 506.684 = $506.68
8. $127.62 $1233 \times 1035 = 1,276,155$; 4 decimal places, so 127.6155 = $127.62
9. $1151.55 $1350 \times 853 = 1,151,550$; 3 decimal places, so 1151.550 = $1151.55
10. $485.22 $501 \times 9685 = 4,852,185$; 4 decimal places, so 485.2185 = $485.22
11. $148.04 $4555 \times 325 = 1,480,375$; 4 decimal places, so 148.0375 = $148.04
12. $164.01 $7810 \times 21 = 164,010$; 3 decimal places, so 164.010 = $164.01
13. $0.99 $8999 \times 11 = 98,989$; 5 decimal places, so 0.98989 = $0.99
14. $152.20 $5637 \times 27 = 152,199$; 3 decimal places, so 152.199 = $152.20
15. $563.63 $8514 \times 662 = 5,636,268$; 4 decimal places, so 563.6268 = $563.63
16. $22.15 $23 \times 963 = 22,149$; 3 decimal places, so 22.149 = $22.15

Lesson 11.3

1. −150.0 $500 \times -0.3 = -150.0$
2. 22 $11 \times 2 = 22$
3. 1200 $60 \times 20 = 1200$
4. 16.0 $40 \times 0.4 = 16.0$
5. −1200 $600 \times -2 = -1200$
6. 3000 $3 \times 1000 = 3000$
7. 3.5 $7 \times 0.5 = 3.5$
8. 20.0 $100 \times 0.2 = 20.0$
9. −160 $80 \times -2 = -160$
10. −100.0 $250 \times -0.4 = -100.0$
11. 45.0 $90 \times 0.5 = 45.0$
12. 160 $40 \times 4 = 160$

Answers and Explanations

13. 13 $13 \times 1 = 13$

14. −4 $1 \times -4 = -4$

15. 3 $6 \times 0.5 = 3$

Lesson 12.1

1. 9.1400

```
       9.14
   5)45.70
     45
     ──
     07
      5
     ──
     20
     20
     ──
      0
```

2. 7.3350

```
       7.335
   4)29.340
     28
     ──
     13
     12
     ──
     14
     12
     ──
     20
     20
     ──
      0
```

3. 7.1727

```
       7.17272...
  11)78.90000
     77
     ──
     19
     11
     ──
     80
     77
     ──
     30
     22
     ──
     80
     77
     ──
     30
     22
     ──
      8...
```

4. −5.9714

```
       −5.97142...
  −7)41.80000
     35
     ──
     68
     63
     ──
     50
     49
     ──
     10
      7
     ──
     30
     28
     ──
     20
     14
     ──
      6...
```

5. 53.2286

```
        53.22857...
   14)745.20000
      70
      ──
      45
      42
      ──
      32
      28
      ──
      40
      28
      ──
      120
      112
      ───
       80
       70
      ───
      100
       98
      ───
        2...
```

6. 5.9857

```
       5.98571...
   7)41.90000
     35
     ──
     69
     63
     ──
     60
     56
     ──
     40
     35
     ──
     50
     49
     ──
     10
      7
     ──
      3...
```

7. 1.2533

```
        1.2533...
   18)22.5600
      18
      ──
      45
      36
      ──
      96
      90
      ──
      60
      54
      ──
      60
      54
      ──
       6...
```

8. −8.9313

```
       −8.93125
   −8)71.45000
      64
      ──
      74
      72
      ──
      25
      24
      ──
      10
       8
      ──
      20
      16
      ──
      40
      40
      ──
       0
```

Lesson 12.2

1. 2.0833

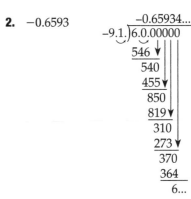

2. −0.6593

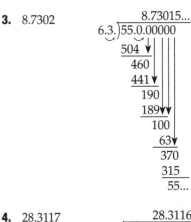

3. 8.7302

```
        8.73015...
  6.3.)55.0.00000
      504
      ───
      460
      441
      ───
      190
      189
      ───
      100
       63
      ───
      370
      315
      ───
       55...
```

4. 28.3117

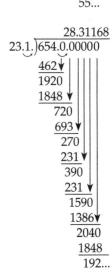

Answers and Explanations

5. 8.0899

```
        8.08988
8.9.)72.0.00000
    712
    800
    712
    880
    801
    790
    712
    780
    712
     68...
```

6. −175.6000

```
      −175.6
−2.5.)439.0.0
      25
      189
      175
      140
      125
      150
      150
        0
```

7. 70.1639

```
       70.16393...
6.1.)428.0.00000
    427
    100
     61
    390
    366
    240
    183
    570
    549
    210
    183
     27...
```

8. 8.0882

```
       8.08823...
6.8.)55.0.00000
    544
    600
    544
    560
    544
    160
    136
    240
    204
     36...
```

Lesson 12.3

1. −3.0000

```
      −3.0
−4.5.)13.5.0
     135
       0
```

2. 2.2800

```
       2.28
2.5.)5.7.00
     50
     70
     50
    200
    200
      0
```

3. 11.0000

```
      11.0
8.1.)89.1.0
    81
    81
    81
     0
```

4. 2.0000

```
      2.0
2.1.)4.2.0
    42
     0
```

5. 1.2800

```
        1.28
3.41.)4.36.48
     341
     954
     682
    2728
    2728
       0
```

6. −3.2000

```
        3.2
−2.11.)6.75.2
      633
      422
      422
        0
```

7. 2.6000

```
       2.6
2.37.)6.16.2
     474
    1422
    1422
       0
```

8. 1.1495

```
        1.14954...
5.55.)6.38.00000
     555
     830
     555
    2750
    2220
    5300
    4995
    3050
    2775
    2750
    2220
     530...
```

Lesson 12.4

1. $5.00

```
     5
3)15
  15
   0
```

2. $11.20

```
     11.2
5)56.0
  5
  6
  5
 10
 10
  0
```

3. $27.38

```
         27.384...
3.25.)89.00.000
     650
    2400
    2275
    1250
     975
    2750
    2600
    1500
    1300
     200...
```

4. $4.35

```
        4.347...
2.3.)10.0.000
     92
     80
     69
    110
     92
    180
    161
     19...
```

5. $8.26

```
        8.263...
5.5.)45.4.500
    440
    145
    110
    350
    330
    200
    165
     35...
```

6. $2.15

```
        2.150...
2.33.)5.01.000
     466
     350
     233
    1170
    1165
      50...
```

Answers and Explanations

7. $13.65

```
            13.646...
6.54.)89.25.000
       654↓|
       2385|
       1962↓
        4230
        3924↓
         3060
         2616
          4440
          3924
           516...
```

8. $961.00

```
          961.0
10.2.)9802.2.0
      918↓|
       622↓
       612↓
        102
        102
          0
```

Lesson 12.5

1.	100	$300 \div 3 = 100$
2.	5	$10 \div 2 = 5$
3.	1.5	$30 \div 20 = 1.5$
4.	33	$33 \div 1 = 33$
5.	631	$631 \div 1 = 631$
6.	2	$2 \div 1 = 2$
7.	3.5	$7 \div 2 = 3.5$
8.	20	$100 \div 5 = 20$
9.	3	$12 \div 4 = 3$
10.	5	$40 \div 8 = 5$
11.	6.5	$13 \div 2 = 6.5$
12.	25	$200 \div 8 = 25$
13.	20	$40 \div 2 = 20$
14.	24	$72 \div 3 = 24$
15.	7	$70 \div 10 = 7$
16.	10	$90 \div 9 = 10$
17.	20	$80 \div 4 = 20$

Lesson 13.1

1. 2:1 or $\frac{2}{1}$

2. 3:2 or $\frac{3}{2}$

3. 25:18 or $\frac{25}{18}$

4. $\frac{17}{32}$ or 17:32

5. $\frac{4}{3}$ or 4:3

Lesson 13.1 (cont.)

1. 6

	Ratio (parts)	Multiplier	Actual Amount
students	22	6	132
teachers	1	6	6

2. 36

	Ratio (parts)	Multiplier	Actual Amount
black	3	4	12
white	2	4	8
red	4	4	16
TOTAL	9	4	36

3. 12 oz peanuts and 6 oz walnuts

	Ratio (parts)	Multiplier	Actual Amount
peanuts	6	2	12 oz
almonds	2	2	4 oz
walnuts	3	2	6 oz
TOTAL	11	2	22 oz

4. 1/2 cup

	Ratio (parts)	Multiplier	Actual Amount
sugar	1	$\frac{1}{2}$	$\frac{1}{2}$ cup
lemon juice	2	$\frac{1}{2}$	1 cup
water	5	$\frac{1}{2}$	$2\frac{1}{2}$ cup

Lesson 13.2

1. $x = 10$ $\quad x \times 15 = 5 \times 30;\ 15x = 150;\ x = 10$

2. $z = 12$ $\quad z \times 6 = 3 \times 24;\ 6z = 72;\ z = 12$

3. $z = 7$ $\quad 14 \times 50 = z \times 100;\ 700 = 100z;\ 7 = z$

4. $y = 280$ $\quad 56 \times 20 = 4 \times y;\ 1120 = 4y;\ 280 = y$

5. $w = 15$ $\quad 45 \times 3 = 9 \times w;\ 135 = 9w;\ 15 = w$

6. $x = 2$ $\quad 14 \times 10 = x \times 70;\ 140 = 70x;\ 2 = x$

7. $r = 9$ $\quad 33 \times 3 = r \times 11;\ 99 = 11r;\ r = 9$

8. $z = 3$ $\quad 72 \times z = 9 \times 24;\ 72z = 216;\ z = 3$

9. $x = 7.5$ $\quad 3 \times 5 = 2 \times x;\ 15 = 2x;\ 7.5 = x$

10. $w = 2.5$ $\quad 700 \times w = 50 \times 35;\ 700w = 1750;\ w = 2.5$

11. $x = 54$ $\quad 36 \times 6 = 4 \times x;\ 216 = 4x;\ 54 = x$

Answers and Explanations

12. $q = 28$ $84 \times 4 = 12 \times q$; $336 = 12q$; $28 = q$

13. −60 meters $\dfrac{-5 \text{ meters}}{1 \text{ hours}} = \dfrac{m \text{ meters}}{12 \text{ hours}}$; $-5 \times 12 = 1 \times m$;

$m = -60$

14. 9 tsp $\dfrac{8 \text{ oz}}{2 \text{ tsp}} = \dfrac{36 \text{ oz}}{y \text{ tsp}}$; $8y = 2 \times 36$; $8y = 72$; $y = 9$

15. 12 hours $\dfrac{3 \text{ hours}}{2 \text{ weeks}} = \dfrac{y \text{ hours}}{8 \text{ weeks}}$; $3 \times 8 = 2y$;

$24 = 2y$; $12 = y$

16. 125 Tbs $\dfrac{50 \text{ Tbs}}{10 \text{ gal}} = \dfrac{y \text{ Tbs}}{25 \text{ gal}}$; $50 \times 25 = 10y$;

$1250 = 10y$; $125 = y$

17. 260 feet $\dfrac{200 \text{ feet}}{50 \text{ mph}} = \dfrac{y \text{ feet}}{65 \text{ mph}}$; $200 \times 65 = 50y$;

$13,000 = 50y$; $260 = y$

18. 1 $\dfrac{y = 3}{x = 12} = \dfrac{y = ?}{x = 4}$; $3 \times 4 = 12y$;

$12 = 12y$; $1 = y$

Lesson 13.3

1. David   Adam: $\dfrac{4 \text{ hot dogs}}{7 \text{ minutes}} = \dfrac{1 \text{ hot dogs}}{y \text{ minutes}}$;

$4y = 7$; $y = \dfrac{7}{4} = 1\dfrac{3}{4}$;

David: $\dfrac{3 \text{ hot dogs}}{5 \text{ minutes}} = \dfrac{1 \text{ hot dogs}}{y \text{ minutes}}$;

$3y = 5$; $y = \dfrac{5}{3} = 1\dfrac{2}{3}$; $1\dfrac{2}{3} < 1\dfrac{3}{4}$

2. 9 widgets per minute

$\dfrac{2700 \text{ widgets}}{5 \text{ hours}} = \dfrac{w \text{ widgets}}{1 \text{ hour}}$; $2700 = 5w$;

$540 = w$; 540 per hour ÷ 60 min = 9

3. $1\dfrac{1}{2}$ miles $\dfrac{2 \text{ miles}}{40 \text{ minutes}} = \dfrac{x \text{ miles}}{30 \text{ minutes}}$; $2 \times 30 = 40x$;

$60 = 40x$; $x = \dfrac{60}{40} = 1\dfrac{1}{2}$

4. \$1.88 $\dfrac{12 \text{ gal}}{\$22.50} = \dfrac{1 \text{ gal}}{d}$; $12d = 22.50$;

$d = 1.875 = \$1.88$

5. 12,600 bricks $\dfrac{5 \text{ people}}{9000 \text{ bricks}} = \dfrac{7 \text{ people}}{b \text{ bricks}}$; $5b = 9000 \times 7$;

$5b = 63,000$; $b = 12,600$

Lesson 13.4

1. 80 cm $\dfrac{BD = 30}{FG = 6} = \dfrac{CD = ?}{HG = 16}$;

$30 \times 16 = 6x$; $480 = 6x$; $x = 80$

2. 6 $\dfrac{3}{9} = \dfrac{2}{s}$; $3s = 9 \times 2$; $3s = 18$; $s = 6$

3. 5 miles $\dfrac{5}{4} = \dfrac{6.25}{x}$; $5x = 4 \times 6.25$; $5x = 25$; $x = 5$

4. 280 miles $\dfrac{1 \text{ inch}}{28 \text{ miles}} = \dfrac{10 \text{ inches}}{d}$; $d = 28 \times 10$; $d = 280$

5. 12.5 feet $\dfrac{2 \text{ inches}}{5 \text{ feet}} = \dfrac{5 \text{ inches}}{x \text{ feet}}$;

$2x = 5 \times 5$; $2x = 25$; $x = 12.5$

Lesson 14.1

A (2,3)

B (4,−4)

C (−6,−6)

D (5,3)

E (3,5)

F (1,2)

G (−2,2)

H (−5,4)

I (9,7)

J (−6,8)

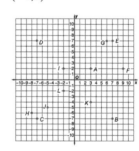

Lesson 14.2

1.

Time	pages Vicki reads	pages Bruce reads
1 minute	$\dfrac{2}{3}$	$1\dfrac{1}{3}$
3 minutes	2	4
6 minutes	4	8

2.

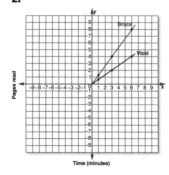

Answers and Explanations

3. (b) Bruce reads twice as fast as Vicki.

4. $0.20 $\quad \dfrac{5 \text{ pounds}}{\$1} = \dfrac{1 \text{ pound}}{d}$; $5d = 1$; $d = \dfrac{1}{5} = \$0.20$

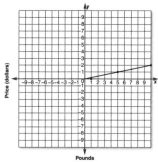

Lesson 14.3

1. (1, 10)

2. 10 miles per hour

3. Below

4. Yes $\quad \dfrac{3}{2} \div \dfrac{1}{2} = \dfrac{3}{2} \times \dfrac{2}{1} = 3$; $\dfrac{3}{1} = 3$; $\dfrac{6}{2} = 3$

5. 3

Lesson 15.1

1. 0.07; $\dfrac{7}{100}$

2. 0.16; $\dfrac{4}{25}$

3. 1.00; $\dfrac{1}{1}$

4. 0.25; $\dfrac{1}{4}$

5. 0.01; $\dfrac{1}{100}$

6. 0.2; $\dfrac{1}{5}$

7. 0.44; $\dfrac{11}{25}$

8. 0.99; $\dfrac{99}{100}$

9. 0.23; $\dfrac{23}{100}$

10. 0.03; $\dfrac{3}{100}$

11. 0.0; $\dfrac{0}{100}$

12. 0.71; $\dfrac{71}{100}$

13. 89% $\quad \dfrac{89}{100} = 89\%$

14. $\dfrac{1}{10}$ $\quad \dfrac{10}{100} = 10\%$; $\dfrac{1}{10} = 0.10$

15. 0.10

Lesson 15.2

1. 50% $\qquad 100 \div 2 = 50$; $1 \times 50 = 50$

2. 15% $\qquad 100 \div 20 = 5$; $3 \times 5 = 15$

3. 46.7%; not simple %
$$15\overline{)7.000} \quad \begin{array}{r} 0.466... \\ \underline{6\,0} \\ 100 \\ \underline{90} \\ 100 \\ \underline{90} \\ 10... \end{array}$$

4. 30% $\qquad 100 \div 10 = 10$; $10 \times 3 = 30$

5. 66.6%; not simple %
$$3\overline{)2.000} \quad \begin{array}{r} .666... \\ \underline{18} \\ 20 \\ \underline{18} \\ 20... \end{array}$$

6. 75% $\qquad 100 \div 4 = 25$; $25 \times 3 = 75$

7. 54.5%; not simple %
$$11\overline{)6.000} \quad \begin{array}{r} 0.545 \\ \underline{5\,5} \\ 50 \\ \underline{44} \\ 60 \\ \underline{55} \\ 4... \end{array}$$

8. 100% $\qquad 1 = \dfrac{1}{1}$; $100 \div 1 = 100$; $100 \times 1 = 100$

9. 3.1%; not simple %
$$32\overline{)1.0000} \quad \begin{array}{r} 0.0312... \\ \underline{96} \\ 40 \\ \underline{32} \\ 80 \\ \underline{64} \\ 16... \end{array}$$

10. 16% $\qquad 100 \div 25 = 4$; $4 \times 4 = 16$

11. 38% $\qquad 100 \div 50 = 2$; $19 \times 2 = 38$

12. 6% $\qquad 100 \div 50 = 2$; $3 \times 2 = 6$

13. 140% $\qquad 100 \div 10 = 10$; $14 \times 10 = 140$

14. 55% $\qquad 100 \div 20 = 5$; $11 \times 5 = 55$

15. 12% $\qquad 100 \div 25 = 4$; $3 \times 4 = 12$

16. 44.4%; not simple %
$$9\overline{)4.000} \quad \begin{array}{r} 0.444 \\ \underline{3\,6} \\ 40 \\ \underline{36} \\ 40 \\ \underline{36} \\ 4... \end{array}$$

Answers and Explanations

17. 35% $100 \div 20 = 5$; $7 \times 5 = 35$

18. 20000% $200 = \dfrac{200}{1}$; $100 \div 1 = 100$; $100 \times 200 = 20{,}000$

Lesson 15.3

1. 0.07 $\dfrac{7}{100} = 0.07$

2. 0.185 $\dfrac{18.5}{100} = 0.185$

3. 33%

4. 67.5%

5. 33.56%

6. 0.0001 $\dfrac{1}{100} = 0.0001$

7. 0.0234 $\dfrac{2.34}{100} = 0.0234$

8. 345%

9. 214.5%

10. 0.003 $\dfrac{.3}{100} = 0.003$

11. 0.3329 $\dfrac{33.29}{100} = 0.3329$

12. 245600%

13. 85.71% $\dfrac{6}{7} = 0.8571 = 85.71\%$

14. $15.43 $\dfrac{15.43}{100} \times \$100 = \$15.43$

Lesson 15.4

1. 20% $\dfrac{1}{2} \times 40 = 20$

2. 40% $\dfrac{2}{3} \times 60 = \dfrac{120}{3} = 40$

3. 9 $\dfrac{50}{100} \times 18 = \dfrac{1}{2} \times 18 = 9$

4. 48 $\dfrac{12}{100} \times 400 = 12 \times 4 = 48$

5. 2% $\dfrac{1}{4} \times 8 = 2$

6. 15 $\dfrac{20}{100} \times 75 = \dfrac{1}{5} \times 75 = 15$

7. 117 $\dfrac{39}{100} \times 300 = 39 \times 3 = 117$

8. 5% $\dfrac{1}{9} \times 45 = 5$

9. 30% $\dfrac{1}{3} \times 90 = 30$

10. 15 $\dfrac{25}{100} \times 60 = \dfrac{1}{4} \times 60 = 15$

11. 9% $\dfrac{1}{3} \times 27 = 9$

12. 9 $\dfrac{18}{100} \times 50 = \dfrac{18}{2} = 9$

13. 42 $\dfrac{120}{100} \times 35 = \dfrac{6}{5} \times 35 = 6 \times 7 = 42$

14. 37 $\dfrac{100}{100} \times 37 = 1 \times 37 = 37$

15. 9% $\dfrac{1}{4} \times 36 = 9$

Lesson 15.5

1. $175.00 $\dfrac{\$200}{\$50} = \dfrac{\$700}{x}$; $200x = 50 \times 700$;

$200x = 35{,}000$; $x = 175$

2. $216.00 $3000 \times 0.072 = 216$

3. $6.00 $100 \times 0.06 = 6$

4. $465.75 $450 \times 0.035 = 15.75$; $450 + 15.75 = 465.75$

5. $350.00 $5000 \times 0.07 = 350$

6. $100.00 $10{,}000 \times 0.01 = 100$

7. $4200.00 $4000 \times 0.05 = 200$; $4000 + 200 = 4200$

8. $16.50 $150 \times 0.11 = 16.50$

Lesson 15.6

1. $625.00   15 months = 1.25 years;

$10{,}000 \times 0.05 \times 1.25 = 625$

2. $588.00   18 months = 1.5 years;

$5600 \times 0.07 \times 1.5 = 588$

3. $2786.63   7 months = $\dfrac{7}{12}$ years;

$2700 \times 0.055 \times \dfrac{7}{12} = 86.625$;

$2700 + 86.63 = 2786.625$

4. $2853.82   37 months = $\dfrac{37}{12}$ years;

$6275 \times 0.1475 \times \dfrac{37}{12} = 2853.82$

5. $35,256.00 $45{,}200 \times 0.195 \times 4 = 35{,}256$

6. $417.54   23 months = $\dfrac{23}{12}$ years;

$2350 \times 0.0927 \times \dfrac{23}{12} = 417.54$

Lesson 15.7

1. $23.82 $22 \times 0.0825 = 1.815$; $22 + 1.82 = 23.82$

2. $7.50 $25 \times 0.3 = 7.5$

3. $59.07 $56.80 \times 0.04 = 2.272$; $56.80 + 2.27 = 59.07$

4. $694.40 $3240 \times 0.06 = 194.40$; $194.40 + 500 = 694.40$

5. 41% $45{,}800 - 32{,}500 = 13{,}300$;

$\dfrac{13{,}300}{32{,}500} \times 100 = \dfrac{13{,}300}{325} = 40.9 = 41\%$

6. 88% $\dfrac{53}{60} = 0.88 = 88\%$

Answers and Explanations

7. $170.00   200 × 0.15 = 30; 200 − 30 = 170

8. 16%   89 − 75 = 14; $\frac{14}{89} \times 100 = 15.73 = 16\%$

9. 60 $12 = \frac{20}{100} \times t$; $12 = \frac{1}{5}t$; $60 = t$

10. $39.49; yes   27.99 + 7.99 + 0.50 = 36.48;
36.48 × 0.0825 = 3.0096; 36.48 + 3.01 = 39.49

Lesson 16.1

1. 144   12 × 12 = 144
2. 10,000   10 × 10 × 10 × 10 = 10,000
3. 343   7 × 7 × 7 = 343
4. 8   2 × 2 × 2 = 8
5. 256   4 × 4 × 4 × 4 = 256
6. 125   5 × 5 × 5 = 125
7. 1681   41 × 41 = 1681
8. 3125   5 × 5 × 5 × 5 × 5 = 3125
9. 279,936   6 × 6 × 6 × 6 × 6 × 6 × 6 = 279,936
10. 83,521   17 × 17 × 17 × 17 = 83,521
11. 0   Zero raised to any power = 0
12. 1   Any number raised to the zero power = 1
13. 12   12 × 1 = 12
14. 1   Any number raised to the zero power = 1
15. 33   33 × 1 = 33

Lesson 16.1 (cont.)

1. 2^8 3 − (−5) = 3 + 5 = 8, so 2^8
2. $\frac{1}{5}$ 5 + (−6) = −1, so $5^{-1} = \frac{1}{5^1} = \frac{1}{5}$
3. 11^7 11 − 4 = 7, so 11^7
4. 54^6 4 − (−2) = 4 + 2 = 6, so 54^6
5. $3^2 = 9$ 2 − 0 = 2, so $3^2 = 9$
6. 8^9 1 + 8 = 9, so 8^9
7. $15^1 = 15$ 5 − 4 = 1, so $15^1 = 15$
8. 8^4 6 − 2 = 4, so 8^4
9. 18^{28} 7 + 21 = 28, so 18^{28}
10. 81^3 10 − 7 = 3, so 81^3
11. 19^{35} 19 + 16 = 35, so 19^{35}
12. $\frac{1}{21}$ 2 − 3 = −1, so $21^{-1} = \frac{1}{21^1} = \frac{1}{21}$
13. $\frac{1}{15^{11}}$ −5 − 6 = −11, so $15^{-11} = \frac{1}{15^{11}}$
14. $10^4 = 10,000$ −8 − (−12) = −8 + 12 = 4, so $10^4 = 10,000$
15. $\frac{1}{17^7}$ 15 − 22 = −7, so $17^{-7} = \frac{1}{17^7}$

Lesson 16.2

1. 6   6 × 6 = 36
2. 12   12 × 12 = 144
3. 9   9 × 9 = 81
4. 5   5 × 5 = 25
5. 13   13 × 13 = 169
6. 3   3 × 3 = 9
7. 1   1 × 1 = 1
8. 7   7 × 7 = 49
9. 2   2 × 2 = 4
10. 10   10 × 10 = 100
11. 4   4 × 4 = 16
12. 11   11 × 11 = 121
13. 8   8 × 8 = 64
14. 15   15 × 15 = 225
15. 3 and 4   3 × 3 = 9 and 4 × 4 = 16, so $\sqrt{12}$ is between 3 and 4
16. 6 and 7   6 × 6 = 36 and 7 × 7 = 49, so $\sqrt{41} \approx$ is between 6 and 7

Lesson 16.3

1. 500,000
2. 4.7823×10^2
3. 8.9786×10^4
4. 6,721,000
5. 0.029731
6. 6.91273×10^5
7. 0.0059178
8. 87,234,500,000
9. 6.664475×10^6
10. 5.123×10^{-4}
11. 8.9×10^0
12. 1.00235×10^2
13. 9.63764×10^5
14. 4.6554×10^0
15. 7.8923×10^2
16. 1.5896×10^{13}
17. 8.999345×10^9
18. 16,973.24

Lesson 17.1

1. A number divided by four.
2. A number plus three.

Answers and Explanations

3. Four times a number plus eight.

4. Nine-tenths of a number minus seven.

5. A number less three, then divided by twenty-five.

6. Eight times the sum of two times a number plus six.

7. Two times a number minus five.

8. Twelve times the result of a number minus five.

9. Seven divided by a number.

10. The sum of eleven plus a number divided by sixteen.

Lesson 17.2

1. Three times a number is less than six.

2. A number minus one is greater than five.

3. A number is less than or equal to four.

4. A number squared is greater than or equal to twenty-five.

5. A number divided by five is less than sixty-three.

6. A number plus nine is less than twelve.

7. Six hundred forty-three is less than the sum of two numbers.

8. A number plus two is less than or equal to fifteen.

9. Four times a number is greater than seventeen.

10. One minus a number is greater than or equal to negative sixty-three.

Lesson 17.3

1. $x = 11$

$$\begin{array}{r} x + 6 = 17 \\ -6 \quad -6 \\ \hline x = 11 \end{array}$$

2. $s = 8$

$$\begin{array}{r} 17 = s + 9 \\ -9 \quad -9 \\ \hline 8 = s \end{array}$$

3. $z = 35$

$$\begin{array}{r} 14 + z = 49 \\ -14 \quad\quad -14 \\ \hline z = 35 \end{array}$$

4. $f > 3$

$$\begin{array}{r} 17 - f < 14 \\ +f \quad +f \\ \hline 17 < 14 + f \\ -14 \quad -14 \\ \hline 3 < f \end{array}$$

5. $c > 22$

$$\begin{array}{r} c - 11 > 11 \\ +11 \quad +11 \\ \hline c > 22 \end{array}$$

6. $y = 2$

$$\begin{array}{r} y + 23 = 25 \\ -23 \quad -23 \\ \hline y = 2 \end{array}$$

7. $102 = x$

$$\begin{array}{r} 107 = 5 + x \\ -5 \quad -5 \\ \hline 102 = x \end{array}$$

8. $k = 28$

$$\begin{array}{r} k + 36 = 64 \\ -36 \quad -36 \\ \hline k = 28 \end{array}$$

9. $u \le 28$

$$\begin{array}{r} 15 + u \le 43 \\ -15 \quad\quad -15 \\ \hline u \le 28 \end{array}$$

10. $37 = t$

$$\begin{array}{r} 59 - t = 22 \\ +t \quad +t \\ \hline 59 = 22 + t \\ -22 \quad -22 \\ \hline 37 = t \end{array}$$

11. $6 = a$

$$\begin{array}{r} 9 - a = 3 \\ +a \quad +a \\ \hline 9 = 3 + a \\ -3 \quad -3 \\ \hline 6 = a \end{array}$$

12. $b > 26$

$$\begin{array}{r} 75 + b > 101 \\ -75 \quad\quad -75 \\ \hline b > 26 \end{array}$$

13. $25 = e$

$$\begin{array}{r} 49 - e = 24 \\ +e \quad +e \\ \hline 49 = 24 + e \\ -24 \quad -24 \\ \hline 25 = e \end{array}$$

14. $d \ge 23$

$$\begin{array}{r} 16 + d \ge 39 \\ -16 \quad\quad -16 \\ \hline d \ge 23 \end{array}$$

15. $w \le 66$

$$\begin{array}{r} w + 15 \le 81 \\ -15 \quad -15 \\ \hline w \le 66 \end{array}$$

16. $q = 58$

$$\begin{array}{r} q - 23 = 35 \\ +23 \quad +23 \\ \hline q = 58 \end{array}$$

Lesson 17.4

1. $y = 5$

$$\begin{array}{r} 2y + 15 = 25 \\ -15 \quad -15 \\ \hline \dfrac{2y}{2} = \dfrac{10}{2} \\ y = 5 \end{array}$$

2. $p < 13$

$$\begin{array}{r} 5 + 5p < 70 \\ -5 \quad\quad -5 \\ \hline \dfrac{5p}{5} < \dfrac{65}{5} \\ p < 13 \end{array}$$

3. $c > 27$

$$\begin{array}{r} 8c + 8 > 224 \\ -8 \quad -8 \\ \hline \dfrac{8c}{8} > \dfrac{216}{8} \\ c > 27 \end{array}$$

4. $w = 84$

$$17 + \dfrac{w}{3} = 45$$
$$-17 \quad\quad\quad -17$$
$$(3)\dfrac{w}{3} = 28(3)$$
$$w = 84$$

Answers and Explanations

5. $6 = q$

$$34 = 10 + 4q$$
$$\underline{-10 \quad -10}$$
$$\frac{24}{4} = \frac{4q}{4}$$
$$6 = q$$

6. $175 = z$

$$42 = 7 + \frac{z}{5}$$
$$\underline{-7 \quad -7}$$
$$(5)35 = \frac{z}{5}(5)$$
$$175 = z$$

7. $x \geq 28$

$$232 \leq 8 + 8x$$
$$\underline{-8 \quad -8}$$
$$\frac{224}{8} \leq \frac{8x}{8}$$
$$28 \leq x$$

8. $15 = g$

$$63 = 3 + 4g$$
$$\underline{-3 \quad -3}$$
$$\frac{60}{4} = \frac{4g}{4}$$
$$15 = g$$

9. $108 = g$

$$12 = \frac{g}{9}$$
$$(9)12 = \frac{g}{9}(9)$$
$$108 = g$$

10. $k > 17$

$$3k + 5 > 56$$
$$\underline{-5 \quad -5}$$
$$\frac{3k}{3} > \frac{51}{3}$$
$$k > 17$$

11. $p \leq 195$

$$49 \geq 10 + \frac{p}{5}$$
$$\underline{-10 \quad -10}$$
$$(5)39 \geq \frac{p}{5}(5)$$
$$195 \geq p$$

12. $y = 34.5$

$$2y + 5 = 74$$
$$\underline{-5 \quad -5}$$
$$\frac{2y}{2} = \frac{69}{2}$$
$$y = 34.5$$

13. $d = 10$

$$8d + 130 = 210$$
$$\underline{-130 \quad -130}$$
$$\frac{8d}{8} = \frac{80}{8}$$
$$d = 10$$

14. $c \leq 99$

$$33 + \frac{1}{3}c \leq 66$$
$$\underline{-33 \qquad -33}$$
$$(3)\frac{1}{3}c \leq 33(3)$$
$$c \leq 99$$

Lesson 18.1

1. 4.17 yd $\qquad$ $12.5 \text{ ft} \div 3\frac{\text{ft}}{\text{yd}} = 4.17$ yd

2. 5280 ft $\qquad$ 1 mile = 5280 ft

3. 4 yd $\qquad$ $144 \text{ in.} \div 12\frac{\text{in.}}{\text{ft}} = 12 \text{ ft}; 12 \text{ ft} \div 3\frac{\text{ft}}{\text{yd}} = 4$ yd

4. 5280 yd $\qquad$ 1 mile = 1760 yd; $1760 \times 3 = 5280$ miles

5. 10.67 ft $\qquad$ $128 \text{ in.} \div 12\frac{\text{in.}}{\text{ft}} = 10.67$ ft

6. 6 miles $\qquad$ $10{,}560 \text{ yd} \div 1760\frac{\text{yd}}{\text{mile}} = 6$ miles

7. 46.5 ft $\qquad$ $15.5 \text{ yd} \times 3\frac{\text{ft}}{\text{yd}} = 46.5$ ft

8. 205,920 in. $\qquad$ 1 mile = 5280 ft; $5280 \text{ ft} \times 12\frac{\text{in}}{\text{ft}}$
$= 63{,}360 \text{ in.}; 63{,}360 \times 3.25 = 205{,}920$ in.

Lesson 18.2

1. 32 pints $\qquad$ $4 \text{ gal} \times 4\frac{\text{qt}}{\text{gal}} = 16 \text{ qt} \times 2\frac{\text{pt}}{\text{qt}} = 32$ pt

2. 132 quarts $\qquad$ $33 \text{ gal} \times 4\frac{\text{qt}}{\text{gal}} = 132$ qt

3. 16 gallons $\qquad$ $64 \text{ qt} \div 4\frac{\text{qt}}{\text{gal}} = 16$ gal

4. $4\frac{1}{2}$ gallons $\qquad$ $36 \text{ pt} \div 2\frac{\text{pt}}{\text{qt}} = 18 \text{ qt} \div 4\frac{\text{qt}}{\text{gal}} = 4.5$ gal

5. 500 quarts $\qquad$ $2{,}000 \text{ c} \div 2\frac{\text{cup}}{\text{pt}} = 1{,}000 \text{ pt} \div 2\frac{\text{pt}}{\text{qt}} = 500$ qt

6. 600 cups $\qquad$ $300 \text{ pt} \times 2\frac{\text{c}}{\text{pt}} = 600$ cups

7. 512 pints $\qquad$ $64 \text{ gal} \times 4\frac{\text{qt}}{\text{gal}} = 256 \text{ qt} \times 2\frac{\text{pt}}{\text{qt}} = 512$ pt

8. 168 cups $\qquad$ $42 \text{ qt} \times 2\frac{\text{pt}}{\text{qt}} = 84 \text{ pt} \times 2\frac{\text{c}}{\text{pt}} = 168$ c

Lesson 18.3

1. 320 oz $\qquad$ $20 \text{ lbs} \times 16\frac{\text{oz}}{\text{lb}} = 320$ oz

2. 10,400 lb $\qquad$ $5.2 \text{ tons} \times 2000\frac{\text{lbs}}{\text{ton}} = 10{,}400$ lbs

3. 128,000 oz $\qquad$ $4 \text{ tons} \times 2000\frac{\text{lbs}}{\text{ton}} = 8000 \text{ lbs} \times 16\frac{\text{oz}}{\text{lb}}$
$= 128{,}000$ oz

4. $12\frac{1}{4}$ lb $\qquad$ $196 \text{ oz} \div 16\frac{\text{oz}}{\text{lb}} = 12.25$ lb

5. 0.3 tons $\qquad$ $3 \times 200 = 600$ lbs;
$600 \text{ lbs} \div 2000\frac{\text{lbs}}{\text{ton}} = 0.3$ tons

6. 27,000 lb $\qquad$ $13.5 \text{ tons} \times 2000\frac{\text{lbs}}{\text{ton}} = 27{,}000$ lbs

7. 3500 lb $\qquad$ $1.75 \text{ tons} \times 2000\frac{\text{lbs}}{\text{ton}} = 3500$ lbs

8. 196.9 lb $\qquad$ $1050 \times 3 = 3150 \text{ oz}; 3150 \text{ oz} \div 16\frac{\text{oz}}{\text{lb}}$
$= 196.875$ lb

Answers and Explanations

Lesson 18.4

1. The hexagon has a perimeter of 108 ft. $26 \times 3 = 78; 18 \times 6 = 108$

2. 30 feet south to get back; $25 + 30 + 25 + 30 = 110$

3. 30 ft $120 \div 4 = 30$

4. 30 inches $5 + 10 + 5 + 10 = 30$

5. 72 ft $20 + 15 + 22 + 15 = 72$

Lesson 18.5

1. 6667 people $1000 \times 200 = 200,000;$ $200,000 \div 30 = 6666.66$

2. 312.5 sq ft $25 \times 25 = 625;$ $625 \div 2 = 312.5$

3. 84 sq ft $A = \frac{1}{2}bh; A = \frac{1}{2}(24)(7)$ $= (12)(7) = 84$

4. The square has an area of 196 sq ft, the triangle has an area of 187.5 sq ft

   $A\triangle = \frac{1}{2}bh;$

   $A = \frac{1}{2}(15)(25)$

   $= \frac{1}{2}(375) = 187.5;$

   $A\square = s^2 = 14^2 = 196$

Lesson 18.6

1. 1000 cu in. $10 \times 10 \times 10$ $= 1000 \text{ cu in.}$

2. $\frac{1}{3}$ cu ft $12 \text{ in.} = 1 \text{ ft}; 8 \text{ in.}$

   $= \frac{2}{3} \text{ ft}; 6 \text{ in.}$

   $= \frac{1}{2} \text{ ft}; V = 1 \times \frac{2}{3} \times \frac{1}{2}$

   $= \frac{2}{6} = \frac{1}{3} \text{ cu ft}$

3. 585 cu ft $9 \times 5 \times 13 = 585 \text{ cu ft}$

4. 37 cu yd $120 \text{ in.} = 10 \text{ ft} = \frac{10}{3} \text{ yd};$

   $\left(\frac{10}{3}\right)^3 = \frac{1000}{27} = 37.037$ $= 37 \text{ cu yd}$

5. 2880 cu in. $12 \times 30 \times 16 = 5760;$ $5760 \div 2 = 2880 \text{ cu in.}$

6. 7560 cu yd $420 \text{ ft} = 140 \text{ yd};$ $162 \text{ ft} = 54 \text{ yd} =;$ $3 \text{ ft} = 1 \text{ yd};$ $140 \times 54 \times 3$ $= 7560 \text{ cu yd}$

Lesson 18.7

1. 129,600 seconds $36 \text{ hrs} \times 60 \frac{\text{min}}{\text{hr}} \times 60 \frac{\text{sec}}{\text{min}}$ $= 129,600 \text{ sec}$

2. 600 hours $25 \text{ days} \times 24 \frac{\text{hr}}{\text{day}} = 600 \text{ hrs}$

3. 50,400 minutes $35 \text{ days} \times 24 \frac{\text{hr}}{\text{day}} \times 60 \frac{\text{min}}{\text{hr}}$ $= 50,400 \text{ min}$

4. 4 days $96 \text{ hrs} \div 24 \frac{\text{hr}}{\text{day}} = 4 \text{ days}$

5. 46,080 minutes $32 \text{ days} \times 24 \frac{\text{hr}}{\text{day}} \times 60 \frac{\text{min}}{\text{hr}}$ $= 46,080 \text{ min}$

6. 2.08 hours $125 \text{ min} \div 60 \frac{\text{min}}{\text{hr}} = 2.08 \text{ hrs}$

7. $\frac{\$27.34}{\text{hour}}$ $3.2 \text{ days} \times 8 \frac{\text{hr}}{\text{day}} = 25.6 \text{ hr};$ $\$700 \div 25.6 = \$27.34 \text{ per hour}$

8. 259,200 widgets $\frac{8 \text{ widgets}}{1 \text{ sec}} \times 60 \frac{\text{sec}}{\text{min}}$

   $\times 60 \frac{\text{min}}{\text{hr}} \times 9 \text{ hrs}$

   $= 259,200 \text{ widgets}$

9. 3 1 century = 100 years.

10. $720.00 $5400 \text{ min} \div 60 \frac{\text{min}}{\text{hr}}$ $= 90 \text{ hrs}; 90 \times \$8$ $= \$720$

Lesson 19.1

1. 3.35 m $335 \text{ cm} \div 100 \frac{\text{cm}}{\text{m}}$ $= 3.35 \text{ m}$

2. 6.235 m $6235 \text{ mm} \div 10 \frac{\text{mm}}{\text{cm}}$

   $\div 100 \frac{\text{cm}}{\text{m}} = 6.235 \text{ m}$

3. 576,100 cm $5.761 \text{ km} \times 1000 \frac{\text{m}}{\text{km}} \times 100 \frac{\text{cm}}{\text{m}}$ $= 576,100 \text{ cm}$

4. 725,020,000 mm $725.02 \text{ km} \times 1000 \frac{\text{m}}{\text{km}} \times 100 \frac{\text{cm}}{\text{m}}$

   $\times 10 \frac{\text{mm}}{\text{cm}} = 725,020,000 \text{ mm}$

5. 3.9 m $550 \text{ mm} \div 10 \frac{\text{mm}}{\text{cm}} = 55 \text{ cm};$ $335 + 55 = 390 \text{ cm}; 390 \text{ cm}$

   $\div 100 \frac{\text{cm}}{\text{m}} = 3.9 \text{ m}$

Answers and Explanations

6. 261,100 cm

$2.611 \text{ km} \times 1000\frac{\text{m}}{\text{km}} \times 100\frac{\text{cm}}{\text{m}}$
$= 261{,}100$

7. 0.132 m

$12 \text{ mm} \div 10\frac{\text{mm}}{\text{cm}} = 1.2 \text{ cm};$
$12 + 1.2 = 13.2 \text{ cm};$
$13.2 \text{ cm} \div 100\frac{\text{cm}}{\text{m}} = 0.132 \text{ m}$

8. 6872 mm

$6.872 \text{ m} \times 100\frac{\text{cm}}{\text{m}} \times 10\frac{\text{mm}}{\text{cm}}$
$= 6872 \text{ mm}$

Lesson 19.2

1. 2100 mL

$2.11 \text{ L} \times 1000\frac{\text{mL}}{\text{L}} = 2100 \text{ mL}$

2. 1.7 kL

$1700 \text{ L} \div 1000\frac{\text{L}}{\text{kL}} = 1.7 \text{ kL}$

3. 3456 mL

$3.456 \text{ L} \times 1000\frac{\text{mL}}{\text{L}} = 3456 \text{ mL}$

4. 350,000 mL

$350 \text{ L} \times 1000\frac{\text{mL}}{\text{L}} = 350{,}000 \text{ mL}$

5. $26\frac{2}{3}$ bottles

$20 \div \frac{3}{4} = 20 \times \frac{4}{3} = \frac{80}{3} = 26\frac{2}{3}$

6. 2,000,000 kL

$200{,}000{,}000{,}000 \text{ cL} \div 100\frac{\text{cL}}{\text{L}}$
$\div 1000\frac{\text{L}}{\text{kL}} = 2{,}000{,}000 \text{ kL}$

7. 375 L

$1500 \text{ cL} \times 25 = 37{,}500 \text{ cL};$
$37{,}500 \text{ cL} \div 100\frac{\text{cL}}{\text{L}} = 375 \text{ L}$

8. 240 cups

$60 \text{ L} \times 1000\frac{\text{ml}}{\text{L}} = 60{,}000;$
$60{,}000 \div 250 = 240 \text{ cups}$

Lesson 19.3

1. 353.654 g

$346 \text{ mg} \div 1000\frac{\text{mg}}{\text{g}} = 0.346 \text{ g};$
$354 - 0.346 = 353.654 \text{ g}$

2. 4.3033 kg

$4{,}300 \text{ g} \div 1000\frac{\text{g}}{\text{kg}}$
$= 4.3 \text{ kg}; \ 3{,}300 \text{ mg} \div 1000\frac{\text{mg}}{\text{g}}$
$\div 1000\frac{\text{g}}{\text{kg}} = 0.0033 \text{ kg};$
$4.3 + 0.0033 = 4.3033 \text{ kg}$

3. 5297.57 g

$2430 \text{ mg} \div 1000\frac{\text{mg}}{\text{g}} = 2.43 \text{ g};$
$5300 - 2.43 = 5{,}297.57 \text{ g}$

4. 14,000 g

$12.34 + 1.66 = 14 \text{ kg}; \ 14 \text{ kg}$
$\times 1000\frac{\text{g}}{\text{kg}} = 14{,}000 \text{ g}$

5. 5.004002 kg

$2 \text{ mg} \div 10\frac{\text{mg}}{\text{cg}} \div 100\frac{\text{cg}}{\text{g}}$
$\div 1000\frac{\text{g}}{\text{kg}} = 0.000002 \text{ kg}; \ 4 \text{ g}$
$\div 1000\frac{\text{g}}{\text{kg}} = 0.004 \text{ kg};$
$0.000002 + 0.004 + 5$
$= 5.004002 \text{ kg}$

6. 300,303,000 mg

$300 \text{ kg} \times 1000\frac{\text{g}}{\text{kg}} \times 100\frac{\text{cg}}{\text{g}}$
$\times 10\frac{\text{mg}}{\text{cg}} = 300{,}000{,}000 \text{ mg};$
$300 \text{ g} \times 100\frac{\text{cg}}{\text{g}} \times 10\frac{\text{mg}}{\text{cg}}$
$= 300{,}000 \text{ mg}; \ 300 \text{ cg}$
$\times 10\frac{\text{mg}}{\text{cg}} = 3000 \text{ mg};$
$300{,}000{,}000 + 300{,}000$
$+3000 = 300{,}303{,}000 \text{ mg}$

7. 14225.8 cg

$142 \text{ g} \times 100\frac{\text{cg}}{\text{g}} = 14{,}200 \text{ cg};$
$258 \text{ mg} \div 10\frac{\text{mg}}{\text{cg}} = 25.8 \text{ cg};$
$14{,}200 + 25.8 = 14{,}225.8 \text{ cg}$

8. 6.565 kg

$65 + 6500 = 6565 \text{ g};$
$6565 \text{ g} \div 1000\frac{\text{g}}{\text{kg}} = 6.565 \text{ kg}$

Lesson 19.4

1. Perimeter: 28 cm
Area: 49 sq cm

$7 + 7 + 7 + 7 = 28 \text{ cm};$
$7 \times 7 = 49 \text{ sq cm}$

2. 8 mm

$48 \div 6 = 8 \text{ mm}$

3. 216 cu cm, 216 sq cm

$6 \times 6 \times 6 = 216 \text{ cu cm};$
$SA = 6s^2 = (6)(6^2)$
$= (6)(36) = 216 \text{ sq cm}$

Answers and Explanations

4. Perimeter 20.8 cm; 19.2 sq cm

$P = 2.4 + 2.4 + 8 + 8 = 20.8$ cm; $A = 2.4 \times 8 = 19.2$ sq cm

5. Perimeter: 40 m Area: 84 sq cm

$P = 14 + 14 + 6 + 6 = 40$ m; $A = 14 \times 6 = 84$ sq m

6. 2500 m

$P = (5)500 = 2500$ m

7. $88.80; perimeter 11.4 meters

$A = 3.7 \times 2 = 7.4$ sq m; $12.00 \times 7.4 = \$88.8$; $P = 3.7 + 3.7 + 2 + 2 = 11.4$ m

8. 900 cu cm

$18 \times 10 \times 5 = 900$ cu cm

9. 35 sq m

$A = \frac{1}{2}bh$; $A = \frac{1}{2}(14)(5) = (7)(5) = 35$ sq m

10. 240 cu m

$12 \times 8 \times 2.5 = 240$ cu m

11. 96 sq m

$A = \frac{1}{2}bh$; $A = \frac{1}{2}(12)(16) = (6)(16) = 96$ sq m

12. 192 sq mm

$A = 12 \times 16 = 192$ sq mm

Lesson 19.5

1. 392° F

$200 \times \frac{9}{5} + 32 = 40 \times 9 + 32 = 360 + 32 = 392$ °F

2. 55.6° C

$(132 - 32) \times \frac{5}{9} = 100 \times \frac{5}{9} = \frac{500}{9} = 55.6$ °C

3. 27.2° C

$(81 - 32) \times \frac{5}{9} = 49 \times \frac{5}{9} = \frac{245}{9} = 27.2$ °C

4. 89.6° F

$32 \times \frac{9}{5} + 32 = 57.6 + 32 = 89.6$ °F

5. 101.1° C

$(214 - 32) \times \frac{5}{9} = 182 \times \frac{5}{9} = \frac{910}{9} = 101.1$ °C

6. 160° C

$(320 - 32) \times \frac{5}{9} = 288 \times \frac{5}{9} = 32 \times 5 = 160$ °C

7. −12.2° C

$(10 - 32) \times \frac{5}{9} = -22 \times \frac{5}{9} = \frac{-110}{9} = -12.2$ °C

8. 113° F

$45 \times \frac{9}{5} + 32 = 9 \times 9 + 32 = 81 + 32 = 113$ °F

9. 23.9° C

$(75 - 32) \times \frac{5}{9} = 43 \times \frac{5}{9} = \frac{215}{9} = 23.9$ °C

10. 194° F

$90 \times \frac{9}{5} + 32 = 18 \times 9 + 32 = 162 + 32 = 194$ °F

11. −26.1° C

$(-15 - 32) \times \frac{5}{9} = -47 \times \frac{5}{9} = \frac{-235}{9} = -26.1$ °C

12. 54.4° C

$(130 - 32) \times \frac{5}{9} = 98 \times \frac{5}{9} = \frac{490}{9} = 54.4$ °C

13. 98.6° F

$37 \times \frac{9}{5} + 32 = 66.6 + 32 = 98.6$ °F

14. 3632° F

$2000 \times \frac{9}{5} + 32 = 400 \times 9 + 32 = 3600 + 32 = 3632$ °F

15. 471.2° F

$244 \times \frac{9}{5} + 32 = 439.2 + 32 = 471.2$ °F

16. 102.2° F

$39 \times \frac{9}{5} + 32 = 70.2 + 32 = 102.2$ °F

17. 176.7° C

$(350 - 32) \times \frac{5}{9} = 318 \times \frac{5}{9} = \frac{1590}{9} = 176.7$ °C

Lesson 20.1

1. 7264 kg

$16,000 \times 0.454 = 7264$ kg

2. 1362 g

$3 \times 454 = 1,362$ g

3. 1814.36 kg

$2 \times 907.18 = 1,814.36$ kg

4. 87.055 L

$23 \times 3.785 = 87.055$ L

5. 0.711 L

$24oz = 3$ cups; $3 \times 0.237 = 0.711$ L

6. Yes. The rope is 45.75 m long

$150 \times 0.305 = 45.75$ m

7. 1.362 kg

$3 \times 0.454 = 1.362$ kg

8. 2.4 pounds of gold 1000 g = 1 kg; 2.4 × 0.454 = 1.0896 kg

9. 30.5 m 100 × 0.305 = 30.5 m

10. 2.9 m 9.5 × 0.305 = 2.8975 = 2.9 m

Lesson 20.2

1. 20.8 gallons 1.75 × 1.056 = 1.848 qt ÷ 4 = 0.462 gal × 45 people = 20.8 gal

2. 27.8 lb 0.15 × 12 = 1.8 kg; 1.8 × 2.205 = 3.969 lbs × 7 days = 27.8 lbs

3. 388.1 oz 11 × 2.205 = 24.3 lbs × 16 oz = 388.1 oz

4. 9.84 ft 3 ÷ 0.305 = 9.8 ft

5. 49.2 ft 15 ÷ 0.305 = 49.2 ft

6. 48.5 lb 22 × 2.205 = 48.5 lbs

7. 164.04 ft 50 m × 39.37 in = 1968.5 in; 1968.5 in ÷ 12 in = 164.04 ft

8. 2,961,000,000 gallons 11,250,000 × 263.2 = 2,961,000,000 gal

9. 3.726 miles 6 × 0.621 = 3.726 m

10. 2608.2 miles per hour 4200 × 0.621 = 2608.2 m/h

11. 118.2 inches; 9.9 ft 300 × 0.394 = 118.2 in; 118.2 ÷ 12 = 9.85 ft

12. Offensive linemen defensive linemen: 110 × 2.205 = 242.55 lbs, so offensive linemen weigh less

Lesson 21.1

1. Soft Boiled

2. Birds and Hamsters

3. Word Meaning

4. Juan

5. 0–3 Years

6. A and D

7. About 45% of the students improved their performances

8. It is getting warmer from 2000–2003

Lesson 21.2

1. Yes, there seems to be a steady increase in visitors with no seasonal ups and downs

2. Northern Hemisphere

3. Month 2 and Month 9

4. No

5. 1800–1810

6. 60 million

7. Good. It got warm by day 6.

8. 46

Lesson 21.3

1. The higher the sales, the higher the profits.

2. Yes. There is an increase in salary with a corresponding decrease in happiness, and a decrease in salary with a corresponding increase in happiness.

3. Males and Females are both living longer.

4. Expenditures are going up. Police are going up faster than the other two areas.

Lesson 21.4

1. No. Non-instruction is only 4% of the total.

2. No. He is more likely to pick blue, green, or red.

3. The manager would need the most employees in January and the fewest in February.

4. Romance and Comedy, or Romance and Sci-fi will equal 50% of the total.

5. 75%. Subtract the percentages that we know from 100%.

6. No. Cutting tools only account for 3% of the total.

7. 91%

8. No. The largest category is Apple at 36%, which is not more than 50%.

Lesson 22.1

1. 2.7 $\frac{3.2 + 2.5 + 2.1 + 3.7 + 2.8 + 2.0}{6}$ $= \frac{16.3}{6} = 2.72$

2. 5 {2, 4, 5, 5, 6, 7, 8} The middle number is 5.

3. 65 43 − (−22) = 43 + 22 = 65

4. 3 The number 3 appears three times.

5. 5 The number 5 appears twice.

6. 9 2 − (−7) = 2 + 7 = 9

Answers and Explanations

7. 15.3

$$\frac{10 + 11 + (-9) + 14 + 22 + 61 + (-2)}{7}$$

$$= \frac{107}{7} = 15.29$$

8. 12   {4, 5, 7, 9, 12, 19, 21, 22, 23}
The middle number is 12.

9. 23.5

$$\frac{-22 - 21 + 44 + 37 + 100 + 2.75}{6}$$

$$= \frac{140.75}{6} = 23.46$$

10. 12 and 13   The numbers 12 and 13 each appear three times.

Lesson 22.2

1. 80   96 − 16 = 80

2. 10, 17, 19, 21, 21, 23, 24, 26, 27, 28, 30, 31, 33, 35, 36, 37, 37, 40, 41, 41, 41, 42, 69

3. 80, 85, 71, 75, 76, 51, 56, 58, 40, 46

4. 45   67 − 22 = 45

Lesson 22.3

1. Botany, Zoology

2. Zoology

3. Range = 40;
Median = 35

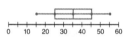

4. Lower quartile 15–25; Upper quartile 45–55

Lesson 22.4

1. 4; Red and Green −2

2.

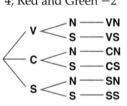

Lesson 22.5

1. Numbers that are even and divisible by *b*.

2.

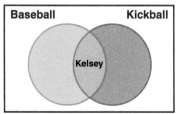

Lesson 22.6

1. All the voters in the United States; people who voted at certain voting sites

2. C   A random sample is best, and C is the most random of the three.

3. A   A random sample is best, and A is the most random of the three.

4. A   A random sample is best, and A is the most random of the three (C may seem random, but people who show up early may not be representative of the whole student body).

5. B   A is not valid because 39 trout and 42 perch are almost the same. C is not valid, because it is an extreme statement (there might be only a few of some other fish and they were not caught at that time).

Lesson 22.7

1. 4.6 $\frac{4 + 6 + 5 + 4 + 4}{5} = \frac{23}{5} = 4.6$

2. 4 $\frac{3 + 7 + 2 + 6 + 2}{5} = \frac{20}{5} = 4$

3. 0.72   4.6 − 4 = 0.6, 6 − 4.6 = 1.4,
5 − 4.6 = 0.4, 4.6 − 4 = 0.6,
4.6 − 4 = 0.6; $\frac{0.6 + 1.4 + 0.4 + 0.6 + 0.6}{5}$

$$= \frac{3.6}{5} = 0.72$$

4. 2   4 − 3 = 1, 7 − 4 = 3, 4 − 2 = 2,
6 − 4 = 2, 4 − 2 = 2;
$\frac{1 + 3 + 2 + 2 + 2}{5} = \frac{10}{5} = 2$

5. 2.78   2 ÷ 0.72 = 2.78

Lesson 23.1

1. $\frac{1}{3}$ There are 4 girls out of 12 students, so $\frac{4}{12} = \frac{1}{3}$

2. $\frac{1}{13}$ There are 4 kings out of 52 cards, so $\frac{4}{52} = \frac{1}{13}$

3. $\frac{1}{2}$ There are 2 cheese pizzas out of 4 pizzas, so $\frac{2}{4} = \frac{1}{2}$

4. $\frac{1}{5}$ George is 1 of 5 white horses, so $\frac{1}{5}$

5. $\frac{3}{14}$ There are 3 dimes out of 14 coins, so $\frac{3}{14}$

6. $\frac{9}{35}$ There are 9 prizes and 35 people, so $\frac{9}{35}$

Answers and Explanations

Lesson 23.2

1.

Outcome	Number	Probability
Win	$\frac{23}{90}$	0.26
Lose	$\frac{14}{90}$	0.16
Draw	$\frac{53}{90}$	0.59

2. 0.59   If she plays one more game, the probability of a draw will be approximately the same.

3.

Outcome	Number	Probability
Win	$\frac{30}{97}$	0.31
Lose	$\frac{14}{97}$	0.14
Draw	$\frac{53}{97}$	0.55

4. 0.55

5. Two times   30 is about twice as much as 14.

Lesson 23.3

1. $\frac{1}{36}$ The probability of each is 1 out of 6,

so $\frac{1}{6} \times \frac{1}{6} = \frac{1}{36}$.

2. $\frac{2}{45}$ There are 5 dimes out of 30 coins,

so $\frac{5}{30} = \frac{1}{6}$; there are 8 pennies out of 30 coins,

so $\frac{8}{30} = \frac{4}{15}$. The probability of both occurring

is $\frac{1}{6} \times \frac{4}{15} = \frac{2}{3 \times 15} = \frac{2}{45}$.

3. $\frac{1}{870}$ $\frac{1}{30}$ for the first, and $\frac{1}{29}$ for the second.

The probability of both occurring

is $\frac{1}{30} \times \frac{1}{29} = \frac{1}{870}$.

4. $\frac{2}{57}$ $\frac{4}{19}$ for the first, and $\frac{3}{18} = \frac{1}{6}$ for the second.

The probability of both occurring

is $\frac{4}{19} \times \frac{1}{6} = \frac{4}{114} = \frac{2}{57}$.

5. $\frac{5}{39}$ $\frac{10}{27}$ for the first, and $\frac{9}{26}$ for the second.

The probability of both occurring

is $\frac{10}{27} \times \frac{9}{26} = \frac{10}{3 \times 26} = \frac{10}{78} = \frac{5}{39}$.

6. Answers will vary. She could use black squares of paper to represent the number of boys and white squares of paper to represent the number of girls. She could draw a tree diagram to represent possible outcomes.

Lesson 24.1

1. A, B, C, D

2. 8 points

3. No. A line must stretch infinitely in both directions

4. $\overleftrightarrow{ZX}$, $\overleftrightarrow{XZ}$, $\overleftrightarrow{ZY}$, $\overleftrightarrow{YZ}$, $\overleftrightarrow{YX}$, $\overleftrightarrow{XY}$

Lesson 24.2

1. 30 line segments

2. $\overrightarrow{BA}$

3. $\overline{BO}$, $\overline{OD}$, $\overline{BD}$, $\overline{AB}$, $\overline{AO}$, $\overline{OC}$, $\overline{CB}$, $\overline{BC}$, $\overline{OB}$, $\overline{DO}$, $\overline{DB}$, $\overline{BA}$, $\overline{OA}$, $\overline{CO}$

4. Ray 33–15, Ray 24–8, Ray 8–24, Ray 15–33

Lesson 25.1

1. Acute

2. Obtuse

3. Right

4. Acute

5. Obtuse

6. Acute

7. Right

8. Obtuse

9. Obtuse

10. Acute

11. Acute

12. Obtuse

Lesson 25.2

1. 50° $40° + \angle Q = 90°$, $\angle Q = 90° - 40° = 50°$

2. 103° $77° + \angle Z = 180°$, $\angle Z = 180° - 77° = 103°$

3. Angle T & angle V, angle T & angle S, angle S & angle X, angle X & angle V

Answers and Explanations

4. F = 120°, $\angle E = \angle G = 60°$;
     E = 60°, $\angle G + \angle H = 180°$,
     H = 120° $180° - 60° = 120°$;
                $\angle H = \angle F = 120°$

Lesson 25.2 (cont.)

1. Complementary: $\angle$ BGC and $\angle$ BGA, $\angle$ FGE and $\angle$ DGE

Supplementary: $\angle$ BCG and $\angle$ BGF, $\angle$ AGC and $\angle$ AGF, $\angle$ BGA and $\angle$ AGE

Vertical: $\angle$ BGC and $\angle$ FGE, $\angle$ DGC and $\angle$ AGF, $\angle$ AGB and $\angle$ DGE

2. Complementary: $\angle$ DFE and $\angle$ CFD, $\angle$ CFB and $\angle$ AFB

Supplementary: $\angle$ AFB and $\angle$ EFB, $\angle$ AFC and $\angle$ CFE, $\angle$ DFE and $\angle$ DFA

3. Yes, they form a right angle.

4. COD = 50°
COF = 90°
FOY = 40°
YOX = 50°
FOX = 90°

Lesson 26.1

1. Acute
2. Obtuse
3. Right
4. Right
5. Acute
6. Obtuse
7. Isosceles
8. Equilateral
9. Scalene

Lesson 26.2

1. Square
2. Kite
3. Rectangle
4. Rhombus
5. Kite
6. Rhombus
7. Trapezoid
8. Rectangle
9. Square

Lesson 26.3

1. Hepatagon
2. Octagon
3. Pentagon
4. Hexagon
5. Hexagon
6. Octagon
7. Heptagon
8. Pentagon
9. Yes. Sides and angle measures are the same
10. No. The bases are of different lengths

Lesson 26.4

1. 5   5 − 0 = 5
2. 5 cm   10 ÷ 2÷ = 5
3. $\overline{AX}$, $\overline{XB}$ radii, $\overline{AB}$ chord
4. $\overline{VY}$ radius, $\overline{WX}$ chord
5. $\overline{WX}$, $\overline{XY}$, $\overline{YZ}$, $\overline{ZV}$, $\overline{VW}$
6. No. $\overline{CD}$ does not go through center point O
7. $\overline{EA}$, $\overline{AE}$, $\overline{EC}$, $\overline{BE}$, $\overline{EB}$, $\overline{CE}$
8. $\overline{AB}$, $\overline{CD}$
9. $\overline{AQ}$ chord; $\overline{RA}$ diameter
10. 100π sq in. $A = \pi r^2 = \pi(10^2) = 100\pi$
11. Circumference 10π sq units; Area = 25π sq units $C = \pi d = 10\pi$; $A = \pi r^2 = \pi(5^2) = 25\pi$
12. Circumference 14π sq units; Area = 49π sq units $C = \pi d = 14\pi$; $A = \pi r^2 = \pi(7^2) = 49\pi$

Lesson 26.5

1. SA = 54 sq in. $2(3 \times 3) + 2(3 \times 3) + 2(3 \times 3) = 2(9) + 2(9) + 2(9) = 18 + 18 + 18 = 54$. For a square, each face has the same area, so you can also say: $SA = 6(3 \times 3) = 6(9) = 54$.

2. SA = 104 sq m $2(2 \times 6) + 2(6 \times 5) + 2(2 \times 5) = 2(12) + 2(30) + 2(10) = 24 + 60 + 20 = 104$.

3. SA = 450.33 sq in. $2(8.85 \times 7.25) + 2(8.85 \times 10) + 2(7.25 \times 10) = 2(64.2) + 2(88.5) + 2(72.5) = 128.4 + 177 + 145 = 450.33$.

Answers and Explanations

4. SA = 125.46 sq ft

$2(9.9 \times 4.2) + 2(9.9 \times 1.5)$
$+ 2(1.5 \times 4.2) = 2(41.58)$
$+ 2(14.85) + 2(6.3) = 83.16$
$+ 29.7 + 12.6 = 125.46.$

5. SA = 856 sq cm

$2(14 \times 12) + 2(14 \times 10)$
$+ 2(10 \times 12) = 2(168)$
$+ 2(140) + 2(120) = 336$
$+ 280 + 240 = 856.$

6. SA = 862 sq m

$2(13 \times 12) + 2(13 \times 11)$
$+ 2(11 \times 12) = 2(156)$
$+ 2(143) + 2(132) = 312$
$+ 286 + 264 = 862.$

7. SA = 478 sq m

$2(11 \times 9) + 2(11 \times 7)$
$+ 2(9 \times 7) = 2(99)$
$+ 2(77) + 2(63) = 198$
$+ 154 + 126 = 478.$

8. SA = 114 sq in.

$2(3 \times 8) + 2(3 \times 3)$
$+ 2(3 \times 8) = 2(24)$
$+ 2(9) + 2(24) = 48$
$+ 18 + 48 = 114.$

9. SA = 370 sq ft

$2(2 \times 5) + 2(2 \times 25)$
$+ 2(5 \times 25) = 2(10)$
$+ 2(50) + 2(125) = 20$
$+ 100 + 250 = 370.$

10. SA = 60π sq cm

$SA = 2\pi r^2 + 2\pi rh = 2\pi(3^2)$
$+ 2\pi(3)(7) = 2\pi 9 + 2\pi 21$
$= 18\pi + 42\pi = 60\pi$

11. SA = 170π sq in.

$SA = 2\pi r^2 + 2\pi rh = 2\pi(5^2)$
$+ 2\pi(5)(12) = 2\pi 25$
$+ 2\pi 60 = 50\pi + 120\pi = 170\pi$

12. SA = 252π sq m

$SA = 2\pi r^2 + 2\pi rh = 2\pi(9^2)$
$+ 2\pi(9)(5) = 2\pi 81 + 2\pi 45$
$= 162\pi + 90\pi = 252\pi$

13. SA = 275π sq m

$SA = 2\pi r^2 + 2\pi rh = 2\pi(11^2)$
$+ 2\pi(11)(1.5) = 2\pi 121$
$+ 2\pi 16.5 = 242\pi + 33\pi = 275\pi$

14. SA = 96.3π sq ft

$SA = 2\pi r^2 + 2\pi rh = 2\pi(4.5^2)$
$+ 2\pi(4.5)(6.2) = 2\pi 20.25$
$+ 2\pi 27.9 = 40.5\pi + 55.8\pi = 96.3\pi$

15. SA = 352π sq in.

$SA = 2\pi r^2 + 2\pi rh = 2\pi(8^2)$
$+ 2\pi(8)(14) = 2\pi 64$
$+ 2\pi 112 = 128\pi + 224\pi = 352\pi$

16. SA = 84π sq cm

$SA = 2\pi r^2 + 2\pi rh = 2\pi(6^2)$
$+ 2\pi(6)(1) = 2\pi 36 + 2\pi 6$
$= 72\pi + 12\pi = 84\pi$

17. SA = 138.125π sq in.

$SA = 2\pi r^2 + 2\pi rh = 2\pi(4.25^2)$
$+ 2\pi(4.25)(12) = 2\pi 18.0625$
$+ 2\pi 51 = 36.125\pi$
$+ 102\pi = 138.125\pi$

18. SA = 600π sq in.

$SA = 2\pi r^2 + 2\pi rh = 2\pi(10^2)$
$+ 2\pi(10)(20) = 2\pi 100$
$+ 2\pi 200 = 200\pi + 400\pi = 600\pi$

Lesson 26.6

1. Volume = 175π cu in.

$V = \pi r^2 h = \pi(5^2)(7)$
$= \pi(25)(7) = 175\pi$

2. Volume = 1125π cu in.

$V = \pi r^2 h = \pi(15^2)(5)$
$= \pi(225)(5) = 1125\pi$

3. Volume = 100 cu in.

$V = lwh = (10)(5)(2)$
$= 100$

4. Volume = 154 cu in.

$V = lwh = (4)(3.5)(11)$
$= 154$

5. Volume = 108 cu in.

$V = \frac{1}{2}l \times h \times H$
$= \frac{1}{2}(3)(6)(12)$
$= \frac{1}{2}(216) = 108$

6. Volume = 17 cu in.

$V = \frac{1}{2}l \times h \times H$
$= \frac{1}{2}(1)(2)(17)$
$= \frac{1}{2}(34) = 17$

Answers and Explanations

Answer and Explanations for Challenge Questions

Unit 1, page 27

1. **B** Find the minimum price: $2.29 - 0.05 = 2.24$. For 2 loaves, the minimum is $4.48. Find the maximum price: $2.29 + 0.05 = 2.34$. For 2 loaves, the maximum is $4.68. The only answer choice between $4.48 and $4.68 is choice B: $4.57.

2. **−12** Follow the order of operations.
$72 \div [3 \times (2 \times 6)] + (-7 \times 2) = 72 \div [3 \times (12)]$
$+(-7 \times 2) = 72 \div [36] + (-7 \times 2) = 72 \div [36]$
$+(-14) = 2 + (-14) = -12$

Unit 2, page 49

1. $\dfrac{7}{15}$ $\dfrac{1}{5} + \dfrac{1}{3} = \dfrac{3}{15} + \dfrac{5}{15} = \dfrac{8}{15}$. Since this is larger than $\dfrac{1}{2}$ pound, she must go up to 1 pound. $\dfrac{15}{15} - \dfrac{8}{15} = \dfrac{7}{15}$

2. $\dfrac{5}{12}$; **20** $\dfrac{3}{4} \times \dfrac{5}{9} = \dfrac{15}{36} = \dfrac{5}{12}$ of the weekend. $24 \times 2 = 48$ hours in a weekend, so $\dfrac{5}{12} \times 48 = 20$ hours.

Unit 3, page 72

1. **9; $0.20** $20.00 - $15.30 = 4.70; $4.70 \div $0.50 = 9.4$, so she can get 9 candy bars for $9 \times $0.5 = 4.50 and she will have $4.70 - $4.50 = 0.20 left on the gift card.

2. **6.55 inches** $48.6 - 22.4 = 26.2$; $26.2 \div 4 = 6.55$

Unit 4, page 99

1. **88; $\dfrac{6}{11}$** Find the multiplier: $40 \div 2.5 = 16$ and then fill in the rest of the chart.

	Ratio (parts)	Multiplier	Actual Amount
Boys	$2\dfrac{1}{2}$	16	40
Girls	3	16	48
Total	$5\dfrac{1}{2}$	16	88

There are 88 students and 48 are girls, so $\dfrac{48}{88} = \dfrac{6}{11}$

Unit 5, page 112 *(left column continues right)*

2. **2.4 hours or 2 hours and 24 minutes** Find each person's individual rate. Kaveri: $\dfrac{6 \text{ pounds}}{2 \text{ hours}} = 3$ pounds per hour. Ron: $\dfrac{6 \text{ pounds}}{3 \text{ hours}} = 2$ pounds per hour. Together, they sort $2 + 3 = 5$ pounds per hour. $12 \div 5 = 2.4$.

Unit 5, page 112

1. **−1** $x^3 = 27$; $x = \sqrt[3]{27} = 3$; $x - y = 4$; $3 - y = 4$; $y = -1$

2. **$x \geq 7.264$** $15.99 + $38.49 = 54.48; $54.48 \div 7.5 = 7.264$. $x \geq 7.264$.

Unit 6, page 130

1. **5** 2875 mm $= 287.5$ cm; $287.5 \div 57.5 = 5$.

2. **10.95 miles** $19{,}272 + 2(19{,}272) = 19{,}272$
$+ 38{,}544 = 57{,}816$ feet.
$57{,}816 \div 5280 = 10.95$ miles.

Unit 7, page 155

1. **32** If the probability of drawing a red marble is $\dfrac{1}{9}$, then the probability of NOT drawing a red marble is $1 - \dfrac{1}{9} = \dfrac{8}{9}$; $\dfrac{8}{9} \times 36 = 32$.

2. $\dfrac{25}{36}$ The probability of NOT rolling a 4 is $\dfrac{5}{6}$. For both to NOT be a 4: $\dfrac{5}{6} \times \dfrac{5}{6} = \dfrac{25}{36}$.

Unit 8, page 174

1. **C** $V = \pi r^2 h = \pi(2.5^2)\, x = \pi(6.25)$
$x = 3.14(6.25)\, x = 19.625x$

2. **C** Find the total area of the pond and walkway and then subtract the area of the pond. Total area: $3.5 + 7 + 3.5 = 14$; $A = \pi r^2 = \pi(7^2) = 49\pi$. Pond area: $A = \pi r^2 = \pi(3.5^2) = 12.25\pi$; $49\pi - 12.25\pi = 36.75\pi$